"Eternal Angel"
7-79

The Israelis

Frank H. Epp

The Israelis
Portrait of
a People in Conflict

Photographs by John Goddard

HERALD PRESS
Scottdale, Pennsylvania

Library of Congress Cataloging in Publication Data
Epp, Frank H   1929-
  The Israelis.

  Bibliography: p. 197
  Includes index.

  1. Israelis–Interviews. 2. Jewish-Arab
relations–1973- –Addresses, essays, lectures.
3. Israel–Politics and government–Addresses,
essays, lectures. I. Title.

DS126.5.E63   956.94′054   80-52
ISBN 0-8361-1924-X

Contents

Preface / 9

Prologue / 11
1. Immigrants / 15
2. Zionists / 32
3. Settlers / 52
4. Soldiers / 68
5. Minorities / 88
6. Spokespersons / 104
7. Believers / 122
8. Critics / 139
9. Activists / 156
10. Israelis All / 173
Epilogue / 189

Selected Readings / 197
Summary of Ninety-six Interviews / 199
Detail of Interviews / 201

*This book is dedicated
to the Jewish people:
those of the past who suffered
and died unheard by the world
and those of the present
still longing to be
more deeply understood.*

Preface

The Israelis: Portrait of a People in Conflict is a sequel and a companion volume to *The Palestinians: Portrait of a People in Conflict*. Though the two books are not identical in style and format, they represent the same idea and the same intent. Both are portraits of people caught up in conflict. Both are intended to give a hearing to two sides of the Middle East war in such a way that these people know they have been heard.

Both books will, I hope, help to resolve the conflict by giving a voice to the people, by sending messages from each side to the other, by highlighting the human dimensions of war and the deep desires for peace on both sides, and by promoting understanding of the situation's complexities as well as its fundamental simplicity.

The two portraits are an attempt to compensate for at least some Western and Christian neglect. The Palestinians waited many years for a proper hearing of their case in the West. In the early 1970's, the most militant and zealous resorted to hijackings and bombings to get the desired attention. Likewise, the Jewish people have felt oppressed, discriminated against, and misunderstood by the Catholic, Orthodox, and Protestant sectors of Christendom for centuries. In this book not only the present anxiety of Israel but also the weeping of Jewish men and women throughout history is heard.

The contents of this volume are based on interviews, conducted for the most part during April-May of 1977 when an election campaign was in progress. We spoke to ninety-six Israelis from all parts of the country. They were resident in twenty-two rural and thirteen urban locations. They represented seventeen different, broadly classified, walks of life. They came from twenty-nine different countries, and various immigration periods. They were from all age groups, from the teens to the seventies.

None of the interviewees was pre-selected. While we were helped by the Israeli government Press Office, by the Israeli Defence Forces, and by Roy Kreider and Paul Quiring, Mennonite representatives in Tel Aviv and Jerusalem respectively, the majority of those interviewed were people we met as we travelled through the country and who in turn

9

nominated others who had a story to be told. No attempt was made to obtain a scientific sampling, though we hoped to talk to a representative group of people (see Summary of Interviews and Index).

Most of the interviews were recorded on tape. The volume of the total material required considerable editing for the sake of brevity. Less than one-third of the words spoken ended up in print, but in the editing every effort was made to retain the heart of what had been said. Anonymity and an opportunity to check the relevant manuscript portion were granted to the interviewee if requested. All the words of each person appear in one place only, and not under various topics as was the case in *The Palestinians*. In the final division into chapters, one of the main points of an interview determined its placement in one of the ten chapters.

The usage of several terms requires some explanation. The name "Palestine," for instance. On the one hand it designates the land area west of the Jordan River as it was administered under the British Mandate. On the other hand the word also refers to the Palestinian state as it exists in the minds of some people today. The term "Palestinian" refers to those Arabs who live in, or lay claim to, a homeland in historic Palestine, although in reality some Jews and other non-Arabs are also Palestinian in this sense. The terms "Israel," meaning the state, and "Israelis," meaning citizens of that state, apply since 1948. While not all Israelis are Jews, the terms are sometimes used interchangeably. Such usage arises from the official status of Israel as a Jewish state and from popular understanding both inside and outside Israel and the Jewish community. This portrait of the Israelis includes a few Arab Israelis who are not Jews, Christians who are not Jews, and a few Jews who are not Israeli in the legal sense of Israeli citizenship. A certain ambiguity of terms which are usually self-explanatory in their context is necessary to reflect the Israeli-Palestinian realities.

This project was assisted by the Mennonite Central Committee offices in Akron, Winnipeg, and Jerusalem and made possible by Conrad Grebel College which allowed released time. John Goddard, the photographer for both volumes and a journalist by profession, was an essential partner and congenial companion in this undertaking. I am much indebted to Jan Kaethler, who, as a special assistant, accomplished not only the monumental task of transcribing nearly a hundred hours of tape but who also assisted in the editing of them. My secretary, Miriam Jantzi Bauman, and other Conrad Grebel College staff also helped to complete the manuscript. My final word of gratitude is to the Israelis themselves whose co-operation and hospitality exceeded my fondest expectations.

Frank H. Epp
Conrad Grebel College
Waterloo, Canada

Prologue

The story of the Jewish people is one of the most remarkable sagas of human history. No other social group has known so much migration and scattering, so much discrimination and persecution, so much miraculous survival and outstanding achievement in so many centuries and disparate cultures as have the Jews.

One of the more dramatic chapters in their 4,000 year history is being written now, in the twentieth century. Depending on one's historic choices, the beginning of this chapter can be the first World Zionist Congress in 1897; the Balfour Declaration in 1917 which gave the British promise that the Jews should have a homeland in Palestine; or the United Nations decision in 1947 to allow the partitioning of the land, thus opening the door to the creation of the State of Israel in May of 1948. Each one of those events led to new waves of Jewish immigration to the area, accounting for the increase in Jewish population from approximately 50,000 at the turn of the century to about 3 million, three-quarters of a century later.

In some ways the twentieth-century Jewish return to the land of Canaan/Palestine/Israel is a repetition of earlier periods in the history of this unusual people. Their first arrival is associated with the movements of the Patriarchs – Abraham, Isaac, and Jacob – nomadic shepherds who proclaimed that Yahweh, a monotheistic deity who looked upon them with special favour, connected them to the land and promised to them and their descendants special blessings if they would remain obedient to His commandments.

Movements including the land of Canaan were not uncommon in the Middle East. Periods of drought and famine led to frequent migrations of whole tribes of people in search of new oases. The migrations of the Patriarchs were part of the common pattern. Jacob, also known as Israel, and his family (eventually actually twelve tribal families) ended up in Egypt in their search for food. There they remained for several hundred years. Under the leadership of Moses, the children of Israel emigrated

11

from Egypt and, after a forty-year sojourn in the desert, returned under Joshua, Moses' successor, to the Canaanite land of "milk and honey."

In the next two centuries the twelve tribal families spread from the hill country, which they occupied at first, into the areas assigned to them. Under their leaders, who were called Judges, numerous battles with the Canaanites and the Philistines extended the land area under the control of the children of Israel, though the Philistines held most of the coastal areas and the plains, and eventually gave to the land one of its historic names, Palestine.

The period of the Judges was followed by the period of the Kings and the Prophets. Saul began the monarchy and the kingdom. David chose Jerusalem as the capital. Solomon built the first temple and developed the kingdom as a Middle East power. This period of glory was followed by internal dissension, and the kingdom split into two parts. Israel to the north was eventually conquered by the Assyrians and many of its people were exiled. Judah to the south succumbed to the Babylonians and, again, a large part of the population was exiled.

Providing an alternate leadership to the people during these times were the Prophets, whose sayings and writings valued righteousness, justice, and peace. Their writings, joined to those of the chroniclers and the poets, were later canonized and became the sacred writings of the Bible.

When the Persian empire became dominant in the area, the Jews were allowed to return to their homeland, to rebuild the temple, and to develop their communities. A period of relative autonomy under the Persians was followed by limited autonomy under the Greeks. The uprising of the Jews against their Hellenist overlords was followed by a period of independence, which in turn was followed by Roman rule. This time the anti-imperial Jewish revolt was totally crushed and the second temple completely destroyed.

An involuntary scattering of the remnant population completed the dispersion of the Jews into the areas surrounding the Mediterranean and the Black Sea. This was not a new development. For generations and for various reasons – commercial and religious – the Jewish presence had become universal, though sparse, in the world as it was then known. In due course, the Jewish community spread deeper into Europe, and several important commercial and intellectual centres were established.

The long-standing Jewish quarrel with Roman authorities was intensified when the empire was Christianized. Forever after in their European experience, the Jews felt discriminated against, ostracized, ghettoized, and persecuted by various Church-state alliances. This was true in Catholic Spain, in Orthodox Russia, and in Protestant Germany and England, to name the outstanding examples. The Inquisition in fifteenth-century Spain, the pogroms in nineteenth-century Russia, and the Holocaust instigated by twentieth-century Germany were times of indescribable physical suffering, social disorientation, and spiritual anguish. Until the modern period, the Arab world and Islam provided the most welcome haven for Jewish refugees.

In the search for a better future, some Jewish leaders pointed in the direction of assimilation with the peoples and nations of Europe. However, when assimilation only intensified anti-Jewish feelings, Zionism, as a distinct form of Jewish nationalism, became an option for survival and consequently the wave of the future. Zionism was identified as a political movement with the first World Zionist Congress in Switzerland in 1897, but it existed long before that time as a religious and spiritual ideal connected to the Messianic hope of historic Judaism.

After the Congress, however, Zionism expressed itself as a deliberate attempt to restore a Jewish homeland in Palestine. The Zionist program was facilitated by the Balfour Declaration of 1917, which gave British blessing to that undertaking, and by the British Mandate government which ruled Palestine until May of 1948.

The resistance of the native Arabs to the Zionist plan was greater than either the Jews or the British had anticipated. The Arabs watched with alarm as the Jewish-Arab population ratios in Palestine changed from one to ten in 1917 to one to two in less than one generation. The bloody clashes between the two societies led to British withdrawal, and the young United Nations, into whose lap the Mandate was dropped, saw no other alternative to perpetual conflict than to partition the land into autonomous Jewish and Arab areas and to internationalize Jerusalem. The Arab majority found the plan unacceptable, and the clashes of several decades became open warfare.

In its War of Independence, the new State of Israel not only established itself but extended its territorial borders beyond the UN plan. The Arab nations, who had tried to prevent the partitioning of Palestine and the creation of a Jewish state, were humiliated, and hundreds of thousands of Palestinian Arabs were rendered homeless. The Israeli state quickly consolidated itself. New waves of immigration rapidly quadrupled the population; agriculture and industry prospered; and an efficient military force arose – a result both of four victorious wars and of a continuing need for national security.

All the successes, however, failed to solve either the age-old problem of the Jews as a minority or the new problems of the Israeli state. Israel was not at peace with three Arab states who insisted that Israel return occupied land. The Arab League as a whole objected to the wedge-like entry of an alien state into their pan-Arabic world, and Islamic societies everywhere protested the Israeli rule of all of Jerusalem. What turned out to be most problematic of all was the Palestinians, who, in their various situations, insisted on the restoration of a national homeland of their own. They could not accept either second-class citizenship in Israel, ruled by military governors in the West Bank and Gaza, or a permanent position as refugees and exiles outside their own homeland.

The long and difficult struggle of the Israeli Jews was characterized by a determination to make Zionism succeed. Enormous sacrifices were made to achieve this end. At the same time, the Israelis struggled with occasional nagging doubts that Israel and Zionism might not be the final or the best answer. This determination and these doubts, expressed in many ways and in varying degrees and prompting many new questions, are at the heart of this portrait of the Israeli people. None of them can be fully understood without reference to their historical experience and to their millennial hopes extending backwards into ancient times and forwards towards better times and a golden, perhaps even Messianic age in the near or distant future.

Immigrants

"Why are we here? Here in Israel a child doesn't have to worry about feeling his Jewishness." –Paul and Sara Grossbein.

Israel, like Canada, is a nation of immigrants. Most of the 3 million Jews now in Israel, or their families, came to Palestine-Israel in the twentieth century as immigrants from about ninety different countries. There were approximately 50,000 in the land in 1900, but of these, several thousand had arrived in the closing decades of the 1800's. All Israeli Jews interviewed remembered a point of arrival going back, in one instance, to the fifteenth century, when ancestors arrived in Palestine. While none of the Israeli Arabs remembered migration or immigration, the wanderings of all the Semitic peoples in the Middle East have been so many since time immemorial that it is proper to conclude, as in Canada, that even the so-called natives have migration somewhere in their past.

The twentieth-century movements, of course, are the most immediate. Whenever and wherever the Jewish people could be persuaded to talk about their past and the circumstances surrounding their immigration, their stories revealed much pathos and tragedy, much discrimination and suffering, much expectation and hope. Somewhat representative of all of Israel's immigration history are the stories that follow.

J. Ben-Yosef, *an official in the Israeli army, was born in the western Ukraine in 1931. He survived pogroms, ghettos, concentration camps, and the flight to western Europe before arriving in Palestine in 1947. He also survived all the wars with the Arabs. Jews must have a national home, he believes, and it has to be Israel. Co-existence with the Palestinians is desirable and possible, but so far the way for that co-existence has not been found.*

The most difficult times started in 1941. On the first day of German occupation–it was in July–a pogrom happened in our town, mainly conducted by the Ukrainian peasants, with the encouragement of the local priest. In the first twenty-four hours about 500 Jews were killed.

15

The Germans restored order and it became quiet, but very soon the Judenrat was installed. Since my father, formerly a teacher but then a book-keeper, was one of the prominent people in town and active in the Zionist movement, the Jews suggested to him that he be a participant in this Judenrat. He refused because he suspected that the Germans used this kind of organization to obtain Jewish assistance in the German extermination plans.

I well remember the German occupation and that we had a very hard living, mainly because of lack of food. We were in danger because every couple of days able-bodied men – my father was then the age of thirty-six – were being caught in the streets searching for food and assigned to forced labour. My father benefited from his good relations with the Ukrainians. He became a newspaper editor and was allowed to leave the ghetto every day to distribute newspapers to German and Ukrainian offices. Thus he had freedom of movement outside the ghetto and could bring back food for the family. I was then the age of ten. We divided the work of distributing newspapers. I took the most dangerous places, because children were less suspect than grown-ups. So I carried newspapers to the offices of the Gestapo.

After the ghetto was closed, the Germans started a so-called "organized action." It meant the execution of the Jews. The first action was in July of 1942. About four to six hundred children and old people were caught in the streets and taken away by train. We suspected that they were being taken to a place from which they wouldn't come back, but we didn't know at that time that there were gas chambers and execution camps. The main action was in October 1942, and it lasted about three days. I remember it began early in the morning. We heard a terrible noise. Since I was known by the Germans in a favourable way, I went out to see what was going on. I was caught and brought to the synagogue, a very big hall, the selected place of gathering. From the synagogue the people were taken to the trains. Since my parents were not among them I tried to escape in order to be with them. I succeeded though not without aid. One of my relatives was a member of the Judenrat. His family was also caught and brought to the synagogue. As an official he remained outside in order to maintain contact with the German authorities. Suddenly I heard his family called out by a German policeman. I simply joined them: a mother, a daughter, and a son.

Then the head of the Gestapo asked my relative, "Is this your family?"

He said, "Yes."

"But you told me that you have a wife and two children; who is the third?"

"No, I told you I had a wife and three children!"

I have him to thank for saving my life. If he hadn't reacted quickly, I would be dead today. Maybe he had a bad conscience, because my father didn't join the Judenrat, and he did. I don't know his reasons. Anyway he saved my life. The next day my parents were rounded up. My father had told me that he would never go to the trains. He would rather resist and die on the spot. And that's what happened. On the way to the train he ran out of the line and was shot by a Ukrainian policeman. I found him dead. From that day, at the age of eleven, I became an independent man. I lived alone.

For a while I joined my relative's family, and we were safe since he was a member of the Judenrat. But not for long. We were among the last to leave after a series of actions. Up to the end of 1942, the Germans in our area took the Jews to the train and exterminated them in a gas camp, which was called Belsetz. Then they stopped because they lacked transportation. Instead, in two other actions which I saw personally in 1943, they took the Jews from the ghetto to dugouts and shot them on the spot.

We Jews in the labour camp were the privileged ones. For about two weeks they didn't take us to work. Then we knew that our end was very near. It's very important to remember one German policeman in the Schutzpolizei, an officer named Molach. He tried his best to save the Jews. One evening Molach appeared in the camp and said, "Tomorrow you are going to be exterminated."

Immediately we considered an escape attempt. We were then a group of about twenty-four people, all men except one young woman and four children. The old border between Russia and Poland, the area where the camp was located, was covered with expansive forests. Someone familiar with the area could wander in the forests for ten or fifteen hours. The man who organized us was once a sergeant in the Polish border police. He knew the area well and assisted those who wanted to leave to hide in the forests. The next morning the Germans came and liquidated all the members of the camp who had chosen not to leave even though they knew that the next day they were going to be killed. I could spend a couple of hours describing our way of living in the forest, how we defended ourselves, how we fed ourselves and so on. In the summer you have a lot of fruits and berries and mushrooms, and in the winter there are animals. And you can steal. In any case, what's relevant is that from this group of twenty-four people, only eight remained alive. The others were killed or died from sickness or food poisoning. This period ended in April 1944, when the area was occupied again by the Russians.

I came out of the forest along with my uncle, who is now living in the States. He was also caught in the big action of October 1942, but he jumped the trains. He told me that my mother and another two uncles also jumped out of the moving trains. They disappeared. We don't know what happened. He escaped, but most of the people who jumped were

17

shot. My uncle was taken into the Russian army. And so I was again alone. In 1944, at the age of thirteen, I became a merchant. I sold vodka to the Russian army. It was a very good business. I remember that my income was higher than it is today.

After the war was finished there was an agreement between the Polish and the Russian authorities that all Polish citizens had the right to leave Russia and go to western Poland, which was independent. So in July 1945 I went, together with my uncle who returned from the Russian army, to the German area of Schlesia which was annexed to Poland. There I discovered that the Zionist organization had started to build and organize kibbutzim for 100 or 150 young people. The average age was about eighteen to twenty. I was the youngest, being fourteen.

We stayed in Poland only about three months. In October we left in the direction of Germany. Our forged papers stated that we were Jews from Greece who spent the war in German concentration camps in Poland, and who were now going back to Greece. At this time there was complete chaos in Europe. People were like wandering tribes, going from east to west, from west to east. A lot of Ukrainians and Russians were coming from and going back to Russia.

So we began our wanderings towards Palestine. It took two years. We started in October 1945 at the Czechoslovakian-German border in Bavaria and arrived in Munich. The German museum was then a camp for displaced persons. We organized an agricultural farm to prepare ourselves for life as farmers in Palestine. Then we left Germany for Italy. We came to the Austrian-Italian border and the Brenner pass. We had to steal across the border by night and march about sixteen kilometres. The snow was up to our knees. In January 1947, we arrived in Italy, Milan first and then Rome. We lived in Rome up to March 1947, and then we went to the southern part of Italy. In two nights we embarked on a small ship with 1,500 people and left the coast of Italy for Palestine. We had a very bad voyage with bad weather. About 100 miles from Haifa, British airplanes discovered us. There was a storm, and the engine of our ship stopped working, and we started to sink. We called SOS, and the British navy approached us with their destroyers. They agreed to tow us to Haifa.

Instead we went to Cyprus, where I spent about nine months, very nice months. We were free to do anything. Of course the food and the accommodation were bad. But we could stand it because most of us were used to even worse conditions. In Cyprus there were two huge camps, with a total of about 50,000 people. I used this time to complete my studies, since I had a very big gap in my education.

In the end of November 1947 the war began in Palestine. I was able to leave Cyprus, because I was young. I came straight from Cyprus to the

18

kibbutz. It was exactly two years and a month since I'd left Poland.

In January 1948, trouble started in the kibbutz. We were attacked. The villages were surrounded and transportation was endangered. And we were supplied only by convoys. A lot of people lost their lives as these convoys passed by Arab villages. It was a hard time, but we felt ourselves free people, all fighting for our independence. This kibbutz was finally occupied, but only three people became Egyptian prisoners. About thirty-two were killed and about sixty were injured. The last night, when we ran out of food, water, and ammunition, we decided to evacuate. In the morning the empty kibbutz was occupied by the Egyptians.

In 1950 I left the kibbutz, mainly because of the political disputes, and joined the army where I stayed till the present time. What motivated a man like me to serve the army? I was determined to be a free citizen because of what I went through. This meant doing my share to defend my country. I wouldn't say that I am a man who sacrifices himself. It would be hypocrisy. I simply don't want to rely on anybody else to defend me. I want to rely only on myself.

Now we come to the problem of the Palestinians. No man of conscience can be apathetic to the sufferings of the Palestinians, myself included. Although I wouldn't say that my conscience is completely easy, I think that we have the right to exist as a country, as a nation, as a state. And I think that we as a nation have suffered a lot. Six million of us were exterminated. I am sure that if there weren't a Jewish state in the world today, all Jewish life abroad would be different. I think that the creation of the Jewish state contributed a lot to Jewish feeling as a people.

Existing at the expense of other people is always a problem. A lot of Arabs left their places. Some of them were expelled by force. But really there's a lot of propaganda. In 1948 we expelled a very small number. Most of the Arab refugees of 1948 were people who ran away of their own free will. When I was in the kibbutz, I saw thousands of people leaving Jaffa, going of their own free will to Gaza, because they were sure that the Arab countries would attack Israel in May 1948 and that we would not last for more than two or three weeks.

In any case it's a problem, because a lot of Jews have been brought to places where Arabs were living in the past. How can you solve this confusing moral problem? It's not so simple. For those who are cynical, it's simple. But for those who are not cynical, it's a difficult situation. Some of us try to explain it thus. We must have a country. Where shall we go? Shall we go to Rhodesia? South Africa? Latin America? The only place that we have any right to claim is this place. The Arabs were sitting here, so we had to beg the Arabs to share this land with us. We had to pay them for every inch of earth we took. A lot of earth was bought between

19

1880 and 1945. Thousands, tens of thousands of acres were bought from the Arabs. But the other land we took without paying; for that we have to pay them.

And we have to suggest to the remaining Palestinians that they settle on the other part of Palestine. Palestine has two parts, historically: the western part of the Jordan and the eastern part of the Jordan. I wouldn't say that there is not a Palestinian nation. If the Palestinians claim that they are a nation, they should be allowed to be called a nation. There are in Africa today nations even younger than the Palestinians. But a Palestinian nation was never mentioned in history. Palestine was part of the Turkish province of South Syria. I would say that an Arab Palestinian, a Muslim, can be assimilated very easily into Syria or Iraq. There is no difference between a Syrian and a Palestinian.

I don't hate Arabs. I think every enlightened man has to fight against the beast in himself. Revenge, for example, and hatred, are primitive beasts in us. And this is the reason why, in spite of what the Germans have done to me personally, I keep very good relations with Germans. And this is the reason that I really don't hate Arabs. I spent years learning their culture and language, their history and religion, and I have some good friends among the Arabs.

I believe that if the hatred will disappear, we can exist here with very good relations, because we have a lot in common. We are both Semitic nations. We speak almost the same language. There is a very great similarity between Hebrew and Arabic. Most of the words have the same roots. And the Islamic religion comes from Judaism. I don't know if we really are historical cousins, as the Bible says, but the roots are Semitic. We can live with each other, if we will not compete, if we will not fight. The king of Morocco made a very important statement last week. He said: If we combine the generosity of the Jews with the riches of the Arabs, we can create a civilization that will flourish in this area, that will become a big power, and so on. This was said by an Arab king and published in the newspapers. So there is really no reason for this dispute. Unfortunately, it is in the domain of emotion rather than the domain of rationality. And it's very hard to fight emotions. I personally don't believe that there will be real peace until the idea of war as a solution dies.

Rachel Kratz, *a primary school principal in Israel, was born in Rumania in 1934. She came to Israel at the age of fourteen. From her painful experience as a member of a minority group in Rumania, she feels she can understand the problems of the Arab minority in Israel.*

I first heard that I was a Jew not from my parents but from our neighbours. They told me that my place was in Palestine not in Rumania. I was in a concentration camp and my family was killed there. In Cyprus I learned the meaning of being a refugee. The moment I came to Israel I felt that I was among my own people, who would look after me, support me, give me a good home, a good education, and make me proud to be a Jew.

I can understand another minority group on the basis of my own experience. In Israel there can be democracy. There can be a place for every minority, for every religion. Every solution can be humanitarian. I am sure we can have a peaceful land where Jews, Muslims, Christians, and other people from all over the world can find a home and a place to fulfil their ideals. Israel can be a cosmopolitan place, but it has to have the colour of a Jewish nation.

Ygal Mochiach *is a technician from Iraq, where he was born in 1940 and where, in his opinion, it was impossible for him to live as a Jew. He feels the Jews must have their own state. The Palestinians are also entitled to their rights, but for them a state may have to await a more propitious time.*

There were 300,000 Jews in Iraq, and 290,000 came to Israel. Israel is my state. I can live as a Jew only in Israel. In other countries it is not possible, not for a long time. Starting in 1947 the Arabs in Iraq thought Jews were Zionists. Many were put in prison. There were public hangings. It is true that Arabs and Jews lived in peace for many generations. But every once in a while someone came along and stirred things up. That's why we must live in Israel.

We are more secure here than anywhere else, more secure here than the Arabs themselves in their own countries. Look at Lebanon. They are all Arabs. There will be peace, but I don't know how long it will take. It is not a problem for Israel. The Arabs did not accept an Arab state. There must be a solution, but it can't be the one proposed by Yasar Arafat. We want peace more than anything else, and we've agreed to pay for it. The Palestinians should have their rights. Maybe in twenty to thirty years they will have a state. Now a state would be like a bomb in this area.

Eugeny Leibovitch *was born in the* USSR *in 1944 and arrived in Israel in 1971. Although he studied economics at university, Eugeny became a seaman. He lives at Yamit, a new Jewish settlement on the shores of the Mediterranean on the Sinai, where Russian and American Jews live together.*

We waited for permission to leave Russia for sixteen years, from 1955 to 1971. And every year we got negative answers. I was absolutely sure that I would not leave Russia. So for me it was a very big surprise, really a miracle. I came directly to Israel, non-stop. When I was still living in Russia, I used to feel like a second-class citizen. I remember once how somebody explained it: if you hear somebody in Israel saying that you are a dirty Jew, you know the meaning. It's simple: you must go and wash yourself.

I'm a professional in the merchant navy. I have been all around the world. Why did I become a seaman? It's because of some kind of Russian complex. In Russia it was very difficult for me to see foreign countries. It was impossible for me to see anything. And now I can do it. I don't have any relatives here. I have some in Canada, in the United States, in Columbia, in South America, in South Africa and in England – all around the world. And now I can visit all of them, if I like. Now it's no problem.

In the Soviet Union there are about 3 million Jews. I think there might be only 10 per cent who want to leave. Most of them are convinced by Communist education. As long as they don't know what it is like outside, they believe the Soviet propaganda and what it says about the United States.

Believe me, Israel is the best place for me. For me to be Jewish I have to be Israeli. If you are Jewish, you are among strangers. If you are an Israeli, you are living with your own.

How do the Americans and Russians get along here in Yamit? I have no problem getting along with the Americans. I don't have a language barrier. I don't feel any difference. They are a little bit naïve, Americans, they don't know anything about life, but never mind, they'll learn. They are very nice people. They can believe anything.

Paul and Sara Grossbein *from Canada live on an experimental moshav, which is only for immigrants from English-speaking countries. There are about fifty families with 110 children. The moshav grows tomatoes under glass and exports them to various European countries. The Grossbeins lived in Toronto before coming to Israel in 1973. Paul was an industrial designer and Sara a law clerk. Paul was born in Canada in 1939; Sara in Israel in 1943. Her Polish-born parents emigrated from Israel to Canada.*

Why are we here? We don't really consider ourselves staunch Zionists. However, in Canada the children do not grow up in a Jewish atmosphere. Here, in Israel, a child doesn't have to worry about feeling his Jewishness. Israel is Jewishness. In Toronto I would have to worry about explaining to my children from early October on what Christmas is and why we don't celebrate Christmas. . . . Or here's another example. Sitting in a Toronto train station I would observe the people and find myself saying, "That man, he's Jewish, he has a Jewish nose." Sitting in a train station here in Israel, just the reverse is true. I don't have to worry about being Jewish anymore. Although I really felt anti-Semitism in Canada, I also had to worry about feeling my Jewishness. And here I feel it less. I argue with my neighbour. He's Jewish, too. I don't have to feel it's anti-Semitic if someone argues with me. In Canada the typical joke is, "Some of my best friends are Jewish." Any Jew will laugh at that, because they have heard it so many times.

How could you live like a Jew in Markham, Ontario, if your son or daughter has to go to get religious training in Toronto? It's impossible! And for the big holy days you have to go to Toronto. I don't care if I'm the only family there, but how will your child feel? How can you explain to him what Hanukkah is, if you only have it in one house in the whole community?

When you live in Israel, you feel the holidays. You're here! You know every holiday, because it's in the streets just like Christmas is in Canada. Purim is like a daytime Hallowe'en here. All the little children get dressed up. Most of them get dressed up as Queen Esther. And you should see how many little Queen Esthers are running around the face of Israel on that day. All over the place the streets are swarming with Queen Esthers. But you don't see this in the Jewish community in Canada. There we quietly go to the synagogue, and there's a service, and that's all.

Schmuel Adler, *thirty-eight, is a civil servant. His parents were born in Poland, lived in Nazi Germany, and were among a select number admitted as immigrants to the US in 1938. Schmuel was born in America, and arrived in Israel with his parents in 1960. From his work in the Ministry of Immigration and Absorption he is able to speak of immigration in general.*

I came from a traditional Jewish family, first-generation immigrants to the United States. I received a Zionist education and joined the Zionist youth movement at a young age and eventually reached the rank of national president. I came to Israel for a one-year leadership program and decided at that time that Israel was my home.

The main idea of Zionism as the Jewish national liberation movement was to bring the majority of the Jewish people who were dispersed all over the world to their own historic country, the land of Israel. At the founding of the State of Israel there were approximately 650,000 Jews here. Since then we've absorbed 1,600,000 immigrants. One out of every two Israelis living today is an immigrant to the country. Immigration

23

into Israel has had a different character since 1968. The mass immigration to Israel from 1948 to 1951 involved immigrants from the displaced persons camps of Europe or from the ghettos in the Arab countries. People came mainly without a trade or vocation. Even though the economic conditions in Israel at the time were very different, there was usually a rise in their standard of living. This was also true for two other large immigrations in 1955-57 and 1961-64, mainly from North Africa and certain East European countries.

Immigration since 1968 has come from two main sources: western Europe and North and South America, and the Soviet Union. Both of these sources have highly urbanized cultures, and almost all of the immigrants, including those who come from the Soviet Union, experience a drop in their standard of living when they come to Israel. Also, previous waves of immigration represented larger families than is the case at present.

The policy of the government now is not to press for immediate cultural integration into the country. And therefore we encourage the immigrants to have their own newspapers in their own languages and to set up their own folklore groups thus allowing the gradual formation of a new culture in Israel. It will take at least two or three generations until there is an Israeli culture. We do not have neighbourhoods for people from one background only, but, on the other hand, we don't have blocks of apartment houses where people from various cultures are mixed. We found that people from various cultures just cannot live in one block of houses together. But, on the other hand, we still want a meeting of the various cultures in the local store, the school, and the clubroom.

As far as Jews from the Soviet Union are concerned I think that their absorption is one great success story. And I have objective facts to prove it. We were unprepared for the immigration from the Soviet Union in terms of available houses and in terms of our knowledge of their thinking, their background, and their professional life. We never expected so many academics and professions. Forty per cent of the immigrants both from the Soviet Union and the Western world were employed abroad in professional, academic professions. Another 20 per cent were in professions based on secondary school training. We weren't prepared for it. In the Israeli population in 1970, only 16 per cent were in these two groups. After three years in Israel, 95 per cent of the Soviet immigrants were in permanent housing and 95 per cent had found employment. Of those in housing, 85 per cent were satisfied with the housing they received and with the neighbourhood they were living in, and 70 to 75 per cent were satisfied with their jobs.

Social integration is still a problem. Only 60 to 65 per cent are satisfied with the social life in Israel. We have financed a number of folklore groups. We finance the publication of newspapers in Russian and the Georgian languages. We are putting out books and translations of various Jewish works. We are also paying for Russian writers to put out works either in Russian or in Hebrew. All this costs a lot of money and we have limited funds.

One of the greatest advantages of our immigration is that we have co-operation between Soviet science and knowledge and Western science and knowledge. Together the scientists can produce great things. And the Israeli government has organized a special fund of $100 million to be used by investors to set up industries and services that can utilize the immigrants' knowledge. It's a new fund. We won't know the results for a number of years. It's a great challenge to see if we can make the synthesis between Western and Soviet science and knowledge.

Less than 5 per cent of the Jews from the Soviet Union have left Israel within their first three years in the country. This is the lowest rate of re-emigration that Israel has ever had during any other previous wave of immigration. About 30 per cent of the immigrants from the United States and Canada returned within three years. That means one out of every three doesn't make it here.

In Israel there is a saying, half joke and half truth, that the Israelis like immigration but they don't like the immigrants. This feeling has existed throughout every immigration.

Lida Sharlin *is a graduate student in philosophy at Hebrew University. She was born in Iran in 1956 and came to Israel in 1965. As a member of a new Jewish settlement on the West Bank near Jerusalem, she reflects on the reasons for and the meaning of her coming to this land.*

My parents were born in Iraq, and we came to Israel through Iran. My parents left Iraq through the desert illegally in 1944. They moved from Iraq to Iran because of the way Jews were treated at that time. They felt it was dangerous to stay. My father was a merchant. My grandparents were religious, but we weren't a religious family. In Iran we weren't quite accepted by the Persian people. I don't know if my parents made a sincere effort to adapt to Persian culture. They already had their own, the Jewish Iraqui culture. They felt quite out of place with the Muslim Iranians.

Being a minority, we found another minority living in Iran, the Christian missionaries. They put up a Christian school in Iran, and that's where we had our schooling. Being a Jew in a situation where you said the Lord's Prayer every morning, went to Church, and said Latin, wasn't very pleasing. You always had a feeling of being inferior. We never said that we felt inferior, but that's the way it was. To put it mildly, being a Jew was a pain in the neck. It wasn't the fault of the missionaries at the school. In fact they gave us the most that they could give. They respected people from different religions. Still the feeling that we were different was there. At home our parents felt that they had to impress upon us that we were Jewish to balance the Christian influence. The more they felt a threat from the Christian side, the more they made us remember that we were different. As a child I grew up with two personalities: one at school, one at home.

Later I also understood that the education I got in the missionary school was not as neutral and international as was suggested by the multinational composition of school attendance. The teachers gave us the feeling that no matter what our religion and no matter what our country we would all belong together. Afterwards, I saw that what they did was get everybody together on the basis of American culture and Christian teaching. They made everybody more or less adopt American culture with cheerleading and hot dogs and everything.

When we came here, I did not feel that Israel belonged to the Jewish people. I did not feel that religion had anything to do with a country. Religion is different from a nationality. You can be a Christian in Israel. You can be a Christian in the States or any other place. By analogy, I thought, you can be a Jew in America, or you can be a Jew in any other place, and the fact that you are Jewish does not entitle you to the land of Israel. That's the way I felt because of the way I was brought up. Now I feel differently.

The difference is that now I see the injustice of the fact that my parents were more or less forced by circumstances to move out of Baghdad, and that now I don't define this land as Palestinian land. I would feel badly if I settled on a place defined as Palestinian land. If this land is Palestinian, then Baghdad and the house that my parents owned was Jewish land. It works both ways. I've finished with the philosophy of turning the other cheek. That's a Christian philosophy. It doesn't belong to me. It's not part of Jewish thinking to turn the other cheek, and to get slapped again. It's part of Jewish thinking to think of your own survival. It's not really egocentric but like the Jewish saying says – I think it's part of the Old Testament – if you're in the desert and you have a little bit of water, and you're holding it, and you have a friend with you, you're not obliged to share it, if sharing means seriously risking your chances to survive. Jewish thinking says, drink the water, you're entitled to it. Save yourself first, and don't feel guilty about it.

There's a big difference between this and Christian thinking, and the way you think has a lot of influence on what you do and what you consider moral and not moral. But the location of a settlement is also important. I would not feel entitled to take an Arab family out of its

26

house, even though this was done to us in Baghdad. It's a different thing settling in a land that's completely desert.

Lionel Pyetan *is a 1938 immigrant from South Africa where he was educated as a lawyer. His parents, in turn, had migrated to South Africa from the Baltic region of Europe. Thus, Pyetan, a journalist by profession, is able to reflect not only on the Jewish search for a homeland but on apartheid and other forms of separation among peoples.*

The Jews of South Africa were largely immigrants from Lithuania and Latvia in the 1870's and 1880's. My own father, for instance, arrived in 1889. The Jewish community around 1930 numbered about 120,000. The biggest concentration was in Johannesburg. The Jewish community in South Africa, a ghetto, I think, like everywhere else, was very largely thrown upon its own resources. True, they were represented in parliament, and they were free, but nevertheless they were thrown back upon themselves, so to speak. Some clubs didn't accept Jews, but the amount of anti-Semitism varied in degree.

It never affected me personally very much. However, I felt that a man has the right to be a whole citizen, not a half citizen. The Jewish people were overly concerned with the effects of things that happened. For instance, if a fellow was caught swindling, they said, "Oh, my goodness, how will this affect Jews?" If someone did something very good they would say, "This is very good for Jews." Then I heard about Palestine, and I thought, there lies the answer. Because in Palestine it won't matter a damn whether Jews swindle or not; I mean, it wouldn't matter to me. If they swindle, we'll put them in jail. And if they're very good, we'll give them medals, or awards, or something. In either case, it's nothing to do with my Jewishness. I can only be judged on what I do. I think that possibility brought me here.

The South African Jews are a wealthy community on the whole. They're very well off. You see, South Africa is the most comfortable country in the world to live in, even today, for a white man. You ask, where do Jews fit into the racial struggle in South Africa now? They are whites. By and large the Jewish community is a white community. It won't matter whether they side with the whites or not. They're whites. In the long run it will be meaningless if Jews stand up and talk about black rights. If it comes to an armed clash, black skins will be against white skins.

Israel is not an apartheid state in the sense that South Africa is. I must answer this on several levels, because one shouldn't oversimplify. The early Zionist conception of settlement which prevailed at the time when the foundations of what we have here were laid was that in settling here no Arab would be displaced by Jews. On the contrary, we hoped to bring blessings to the Arab world by raising their level to our own general level so that we could all live happily and contentedly together. This was the basic ideology; this was the ideology that was written into our declaration of independence.

Now, what is the reality? The reality is that this was probably a mistake – at least it was badly handled – because the Arab reaction to it was, "Well, who asked you? Who asked you to come and bring us blessings and raise our level, and so on? Who are you? What do we need you for?" So you had, from the beginning, an established hostility. As long as you have an established hostility, you don't have any togetherness. This hostility existed before the state was proclaimed.

I'll tell you a story. You know, where I lived, which is now a suburb of Tel Aviv, we had three Arab settlements. The people were very nice. We knew them, and we lived with them very well. I had a friend there, a fellow called Abed. It was in those months just before the actual outbreak of war. The largest Arab village, where Abed lived, was semi-evacuated already in February. But before they all left, they had a celebration. And you could hear it. A big celebration. Arab propagandists had come from Jaffa, you see. Abed told me afterwards: "You know, we had this party, and there's the war, and the Jews are all going to be thrown into the sea and we will divide up your houses." They knew us by name, these people. They did business with us, they sold us vegetables. I bought fish from Abed, and so on. We had ordinary relations with them – we were neighbours. He used to come past my house, drop his kid there to play with my kids, and then go on to Herzlea and pick up his kid on the way back. But it didn't worry him in the slightest that I would be thrown into the sea, and somebody – maybe even himself, I don't know – would thereafter occupy the house of the late unlamented Mr. Pyetan. Now, you see, this is the background of separation.

The beginning of my education and understanding of what was happening with the Arabs in this country was one day when I was told, "Go down to such and such a village because it looks as if the Arabs are going to pull out." In the village there were three or four state houses, large villas occupied by very rich people. The rest were small and very humble places. These four houses were empty. There wasn't anything in them. They had been evacuated in good time. These people had taken out all their possessions and left. In the other houses there was still food on the table. You see, at the last minute they were told, "Get out, quickly." They'd been told to run at the last minute while the rich people had left and looked out for themselves in good time. They were very well off;

28

they had money. They were not the refugees about whom we are now hearing all the time.

The problem with the present situation has to do with apartheid. It is a sort of apartheid, not an imposed apartheid, but a willingly accepted apartheid by both sides. The Jews are not anxious to generate intermarriage with the Arabs, and the Arabs are not willing to mingle with the Jews. So, in other words, you do have two separate communities. There is a village in which there are about sixty or seventy Arabs with Jewish wives. The other Arabs are not very happy about it. Of course, these girls are nearly all from the Oriental Jewish community and speak Arabic. And there's really no cultural barrier, because the villagers are simple peasants, and these girls came from poor and probably minimally educated families. They have the same customs. They speak the same language. There is only a religious barrier. I think, though, that all the children are brought up as Muslims. I think that if a girl is already willing to go and marry an Arab his religious side will not worry her too much. But now, there are very few cases of Jewish boys marrying Arab girls.

Moshe Bar-Ami *of Tel Aviv is a political party representative. He was born in Germany in 1930, and came to Israel at the age of twenty. Fascism in Europe and anti-Semitism in the US prompted his migrations.*

My chosen name, Moshe Bar-Ami, is symbolic of my feelings for my people and of my own attitude towards life. The name Moshe is a Hebrew word which means "to be pulled out of." I chose that name because I was pulled out of that cancerous water which is fascism, twice in my life – at the age of three from fascist Germany and at the age of seven from fascist Italy. I found refuge in the United States of America. The name Bar-Ami means "a son of my people," and that's the way I feel.

My father immigrated to Germany from eastern Europe. He was an actor. In 1933, a friend of his who had joined the Nazi party warned my father that the Gestapo was going to pick him up as one of the anti-fascists and take him to a concentration camp. He warned him three hours beforehand, and my father was able to escape. We went to Italy and lived there until 1937, when work permits were taken from the Jews. My father, seeing that the same future that would have awaited him in Germany now awaited him in Italy, sought refuge elsewhere. My mother's sister presented my parents with an affidavit which permitted us to come to the United States. And thank goodness for that, because otherwise we would not be here today. Thirty-five members of my family, a number of them from northern Italy, were taken from Europe to Auschwitz, where they were exterminated.

29

In January 1938 we arrived in the United States of America. My father found a job washing dishes at the Lexington Hotel in New York City where he received the salary of $12 a week. I suffered from malnutrition, something which has left its mark on me to this present day. That's one reason why I'm not able to do physical labour.

Yes, I suffered from anti-Semitism in the United States. There was not one day when I was not beaten up either physically or mentally by my fellow pupils at school – by the non-Jews and even by the Jews themselves. I think there was a psychological reason for this. Being different, being an immigrant to the United States, I made a greater effort than they to master the English language, and therefore, I was one of the outstanding pupils. The Jews, I imagine, beat me up in order to show that they too were Americans.

Although I found refuge in the United States, and though I tried to be as American as all the other Americans, there was always an undercurrent that led me to feel that I was different. My brother had gone to Palestine at the age of sixteen in 1946. His letters and some of my own experiences led me to believe that Zionism was the answer to the Jewish question. In 1946 I joined the Labour Zionist movement, which today is the Israel Labour party. From that moment on the Zionist feeling was deep within me. My parents and I joined my brother in his kibbutz. From my first contact with the Israeli authorities, I felt that my immigration was not looked upon favourably. At that time, anyone who was not able to do physical labour was looked upon by the Zionist authorities as a parasite. This naturally left its negative mark upon me, but it certainly did not change my attitude towards Zionism. I felt then as I feel today, that Zionism was the liberation movement of the Jewish people – Zionism meaning the territorial concentration of the Jewish people in their homeland, in the homeland of their forefathers. The thing that kept me alive spiritually was my musical activity. Up to the present I have been a choir singer and, thanks to my love of music, both vocal and instrumental, I have met some of the most wonderful people.

I am not a religious Jew in the sense that it is understood here. In my opinion, religion is not a mantle which can be placed on someone as the religious authorities in Israel seem to feel it must be. Religion is a belief, whether one calls it religion or philosophy. It is something which must come from living or it isn't there at all. I would say that my people have contributed the greatest piece of literature the world has ever known: the Bible. It has been a shining light not only for Judaism and Christianity, but for Islam as well. I feel that being here, my personal being here and our being here, are something very, very positive, and I think that the potential we have, both the Jews and the Arabs, and the contribution which we can make, has yet to be seen.

Tanja Samoilova *was born in 1951 in Riga, the capital of the Latvian Republic in the USSR. She migrated to Israel in 1973 with her parents and one brother. She is an M.A. student in linguistics and knows Russian, Hebrew, English, and German. Freedom and Jewish identity are very important to her.*

The main reason for leaving the Soviet Union was the lack of freedom. It was so suffocating there. When we came to Israel we all liked it here so we stayed. From the point of view of culture and education I am a typical Russian. I didn't get a Jewish education, nor was I introduced to Jewish culture. But I know that I am a Jew. Jewishness is something in the mentality. I am not a religious Jew. I am an atheist. Communist atheists are very aggressive, and Jews, atheists or not, are more flexible.

In Israel I was very surprised at the sight of people expressing themselves so freely. It was something special for me, and I appreciated it. There were many other things. People who have lived here for a long time are different. In the beginning there was a lack of understanding between me and other people. But I don't think this point is crucial because all immigrants have this problem. It hasn't anything to do with Israel specifically.

Israel has two main problems: the preservation of the state, and economic difficulties. There is a lack of organization and too many strikes. People lack responsibility for their actions.

I think I could always recognize Russian people. They have something basic in common. They lack initiative, not because they are such people, but because they come from such a society. The structure of that society offers you all the solutions. You don't have to think: you get everything ready-made. When you come here, and you encounter the freedom of choice, you don't know what to do with it at first. Sometimes you remain passive. I think this is one of the reasons why the immigrants are discontented. They wait for things to come to them, and it doesn't happen. The Israeli approach is unbounded by restrictions. I think it's healthier. I prefer Israel to Europe. I think it comes from the fact that in Europe non-Jewish people make Jewish people feel different. It doesn't come from the Jewish people themselves, because many Jewish people want to assimilate with other people. Many don't want to be Jewish. They want to be like the others, but they don't succeed.

All the nations must have a state to make them feel secure wherever they are; a state where they can feel free. The Russians have Russia, the French have France. The Jews must have a Jewish country, at least now in the present state of affairs. Maybe sometime in the indefinite future they won't need it. Now I think it's important, because things are not ideal, not perfect. Now the Jewish state is a necessity.

Anglo-Saxon culture, French culture, Russian culture. But, in spite of these differences, we can say that there is a Jewish nation in the world. Because if there is no Jewish nation in the world, what about all the Jewish social and cultural institutions? What about the political aid the Jews are giving to Israel? What about the involvement of the Jews in New York and in London in the plight of the Jews in Russia? And their connection to Israel? Yet they are not religious Jews. So you have no choice except to speak about a feeling for being Jewish – and that is something that is hard to explain. It's a feeling. It's not a territory, not a political frame, not even any economic interests. It's not a religious feeling, just a feeling. Jewish unity is based mostly on that feeling and on those Jewish institutions which are operating in Jewish life.

Now, what does it mean to be an Israeli? This is not less complicated. I am first a Jew. I don't think that I, and my friend from the Arab minority here, are members of the same nation. We are members of two nations. We are citizens of the same country. We have the same rights as citizens of the country, but I make a distinction between being a member of a state and being a member of a nation. Now I would say something more. I believe that this country, Israel, is a Jewish country. This is the country of the Jewish nation. It belongs to the Jewish nation. On the basis of principle this state should be, now and in the future, a Jewish state. This has been the ideal of Zionism. That is why we came here to the country. That is why we have suffered here almost a hundred years. That is why we are sending our sons to the army. This should be a Jewish state.

We have in Israel one and a half million Arabs – but our state cannot be a state of two nations. The annexation of the territories threatens to make this country a bi-national state. I think that a bi-national state is not only a problem politically but also the antithesis of the Zionist ideology, and so politically, we must go back to the plan of partition. Of course, I would like all of the West Bank, this historical Eretz Israel, to be a Jewish land, but history is sometimes cruel. Here, on this historical Jewish land, are living one and a half million Arabs, and we have no choice now. We must go back to the plan of partition. The Arabs are citizens here. And I think they should belong to the Arab nation. They should not belong to the Jewish nation. As a Zionist, believing in Zionism, I think that they should have some kind of Arab Zionism. They can live here in Israel as a minority, if they are happy to live here as a minority – even though to be a national minority is always a problem. But if they are happy, let them live here. Still, they are part of the Arab nation, or let us say, of the Palestinian nation.

Yeshria Leibowitz *is a biologist-philosopher at Hebrew University. He came to the Jewish homeland from the USSR fifty years ago. For him Zionism was a desirable thing, meaning moving Jews from under the goyim (Gentiles), and a necessary thing, meaning political and national independence for the Jews. But Zionism solved few of the real problems facing the Jewish people.*

What is the meaning of Zionism? You are speaking with a man who was Zionist from childhood. I'll give you in a nutshell what is the meaning of Zionism. We are fed up with being ruled by goyim. Zionism is not the solution to the problems of Judaism. The one and only problem solved by Zionism is the political and national independence of the Jewish people. But all the problems of the Jewish people stay just as they always were. There is no unanimity among Zionists concerning any other problem. There are among Zionists socialists and capitalists, there are democrats, and there are even some fringe fascists. There are deeply religious Zionists; there are atheistic Zionists. They are all Zionists. The common idea is the national and political independence of the Jewish people.

The Jewish state is not a framework for ideological unity. It is the arena of very deep internal quarrels, maybe enough for civil war. It's possible. After all, what was the greatest happening in the great political history of the great American nation? A civil war. What was the greatest fact in the very great history of the English people? The revolution of 1642 to 1648, the war between the Roundheads and the Cavaliers, the beheading of the king. A state is not a framework for unity. No problems have been solved by the state, not even the problem of the essence of the Jewish people.

Being a Jew is a status; it's not an idea. I accept this status. Status is a legal notion. I certainly distinguish between Jews whom I approve of, and Jews whom I don't approve of, but both of them are Jews. I may approve of a soldier who is brave and obeys orders and disapprove of a soldier who is a coward and disobeys orders. But both of them are soldiers. There are today about 14 million people who are Jews, according to the laws of Judaism. There are many among them who reject Judaism, many; it makes no difference whatsoever to their status as Jews. If the law of the state says someone is a soldier, no matter how disobedient he is, he is still a soldier. The laws of Judaism make Jews. Judaism is very ancient law. It's not an innovation. And I know it's rejected by very many Jews, and that's a great problem of the Jewish people nowadays.

The State of Israel is nothing but the Jewish people's instrument of political and national independence. For the last thirty years the State of

35

Israel has been safe-guarding the political and national independence of the Jewish people. The State of Israel didn't solve any problem for Judaism; it didn't solve the social problem, nor the cultural problem, nor the educational problem. As a matter of fact, there is no security in the State of Israel. We have to make the greatest efforts to maintain the state, and its existence depends not only on the maximal efforts of the Jews, but also on powers beyond our power. The state is not an instrument for forming real values, just a necessity. It's necessary to have an army, but an army is an abomination. It's necessary to have a flag, though a flag is something ridiculous.

I wrote the article "Jesus" in the Hebrew Encyclopedia, an article of forty pages. Jesus is not an internal Jewish phenomenon. He has nothing to do with Judaism or the history of the Jewish people any more than Krishna, or Buddha. Jesus is a factor of universal history, who decided human history for a few thousand years. The same goes for Buddha and Muhammad. Both are absolutely foreign to Judaism. About the historical Jesus, as a matter of fact, we don't know anything. He left no traces. The Jews know about him only from the Christian sources, and therefore even his existence is doubtful. He may be a mythological figure. Even if he existed, his existence is of no relevance to the history of the Jewish people, although the figure of Jesus is certainly a fact of universal significance as the great opponent of Judaism. Jesus is the single abrogation and rejection of Judaism. In fact, the meaning of Christianity lies in an abrogation of Judaism. If Christianity doesn't reject Judaism, it ceases to exist. The claim of Christianity is that Christianity is the real Judaism. No Christian can accept the existence of Judaism after the year 33 as legitimate.

Menachem Brinker *was born in Jerusalem and educated in both religious and secular schools. For seven years he was a member of the Nachal, a special unit within the Israeli army, whose members work on a kibbutz. Now he is attached to Hebrew University as a philosopher. He edits* Emda, *a monthly paper which defines Zionism for the "doves" of Israel who are organized as the Movement for Peace and Security.*

Both my parents were Zionist, though in different ways. My mother was and is very orthodox. My father was traditional, but not religious. With a Jew there is not one single way to define religiosity or orthodoxy. My father used to go each Saturday to the synagogue. He never drove his car on Saturday and never smoked on Saturday. He ate kosher, but he was not orthodox. I was educated as a religious boy, but I lost my faith in my adolescence. It's hard to describe, but there came a day when I felt that, though connected culturally to Jewish religion, I wasn't a believing man. I have opinions, preferences, attitudes, but I wouldn't say that I have an overall belief.

In our magazine, we interpret Zionism as the normalization of the Jewish people. By that we mean that the Jewish people should be somewhere in the world a people sovereign over a certain piece of land. Normalization allows the Jewish state to give personal security to the Jew, a feeling of equality with others without any need to move through assimilation and self-denial. These aims of Zionism can't be achieved unless there is a peace. Therefore, peace is not only an idea of the Israeli state, it is not only a thing desirable in itself, but it is also the only thing that can fulfil the Zionist idea. All other questions, like territory, are secondary elements in Zionism. At this point we have a quarrel with those who interpret Zionism as the maximal hold of the greatest number of territories in the historical Eretz Israel. You see, we emphasize the secular rational element in Zionism above the mystical irrational element. We try to draw a line of demarcation, which would separate completely and absolutely Zionism as a modern national movement from Messianic aspirations. Zionism is not to be looked upon as the beginning of the redemption of the world by the redemption of the chosen people. Instead, it has to be interpreted in secular terms.

The Jew is faced with two alternatives: either he has to deny his origins in order to gain equality with other people or he has to suffer persecution and discrimination. The only way to avoid both persecution and self-denial is to have a modern state, and this is what Zionism is about, according to us. So we start with Zionism on a more abstract level of debate. Then we go down to the question of the territories: are they really needed for strategic purposes? They are not. What many people want to achieve by ownership of the territories might be achieved even better by demilitarization of those territories. We emphasize next that in Zionism there is a universal element, the right of every people to self-determination, and this universal element makes it almost obligatory for Zionists to attach the same principle to the Palestinians as it does to the Jews. As Jews we were always offended when non-Jews told us, "You are not a nation, you are not a people, you are just a religious sect, a religious community, or a quasi-national community." We always said, "It is for us to decide whether we are a nation or only a religious community." And now we approach the Palestinians with the same attitude that non-Jews gave to the national Jews at the beginning of this century. It is not for us to decide whether they are a nation or not. It is for them to decide. If they decide that they are, then they are entitled to the right of self-determination in the same way that we Jews are entitled to it. All the rest are questions of a pragmatic nature to be discussed in the process of negotiation. They are questions of a pragmatic not an ideological nature. Ideologically, Zionism must be ready to compromise over the historical land of Israel with the Arab Palestinian people. The rest is to be decided in the context of peace-making negotiations.

Now, there are many people who are afraid that once the Jewish people become secular they will also become assimilated. We don't think so. Assimilation is a double concept: it means that you are leaving an historical existence, and it also implies that you are joining, being assimilated into, another entity. A secularized Jew may be leaving something, but he is not leaving everything. When a Jew becomes secular he is still identifying himself as a Jew and feeling national ties to other Jews – ties of Jewish solidarity, of Jewish expectations of the future, and Jewish reminiscences of the past. If he feels in this way, there is no danger of assimilation. Being assimilated also suggests accepting someone else's culture, language, and habits, but we don't feel that this can happen to the Jewish people in a secular Israel. We are not afraid of assimilation.

We also feel that religious belief is to be left to the individual conscience. You cannot encourage religion on a national basis, and you cannot discourage religion on a national basis. We don't like the idea, but for the sake of the Jewish people we must encourage Jewish religion wherever we encounter it. We don't want to impose secularization. We don't want to impose religious convictions and ways of life. It's for the individual to decide whether the religious elements in the Jewish tradition are forceful for him, whether he really feels himself attached to them or not. But the danger of assimilation is small. Shall we be assimilated into the Arab Middle East world? There are no signs of it. There are 3,400 Arabs who are married to Jewish wives in Israel. The fact that intermarriages between Jews and non-Jews is lower in Israel than in any other country proves that Israel is the last place that you might anticipate assimilation of Jews into the non-Jewish world.

I believe it is possible for Arabs and Jews to live together. Yet there is no way to prove this unless you attempt a political settlement. The argument of rightists in Israel is that Islamic society will never tolerate within it another national and religious and political minority. We say that the attitudes of Arab politicians today cannot be derived from Islamic culture and ideas, just as the behaviour of Israeli politicians today cannot be derived from the Bible or from the Talmudic literature. Our opponents always say that there is never a chance to have a true peace between Israel and its Arab neighbours, and therefore we must go on fighting, annexing the territories, not giving up, not giving concessions, and so on. We say, if you speak about true peace in the sense of true love, if you speak of true peace in the sense of Messianic ideals, perhaps it is true that we can't get together for the next couple of generations. But this ideal cannot be the beginning of the process. We say political settlement is the beginning; psychological acceptance by the Arabs of the Israeli state is the end. And we blame the right for putting the cart before the horse, when they postulate the need for total change in Arab psychology towards Israel. We say there are many countries in the world which hate each other, yet they don't make war against each other. They accept each other as a part of a political arrangement. What about the Soviet Union and the United States? Do they like each other? Is it true peace in the sense of true love? For us peace means first of all a political settlement, ending terrorist activities and people shooting at each other. Love and acceptance we work at from the minute we get a political settlement.

Now, on a different level, which is perhaps the deeper level of the conflict between Israelis and Arabs, the main factors are illusions, psychological illusions, which have elements of truth in them but are exaggerated beyond recognition. There is the Jewish illusion that the Arabs are continuing European persecution – that they are the last link in the long chain of anti-Semites who want to destroy the Jewish people. Then there is the Arab illusion that the Israeli, the Jew, is the last link in the chain of European colonialists who are more developed technologically, and who come to exploit or to take advantage of peoples who are less developed. There are some facts here, but it is mostly illusion. Now these two myths which give the conflict its psychological depth – the ambience of fear in the Israeli camp and deep hatred and humiliation in the Arab camp – these feelings must be fought for a long time. And this means that the Israelis should stop putting new settlements in the West Bank and in the Gaza Strip, because any Israeli settlement, besides the fact that it creates obstacles for political settlement in the short run, also contributes to the myth that the Israelis will never satisfy themselves with what they have and that they are going to exploit the Arab people. In the same way, we say that Arabs should stop making propaganda against Israel, and educating their children against Israel in the very first classes at school. But first must be the political settlement, then the deep psychological work. We start with a political settlement without much love, maybe even without full trust. Then you gain more and more trust to work on the psychological level, on the deepest level of the conflict. That's the way we envisage pacification.

Dan Meridor, *a private attorney, was born in Palestine in 1947. He grew up in Jerusalem. His mother and father, born in Austria and Russia respectively, came to Palestine in 1935-36. His father fought to expel the British from the land and was sent to the detention camps in Africa for some years.*

I think Zionism is the most beautiful national liberation movement that ever existed. It is a phenomenon of a people who withstood 2,000 years of persecution, and who were killed and massacred for centuries. They were driven from one country to another, never having any secure place, and yet they refused to disappear. The nations who suppressed them, like the Greeks, the Romans, the Babylonians, don't exist anymore. Their empires and the territories are gone, but this people still exists.

Eretz Israel is a biblical and Hebrew expression for Land of Israel commonly used in every-day life. The dimensions of land under Jewish sovereignty in Eretz Israel change from generation to generation. The land that was promised to Abraham was very wide. In the days of King David and King Solomon, it was wider than today. At other times it was very small, smaller than what we have today. My opinion of the borders? Sinai is not a part of Eretz Israel. I am concerned with what we have now from the Jordan River to the Mediterranean Sea, including Jerusalem, Nazareth, and Bethlehem. This is Eretz Israel for me today. I don't think the Golan Heights should be included. There is room for flexibility.

It is true, Zionism and the State of Israel caused an inconvenience to a very small part of the Arab people. There was never an independent Arab state here and there was never a Palestinian people in history. Even in the beginning of the Arab objection to Zionism they spoke of Syria, not of Palestine, never. I don't think you can compare the two situations. One is injustice, which caused the suffering of a people for 2,000 years, and the other is inconvenience. We didn't deprive any Arabs of any rights. They didn't have any national home here that we took away. Every Arab should have civil rights like every Jew, as well as community rights in religion, culture, and education.

Yoni Yuval *is an army officer and an agriculturalist. He was born near Lvov in Poland where the population was mixed: two-thirds Ukrainian and one-third Polish and Jewish. He thinks Zionism could have succeeded better a century or two earlier.*

The tragedy of Zionism is that it came 200 years too late. When nationalism was at its beginnings in Europe, the right of conquest was a fact of human law. If Herzl's Zionism had emerged 200 years ago the situation could have been different. We are now being lectured by nations who behaved a century or two ago as we do now.

I can compare the Middle East dispute to three people in a train, two sitting, one standing. The third wants to sit down. He pushes the others and sits down. We have been standing on our legs now for 2,000 years. Our legs are swollen from the Inquisition, pogroms, and the Holocaust. Now we are pushing by force to sit down. The bench is once again ours.

Sinai Okrent *was born in 1921 and came to Israel from Poland in 1948, the year the State of Israel was established. He lives at Kibbutz Lohamey-Hgetaoth. Freedom and fulfilment for the Jews are essential goals of Zionism.*

If you ask me what it means to be a Zionist, I'd say it means to do everything possible to absorb as many Jews as possible. This is the only place where they can live as free people. To be a Jew means not only to live and be well off somewhere, but to live your life freely without anybody questioning your nationality or trying to label you. You no longer say this or that or do this or that because you are a Jew. Here, whatever you do, you do it because you think so and because you are a human being and no more. Since I was born a Jew, I want to stay a Jew, a proud Jew, a free Jew. There has been too much oppression in my life for me not to be proud that I am free now and I'll educate my children to know what it means to be free and not a minority. Actually, they never knew it because they were born in a free state. When you have to choose between going down again on your knees or standing up to fight, then you prefer to fight. I'm sure that whoever knows enough to appreciate freedom knows also to stand up and fight for it. It makes no difference whether somebody is a Jew, an American, a Frenchman, or an Arab. This is what it means for me to be a Jew.

Mel Heftler *left his hotel in New York, the largest hotel in the world to cater to religious Jewry, to come to Israel and work for the Central Hotel in Jerusalem. He believes all 14 million Jews in the world should go to Israel. That would make Zion complete.*

I believe that every Jew belongs in the State of Israel because of a religious commandment. This is what the Almighty told us to do. So we went ahead and came here. I'm an orthodox Jew, and as an orthodox Jew I believe that God gave us the Bible. In it he gave certain rules and standards of living that he wanted people to follow. Among these things

41

is what's called *mitzvah*, the commandment for every Jew to reside in the Holy Land. Yes, I do think every Jew in the world should come here, without exception. That is Zionism. The truth is that most of the country, including Jerusalem, is uninhabited. There is so much vacant space in this little land. Fourteen million is not a hell of a lot of people. It really wouldn't be that difficult to find room for them all.

Why don't they come? Some people don't come for safety reasons. There's fear of war and physical danger. Some people don't come for financial reasons. It's extremely difficult to make a living. Some people don't come because of language difficulty. They're afraid to start all over again. Some people don't come because others have frightened them with tales of hardship. For example, we moved into a new flat and discovered that there was a two-year waiting list for a telephone. This is foreign to an American. It's a very difficult adjustment to make. And yet it's small. I'm not talking about anything big. Some of the most difficult adjustments are in education. The West, especially, has one of the highest standards of education, particularly for orthodox Jewry, with a well-developed network of parochial schools. This country is in an infant stage in everything, including education. It's extremely difficult to make that adjustment.

I don't really believe that the 1,500,000 Palestinian Arabs object to anybody coming into the land. On the contrary, our coming into the land has only helped everybody who's here. The land is big enough for all Arabs and all Jews, and in the past has had Arabs, Jews, Romans, Turks, and Christians without any particular problems. I happen to think that if everyone was let alone for a little while, then things would just take care of themselves. I'm a great optimist. I think that the common man solves most of his problems by just doing, instead of sitting and discussing the political implications.

There is a great diversity among the Israeli people, but there are a number of things that tie them together. Chief among them is religion and Zionism. Until the most recent generation, most people within the country were religious to some degree or another. Those that weren't religious were not anti-religious. They just didn't accept the faith and that was it.

Another thing that ties them together is the rest of the world. The rest of the world points a finger at them and says, "You are you." And there's the physical tie. People who are in the same place are automatically tied together. Personally I have never experienced anti-Semitism in my life. The term "anti-Semitism" has been overworked and misapplied. My personal experience has never been more than people not getting along together. If they happen to be Jew and Gentile, we call it anti-Semitism.

If they happen to be Gentile and Gentile, we give it another name.

What am I excited about? I really believe that everybody here has an opportunity to contribute. If you do something here you see the results. Any changes that you make, you can touch with your fingers. It's something that really exists. For 2,000 years we've been saying, "Next year in Jerusalem." Next year has come, and that's exciting.

Rachel *is a hotel telephone operator and knows several languages. She was born in Belgium in 1918 and came to Palestine in 1933 at the age of fifteen. As a Zionist, she loves her country, but she is very concerned about the present state of affairs in Israel. She is married to an Arab, a Muslim. The daughters are Jewish, the sons Muslim.*

Yes, they sent me here from Belgium at age fifteen. My mother was a strong Zionist. My father didn't object to sending me. I was a quiet girl, but I was a spoiled girl. I could turn my father on my fingers, and I could have everything that I wanted from him. I went to a school for girls. And then to Jerusalem. I took a small flat, got married, and brought up my children. What did my mother understand Zionism to mean? She understood that we were all to come here. My father was stubborn. He was wealthy and his business was there. He didn't want to come. So he stayed and died there. My mother came after 1948. She came with empty hands.

I have been a Zionist. I love my country. But after so many years of success, our country is going downhill. We are burning ourselves alive. It's not the fault of the government; absolutely not. But the government is too weak concerning the people who are making strikes or concerning the business part of the country. They are not severe enough with all these people. No one should be allowed to make strikes, starting with doctors, nurses, people in the port, and so on. We are in such a bad financial position. Every few days there is a devaluation of the money. The money has no value any more. It's just a piece of paper. People are earning very little. Prices are going higher. The rich don't feel it, the poor feel it. And we have people who are struggling for their daily bread. The people who are striking are those with money. A doctor is making good money; a nurse is making good money. It's just *à la mode*, as we say, to make strikes. Everyone says to me, "Oh, they have it everywhere." Everywhere is not Israel. We are too small a country to take part in strikes.

I have been a pioneer. I'm still a pioneer. I love my country, and I wouldn't leave my country for anything in the world. I've been in the

States. They offered me a wonderful job there, for one year. I refused. I would never decide to stay there, not for anything in the world. This is my country. But it's hard to be enthusiastic. I have experienced the time when the country was built up. It is now being destroyed by our own hands. The prices are too high, the rent is much too high. I think that the only thing that can save us again is a war, but a war started by the Israelis, now and not tomorrow. If they don't do it today, it will be too late. And we don't need this misunderstanding among the members of the parliament. It's a shame for us, all these arguments with one another.

I am not religious. I respect religion. I respect those at the place where I am working. I won't do anything against it. But for myself at home, absolutely not. I am married to a Muslim. We never argue about politics. We never talk about religion. My kids are going their own way. My son considers himself an Arab. My daughter has been in the army. My other daughter married a Jewish boy. Our household is half Arab and half Jewish. My son is going to the mosque. I have nothing against it. He has an Arab wife. I have a wonderful daughter-in-law. I have wonderful grandchildren, four girls. As I said, we never argue politics or religion. And I think that's the best way to keep quiet in the house.

Sure, Arabs and Jews can live together, absolutely. In our house, privately, we have no problems whatsoever, because we try to avoid it. We are just human beings. We would have been just a French family or an American family had we lived abroad, and not a Jew and an Arab like here. This is the most awful thing in Israel –to be identified as a Jew, a Muslim or a Christian. It is a very big mistake for the minister of religion to make such a big fuss about who is Jewish and who is not Jewish. They are all human beings. I was educated in a very religious house. My father always tried to teach us that a human being is a human being. The colour of the skin or religion doesn't make any difference. This idea –I took it from him –I am trying to give to my children.

The Jews always had to fight and to struggle. Now that they are in their own country they are struggling against each other. We have thieves now. We never knew what it was to have a key in the house. Now we feel that we are in prison when at home. It is not safe today. The Zionist dream has gone sour.

Sara Rahabi is an unusual Israeli in several ways. Born in Jerusalem in 1926, she heard much of the Russian and American background of Jews from her parents. Their ideas of Zionism influenced her. Though her mother, Golda Meir, was much involved in politics –eventually she became Prime Minister of Israel –daughter Sara chose to pioneer on an

*agricultural kibbutz, named Revivim, in the Negev. By marrying a Jew
from Yemen she also helped to build bridges between the so-called
Ashkenazi and Sephardic Jews.*

My parents were educated more or less in the United States. Still, I think
that their spiritual background was more the revolutionary movement
from Russia, both in social and in national terms. They were Labour
Zionists in their outlook, especially my mother. I don't think my father
would define himself as a Zionist. He didn't believe in the Zionist
future. He didn't think that this could be a solution to the Jewish
problem. He was a socialist, and although he probably believed that
socialism would solve the Jewish problem throughout the world, he had
little or no hope for a solution in Palestine.

My mother, on the other hand, was very insistent on this point. Being
a Zionist meant not only formal membership in the Zionist movement,
but also the realization of the idea by coming to Israel. She was expelled
from Russia in 1917 and went to America and met with Jewish communities. That was a decisive experience for her when she was a youngster.
So she and my father came to Palestine in 1921 and joined a kibbutz.
They stayed for two or three years. But then my father became sick and
for these reasons and others – he was much more individualistic than my
mother and kibbutz life didn't agree with him – they moved to
Jerusalem, where I was born.

When I was about three years old, the family moved to Tel Aviv. I
went to school there, was educated, and joined the labour and youth
movements. There was no conflict between me and my mother, because
she was altogether identified with the movements. Later, at the age of
seventeen or eighteen, I joined an organization which was a preparation
for kibbutz life. The procedure was more or less like this: the youngsters
from the city were organized in groups and sent out for a year or two to a
kibbutz, where they received training in kibbutz life, in agriculture, and
physical work. Afterwards they founded a new kibbutz or were sent by
the movement to supplement an older kibbutz that needed more people.
That's how I came to Revivim. The group here was very small and
needed to grow. So we were sent here in 1945, I and thirty of my friends.
And I've lived here almost thirty-two years.

My husband and I went to Moscow for a year and a half in 1948-49
when my mother was ambassador to the Soviet Union. We were just
married. It was a very important experience, I think.

You know, we talked about what it means to be Jewish with our
friends just a few weeks ago. It's an odd question for us. An Englishman,
for instance, doesn't ask himself five times a year: In what sense is he
English? Why is he English? Why does he live in England? He knows

45

what being English means. We know what being Jewish means and we don't have to talk about it anymore.

I think the Jewish movement was conscious of the fact that Arabs were living here, and we were perfectly prepared to live in peace with them. Jewish people have no other place we can call our own. The Arabs have all these countries. It's just a question of goodwill on their part, I am sure, and this problem can be solved. It can be solved by their accepting the fact that we have no other homeland. This is our place – and there is enough land for them and for us. I don't think they should be given a separate Palestinian state, because the purpose of such a state would be to threaten our life here, our state. We agreed to the borders of 1947, which were ridiculous. They began the war; that's it.

These are critical times for the State of Israel. People are somewhat shaken in their sense of justice. I think that we are perfectly humane when we say that there is room for both peoples, both nations, to live here and to prosper, without Arabs thinking that we took something away from them. But it's fashionable now to say that we are reactionary, that we are like South Africa. Some young people in this country, with very good intentions, are somewhat influenced by these views.

I'm not like those who say that we shouldn't give back the occupied areas. I think we can compromise. We can give back part of what we took in 1967. But we should give it back because we want peace, not because we are in the wrong. I think that we have a right to this country. We have historical ties to it. But I am realistic. If they want peace, we can compromise.

I think the periods when my mother was happiest, according to her own evidence, was when she was in a kibbutz. Later on she was sorry that she was not living in a kibbutz anymore. It was a sacrifice that she made, I think, for my father. As for her public activities, the most rewarding was the period in Moscow and the meeting with Russian Jews after so many years of isolation. Before the state was formed, she was a member of the Histadrut, and in 1946, I think, there was a moment of severe conflict between the Haganah and the British. Most of the Jewish leadership was arrested, including Moshe Sharett. She was called to take his place in Jerusalem while he was in prison camp. But from then on, more or less, she didn't go back to the Histadrut, but continued working with the Jewish Agency.

In modern terminology, you would say that, if there were hawks and doves in those days, she was among the hawks. She was an activist and follower of Ben-Gurion. I think those were Ben-Gurion's greatest days, when he and others worked for the establishment of the state. He foresaw the war with the Arabs and prepared for it, with arms and the Haganah.

Moshe Bichovsky, *a young agriculturalist in a kibbutz, was born after the State of Israel was founded. He believes that Zionism has given the Jews a home and that they have no other. An exchange of populations, he thinks, would resolve the conflict between Arabs and Jews.*

The Jews have a long history. It began, as we believe, 5,000 years ago. If you read the Bible you know that it is the oldest story in the world, beginning in the time of the fathers Abraham and Isaac and Jacob. We believe the country belongs to our nation. It is written in the Bible. The country stretches from the mountains to the sea, and from the mountains in the north, which means the Lebanon mountains, to the desert, the Sinai.

In the beginning of the Christian era, all the Jews who lived in Israel were dispersed all over the world, most of them in Europe. After that to return to Jerusalem was a dream in the minds of many, many generations. It was called Zionism. At the end of the nineteenth century people started migrating to Israel again to make their dream a fact. I cannot say why it happened in the nineteenth century, and not in the sixteenth century, but this is the way of history. That is what you call Eretz Israel.

For me, I am one Jew from a very big nation of Jews who now live all over the world. I believe that this place must be the place of the Jews in the world. I believe that one day most of them will go to Israel, because history says that our story is not so good in other places. We remember the Inquisition in Spain in the fifteenth century; we remember the Jews destroyed by the Nazis in the Second World War. Anti-Semitism is a part of our history, and to prevent it we must be a nation like all the other nations in the world.

If more Jews migrate here, will more Arabs have to leave? No. We have enough room for many more people. Many, many Jews from the Arab countries came to Israel. At least a million Jews from Egypt, Yemen, Syria, Iraq, and North Africa came to live here. The best resolution would be to make an exchange of populations – the Jews come here, and the Arabs go out. But it must not be by force; it must be by choice. In Europe, there were some nations who did that. I'm thinking of Turkey and Greece. The Greeks in Turkey came to Greece, and the Turks in Greece went to Turkey.

Robert Smallman *has lived in Yamit, the new Sinai settlement, for three years. He came from the US with fifteen other families to found a new way of life. Anti-Semitism and Zionism motivated him.*

My main reason for being here is because I'm a life-long Zionist. I was active in most of the organizations on the west coast prior to coming here. I see Israel as a cultural renaissance for Judaism. What do these fifteen families want? Well, I think they came here to become a part of something new, something dynamic, and to find a way of life where being a Jew has meaning. I don't believe discrimination is a reason for them coming here, although I have personally felt anti-Semitism many times in the United States. In my childhood, I remember once being beaten and tied for being a Jew. I've had many experiences of being called a dirty Jew.

Yamit was established about three years ago. The people here believe that they are helping to develop another new area for Israel. The community includes recent immigrants from the US and the USSR and about 250 Israelis.

What do Russian and American Jews have in common? We're Jews, first. We have a very good relationship regarding operations in the community. In fact, some of the Russians are in business with some of the Americans. Two partners in the market are a Russian family and an American family. I haven't felt any carryover of the East-West conflict. My only complaint is that I can't communicate with them, because my Hebrew is too poor and I don't speak Russian. But otherwise, we feel no conflict. Sometimes I think that they have a certain advantage over us because they are used to a socialist type of system, and we're more oriented towards a capitalist type of system. Israel is a socialist country, and it's difficult at times. I think Israel is heading towards more capitalism, but it's still basically a socialist state.

No, Yamit isn't sitting on what was Egyptian land. That's a fallacy. It's something I feel very strongly about. The Sinai was never Egyptian territory, historically. When Egypt became a state, Sinai was under the British Mandate. At no time was it ever Egyptian. The idea of giving it back is wrong. I think someday we'll have some kind of a compromise with the Palestinians. A Palestinian state on the West Bank should be part of Jordan. This is the only logical thing that I can see.

Jonathan Segal *is a student in Jewish history at Tel Aviv University. He was born in the US in 1952 and came to Israel with his parents in 1961. In Israel he has found his Jewish identity and also the peace movement.*

My parents were long-time Zionists in America. It was quite natural for them to come here. I was nine years old. I was not consulted, but now I understand that it was quite a natural step for them to take. Coming here, I suppose I experienced what any kid who is taken from one environment and put into a totally different one would experience. I was the new kid in the school and in the neighbourhood, and not knowing the language of the other kids, I was a little bit of an outsider for the first couple of years.

One advantage I had was that in America I had gone to a Jewish elementary school the first few years. So I knew some basics of Hebrew, and after two years or so, by sixth grade, I was already one of the crowd. In high school, I was influenced by the Israeli peace movement. At that time there were all kinds of political events which influenced me. There was continual blood-letting on the border, which was the war of attrition with the Egyptians. Every day you could see in the papers pictures of soldiers who had been killed the day before.

In 1972 I joined the army, and there, too, my political thinking developed. I read a lot and exchanged ideas with other people. In 1973, during the war, I was in the army as a medic. I had already identified with the opposition to the government policy before the war. But after that experience I stopped being a nice, liberal do-gooder. I became much angrier, perhaps more radical in my thinking. And when I got out of the army and into the university, I started looking for political activity. I found the Moched movement, which has both a program for peace and is socialist. It's one of the political parties that makes up the Shelli. Shelli is a youth organization composed of at least four diverse groups: Moched, the Black Panthers, and two others. The peace movement that I belong to believes in a peace which the Arabs will recognize, without any ifs, ands, or buts. And Israel has to recognize the Palestinian people and their right to self-determination in a state of their own in the occupied territory.

I think I have a pretty strong commitment to both Judaism and Zionism. I think any conflict of identity which I might have had, say, before the war – I was partly American, and only partly Israeli – is gone. The war strengthened my identification with Judaism and Zionism. I thought to myself, "This country is the only country I would fight for." Certainly, more than America.

What is it in Judaism that I am committed to? The people. To me, the heart of Judaism is the Jewish people. And my concern is for the people's well-being and survival. No, I am not a religious Jew, but I come from a family with respect for tradition. In my house we keep kosher, and we have the ceremonies. There are theological concepts in Judaism that appeal to me particularly. For example, if you take the theological concept of the oneness of God, of the Fatherhood of God over all men, I think that implies brotherhood. To say that all men have the same Father is to say that all men are brothers. And, of course, that is in common with all monotheistic religions. They have a lot in common. And, if you read the Hebrew Prophets, like Isaiah and Amos, you find a lot of the principles of equality and of promises to the have-nots.

49

Yes, I think that Jesus was a Jew. I don't think there is any question about it. Of course, I think that Jesus had a lot of concepts in common with many of the Jewish Prophets. I'm not sure that after Jesus the Christian Church developed as Jesus would have wanted. I don't think that he was the Messiah, the Christ.

Michael Brot *was born in Poland and was taken to Belgium by his parents. In 1940 the Germans came and the Brot family fled first to France and then to the US. Michael was drafted and spent four years overseas with the American army. In his opinion the implementation of Zionism has happened too fast.*

I have been a Zionist all my life so it was natural for me to come here in 1950. First I lived in Jerusalem; after that I came to the kibbutz, and that's my life. Now I'm a farmer.

I would like to have boundaries to keep back the Arabs and separate them from the Jews. I wouldn't like to have so many Arabs in this country that we would be a minority in ten or twenty years. Boundaries would also prevent us from having two kinds of population, one with full rights and one with less rights. That is the way the situation is now. We just can't help it, because we are at war. If we had peace, the boundaries could come to an end. The Arabs could then come and go as they please. I don't hate the Arabs. I like them.

But there are two things that would prevent peace: our religion and the Arab religion. Everybody claims what belongs to them from the Bible. This is something I don't understand. I don't believe in any holy places. Actually, the holiest thing there is in the world is a man's life. I would give you all the holy places of Jerusalem for one man's life. My religion is inside me. The highest thing that can be is a man's life, as far as I know. That includes an Arab life. Maybe Jerusalem is a holy place. Without Jerusalem there wouldn't be a State of Israel.

I believe in Jewish history. I read a lot of the Bible. But I am not religious. If you ask me, what's my religion, I say agriculture: that's my religion. All over the world we always had a lot of merchants. We never had any agriculture. If you look at the history of this country–if this country has done something–it's in agriculture. Agriculturally we are tops all over the world.

What does it mean to be a life-long Zionist? I had my education at home. When we said "next year in Jerusalem" we meant it. We couldn't see any other solution for Jewish people, except to build our own country. It went wrong in one thing. We went too fast. Every idea that comes true in ten or twenty years is a little bit too fast. This idea of Zionism should have taken a little bit longer. I believe that it will take a few generations to straighten things out; it's gone too fast. It is not enough to live in Zion to be a Zionist. We should have a few more people ready to give everything they have for this country. Some just want to use it. A lot of people think that a country is built for them –like Kennedy said in his inaugural speech. He wanted the American people to give more to America and not to take so much. In other words, if you only think of what you can get out of the country, you've got yourself a problem.

I believe that this problem could be solved in two years. I believe the Palestinians are entitled to their country. That's what you would like to hear, and I believe it. But it all depends. If they'll get it in their minds that Israel is going to stay, the problem is easily solved.

I know something about the Palestinians. There are two opinions over there. Among the PLO, some of them say, "We have to destroy all the Jews." But there are others who say, "Wait, we still have time; first of all let's take what peace is coming to us now; we'll wait for a chance of it." Most probably the chances are that they are going to be a lot more than us in population. They have a lot more money. Maybe they'll get more education. Nobody can tell you what's going to happen fifty years from now. But war will be no solution, not for them and not for us.

Settlers

"One of the things which makes the kibbutz very dear to me is that you have to act as an idealist and not only think as an idealist." –Herbert Rokotnitz

The present era of Jewish settlement in Palestine-Israel is now nearly a century old. The first kibbutzim were established near the end of the nineteenth century by immigrants from Russia, who settled in the Jordan valley just below the Sea of Galilee. Every decade since then has known agricultural pioneering in some part of the land. The extent of the settlement was related to the number of immigrants in a given period.

The land area available for settlement has constantly expanded. Early acreages were purchased from Arab landowners or reclaimed from centuries of relative disuse. The establishment of the State of Israel and the flight of the Palestinian refugees opened up new areas which were appropriated. Military conquest in 1948-49 and again in 1967 exposed all of Palestine, plus the Sinai and the Golan Heights, to the settlement plans of the state. Currently, the West Bank is the scene of the most vigorous Jewish settlement activity. Every new Jewish settlement, of course, is of consequence to the Arabs, who feel their land slipping away dunam by dunam and village by village.

The new settlements usually begin with the identification of a security area by the military governor. In the name of Israeli national security, an area is appropriated and cleared of Arab settlers. Gradually, the military settlements become civilian Jewish settlements which are "legal" and authorized by the Israeli state. Some settlement attempts are illegal in the sense that Israel has not approved the initiatives of certain zealous groups.

Dov Shalgi *was born in Germany in 1914. After finishing high school in 1933 he studied Jewish theology with the intention of becoming a rabbi. He came to Palestine in 1940, intending to continue his studies, but changed his mind and joined one of the first kibbutz settlements to be founded, Kfar Giladi.*

This kibbutz was founded in 1916. It was one of the first. The founding members, twenty in number, belonged to a forerunner organization of Israel's Defence Forces. The name of that organization was HaShomer, meaning the Watchmen. The members of this organization had in mind two tasks: to guard Jewish land and the borders of this country, and to create settlements of a particular kind, which later became known as kibbutzim. Kfar Giladi, the Village of Giladi, was one of the first settlements to be founded by the HaShomer organization. Out of this beginning of twenty people in 1916, the kibbutz now has a population of about 700 people, of whom 400 are members. The others are children up to the age of eighteen, and people who are here as temporary residents, mainly young people from all over the world who come here as volunteers.

The kibbutz is based on socialist principles, of which I would like to mention a few. First, all means of production are and remain the property of the community. Second, the kibbutz provides its members with their needs, and the kibbutz members work for the benefit and development of the kibbutz. Each is provided with necessities according to his or her needs, and each contributes in accordance with his or her abilities. Older people cannot work as long and hard as younger people. We have a staggered work day, and older people work fewer hours than young people. We all work and also earn money. The profit motive has not been eliminated. The money we earn goes into the kibbutz fund. We know nothing of salaries, wages, dividends, or shares; in other words, there is no possibility of amassing private riches. The members have no private income of any kind. All members of the kibbutz get an equal amount of cash money per year. This is equal for all members of the kibbutz, regardless of job, position, or seniority.

This is one of 254 kibbutzim with a total population of about 110,000. In other words, the kibbutz population represents 3.5 per cent of Israel's Jewish population. This kibbutz covers about 2,000 acres – 8,000 dunams. But that includes non-arable land – the land in the hills to the west. The land was acquired during the early years from Arabs who were willing to sell the land to our people. There were always Arabs who were willing to sell part of their land for good money. Now, land can only be acquired by the state.

All of these 254 kibbutzim are basically agricultural settlements. In recent years two-thirds of them have added non-agricultural operations, of which we here in Kfar Giladi have three. One is a guest house, with 130 rooms. It caters to Israelis and tourist groups all through the year. We have a stone quarry operation. The original idea was that the kibbutz members should perform all duties and jobs. This dream has not come true. We had to take in vast numbers of hired labour, which is contrary to our principles. Last, but not least – with elderly people in mind, we have recently opened a new plant to produce spectacle frames. By the way, the rule here is once a member of the kibbutz, always a member of the kibbutz, regardless of age or state of physical and mental health. We are provided with all our needs from the very first day of our lives to the very last day of our lives.

This is not a religious kibbutz. Out of the total number of kibbutzim, roughly speaking, 10 per cent are populated by orthodox Jews. In these so-called religious kibbutzim, religion is part and parcel of their way of life. In other words, in the vast majority of these kibbutzim religion remains a matter of private attitude and approach. We have a synagogue but the kibbutz does not organize religious services. This is left to private initiative. People may, of course, go and pray. But officially we have nothing to do with established religion.

For me, to be a Jew means to belong to the Jewish people, to be imbued with the heritage of the Jewish people, especially the cultural heritage. Jewish religion is one expression of Jewish life, but not necessarily the predominant one. We consider the sacred books as part of our cultural heritage, in other words, as literature, and accordingly the Old Testament or the Jewish prayer book are taught and treated as Jewish literature. All kibbutzim consider the small family unit, parents and children, as the basis of Hebrew society. The kibbutz, perhaps contrary to expectation, is not a paradise on earth. Nor are the kibbutz people angels, semi-saints, or holy people. We are very normal people with many problems and difficulties, and with certain achievements. Perhaps the main achievement of the kibbutz way of life is the children's education, which in my humble opinion is superb. I wouldn't say that all our children are perfect human beings, far from it – but generally speaking, our educational system has brought about wonderful results.

The kibbutz is no longer directly involved in the defence of the country. This is the duty of the Israeli army. We put out night guards, not necessarily against the enemy but rather to protect the kibbutz against thieves. As for Jewish-Arab relations, this, in earlier days, was one of the finest examples of helping your neighbour. The very first settlers made it a principle to instruct and to help their Arab neighbours who then lived under terrible conditions in an area with malaria-infested swamps and with no medical care. Our people had access to medical equipment. They provided the Arabs with treatment against malaria.

In the first stage of settling here, the Jews learned from their Arab neighbours how to plough the fields. They had no experience in agriculture. Jews were not allowed to be farmers in Czarist Russia. Later, when Jewish agriculture prospered, the Arabs learned modern techniques of agriculture from their Jewish neighbours. The relations were excellent until 1948, and then, much to our surprise, they all left one morning. Nobody told them to leave.

As far as we know, as far as we feel, there is no hatred on our side, on the Jewish side, towards the Arabs. I do not want to imply that our feelings towards the terrorist groups are very positive ones. They have caused us a lot of trouble and misery with their activities. But if we consider the relations between the Jews and the Arabs, I would say that, on our part at least, there's very little feeling of hatred, of enmity, of animosity.

Herbert Rokotnitz *was born in 1915, grew up in Germany, and came to Palestine in 1934 hoping to realize some of his socialist ideals in the kibbutz. He feels that normalization of Jewish life, which came with the state, militated against idealism and the pioneer spirit.*

Until Hitler came to power, I had never heard about Palestine or ever considered going there. In 1933 my parents had to leave Germany to escape a concentration camp. The only destination open to them was Palestine. They came here as tourists and couldn't take my sister and me. I was seventeen and my sister was thirteen. So we stayed behind for another year until they arranged somehow for legal status.

In the meantime both my sister and I joined the Zionist youth movement in Berlin. This influenced me for the rest of my life. I decided to join a kibbutz and come to Palestine. It was the most decisive year in my life, because the ideas I adopted then have carried me through until today. When I came here, I went to an agricultural school. Since then I have had a lot of different occupations, not all important in our context. I had an interesting experience of some years with the Palestine Police Railway Department under the British Mandate. For three years I guarded the railway line from Constantinople to Cairo – not as it is today, only Haifa-Tel Aviv. I was sent there by the Haganah. In Tel Aviv I was a diamond cutter for four years, and again acted in the Haganah. I came to Kibbutz Givat Hayim in 1948 with my wife and small son. It's quite remarkable to remember how primitive this place was when I joined it compared with the state of affairs now.

The early thirties were a time of very extreme idealism. This was not only in Germany – but in Germany especially there was among most of the people a tendency either to be extreme right or extreme left. I read a lot and was quite a Jewish intellectual in those days. I started out quite moderate but drifted more and more to the left. I always had an antipathy for ideas that wouldn't do anything about the human situation. I mean, if I thought about Communism, I would have liked, when I was fifteen or sixteen, to do something about it. I quite despised the Jewish intellectual societies which dealt in ideas very easily, but didn't do anything about them. When I joined the Zionist youth movement a way was shown to me to realize my ideas. And this came to me like a revelation. I was extremely happy, and I remember that year as one of the best in my life. It was actually Hitler's first year in power and most people have very sorrowful memories of those years. But compared to most other people in my age group, all of us who are here in Palestine have something to show for the years which went by. It's a success story, if you compare our ideas then with what we succeeded to do with them.

But now we have deviated from several basic ideas that made us strong. Once, the main point was that we worked ourselves and now more and more we rely on the work of others. The building trade, for example, depends completely on Arab labour. If you talk about orange-picking it is the same. The whole idea of Zionism and of the building of the State of Israel was that we ourselves would do the work from the bottom to the top of the ladder. But now the bottom is already not Jewish. And this is a big danger. It represents a return to the type of Jewish people we were before we came here. We may all end up being professors and journalists and doctors and so on. The whole idea was that we would normalize the Jewish people to be everything – not only the nationally weak top strata of the economy. Since 1967 there are tendencies in Israel which go in this direction very strongly.

There is one member of my kibbutz, a very well-known Israeli politician, who became very unpopular years ago by saying that we should leave the territories without any negotiating – not for political reasons, not because of what the world or the Arabs would say, but simply in order to avoid being contaminated by Arab neighbours. As long as we keep the territories, he said, we are responsible for their well-being; as long as we are responsible for their well-being we have to provide them with work; as long as we have to provide them with work, we have cheap labour; the moment we start to work with cheap labour, it turns us into something different from what we dreamt to be, and there we are. Now we have tens of thousands of people from over the Green Line who have already been working here for the last ten years. It was very good for their economy, but in my eyes it was very bad for our ideological well-being and for the future of Israel.

I would say, looking back over thirty years, that I have a very bad opinion of the Arabs. We are lucky that we came into the Middle East, and not somewhere else, because a more inefficient group of people than the Arabs would be hard to find. Judging from the hostility that surrounded us from the very first moment I came here, any other group of states or any other nation would have been far more effective in defeating us than the Arabs. So we are lucky that they are our opponents.

I still am very much a Zionist. A socialist also, although I went through many shades of socialism in my life, starting with Stalinist socialism and ending with social democracy today. I definitely think that socialism is the proper way to make life together between people and life together between nations more agreeable and peaceful. Am I still an idealist? I think even more so than when I started. One of the things which makes the kibbutz very dear to me is that you have to act as an idealist and not only think as an idealist. This was one of the biggest advantages of our generation: our slogans had to be worked at. This type of idealism is very much needed today.

After many years I now see that we were right in one thing, namely our claim that having a state doesn't solve everything. Both the Jewish people and the State of Israel are not normal. We are not a normal people and we are not a normal state. We can't expect our newly founded state to solve all our problems. We need a voluntary approach. We need idealism and the special forms, like the kibbutz and the moshav, things which came into being during the pre-state period. Ben-Gurion and his party said, "We have the state, now we have to be normal." This approach of pushing to be normal did a lot of damage to the pioneer spirit which is necessary to achieve our common ends. The moment you say "normal" and "state" you can't expect people to forego careers and money. In a normal state you want to earn as much as possible and raise your standard of living. A normal society, a normal army, a normal educational system, and everything normal does away with the spirit that brought us up to 1948, and in a way it's self-defeating.

Zechria Rahabi's *family arrived in Palestine from Yemen in 1907. Most other Yemenite Jews arrived after the State of Israel was founded. With his wife, Sara Meir, the daughter of Golda, he became a pioneer on a kibbutz in the Negev. He compares life then and now.*

Now we are 600 people counting children and newcomers. We have a huge fruit farm with peaches, pears, and apricots. During the last few years we've started with avocados. In the winter we grow vegetables for export: green peppers, corn, and sugar beets. We also have a citrus orchard near the Gaza Strip. We collect sewage water from the town, and use this water for irrigation.

Maybe the whole Negev will be green some day. I hope so. It depends on the amount of water available and on more Jewish youngsters. It's a nice land here. If you know how to cultivate it you can get wonderful products. With knowledge and water, everything is possible.

Twenty years ago we used to work ten days for one dunam. Now we work one and a half days for one dunam. With machinery, with the knowledge, with the change in the system of irrigation, it's not so hard now.

Before, we didn't have enough tractors, and we had to build trenches with our hands. We used to build trenches with axes and shovels to defend ourselves because of the danger from the Egyptians. We didn't want to leave this place. It was our home. We had twenty-five members altogether in 1948-49. I remember this period as really hard work. But now all this work can be done in one week.

The young people have a pioneering spirit, but in a different way than our way. My son used to say, "Look at the kibbutz, it's a wonderful thing that you built. But look around us also. We're developing new areas, so why should I stay here? You have done everything." Perhaps they are right. They have to pioneer in a different way.

Haim Yshby *has known Arabs all his life and he isn't optimistic about good relationships between Jews and Arabs for at least a generation. His parents were among the Jews of Jaffa expelled by the Turks in 1914 for fear that they might collaborate with the British. Haim was born in a Jewish refugee camp near Alexandria in Egypt and since 1937 has lived in Kibbutz Maoz-Hayim, established in an area always claimed by the Arabs.*

When we started this kibbutz, we lived in tents and barracks. It was a war situation. We had problems with the Arabs from 1936 until 1939. They protested our taking of water from the canal. They put their cows and sheep to graze on our fields, which they said were theirs. Sometimes we fought with sticks and dogs. These conditions continued until the War of Independence in 1948.

When I was a boy, we lived in the same house with Arabs. And my mother was a seamstress to the Arabs. She had a hand machine; not an electric one. She went from one house to the other to make clothes for the Arab women. All my friends were Arabs. The trouble with the Arabs started in 1921 when I was four years old. They knew it, and they said to

58

my mother and father, "Take your children, and go somewhere because tomorrow there will be trouble." And that was exactly how it was. After one or two days there was trouble in that area. Many Jews were killed. The Arabs called the Jews, in slang, the death people. They were sure that one day all the Jews would be killed by the Arabs, and there would be no more Jews here in Palestine. It would be an Arab country.

The future? I don't want to say that I'm a pessimist, but I know the Arabs very well, and I don't believe that our generation will come anywhere near peace. They must recognize that they lost all the wars. And we must talk. I cannot say that all the Arabs wanted the war and the fighting. I'm sure that the real population of these villages wants to live quietly and work in the fields. But there are terrorist elements and they are the dominant factor in this. After the war of 1967 the terrorists came to this area, and we had a terrible three years. Every day they would shoot and bomb all the settlements along the border. For three years our children lived in the shelters, day and night. They slept there until September 1970.

Migaf Kwiat, *born in Israel in 1945, went to Australia with his family in 1952. He returned to Israel in 1965 and is now helping to build a new, government-sponsored settlement called Pearim on the West Bank. He is a mechanical technician.*

In essence the settlement, which is six or seven kilometres east of the former Green Line, has existed for the past three and a half years. Unfortunately, the government wasn't very positive until recently. The idea originated in Ramat Gan with people my age who belong to the Gush Anunim movement. They got together and decided that one of the sure ways of avoiding another war was to settle the West Bank with Jews. We also wanted to avoid the situation we had after the 1956 war, when we had to return certain territories. The world knows what happened after that: two wars, one in 1967 and one in 1973.

What is Gush Anunim? It's the name of a religious movement. In Hebrew, Gush means "great," Anunim means "place." Gush Anunim was formed after the 1967 war. Its main aim was to settle the land of Israel as it is defined in the Bible itself. That's what's been going on since 1967, since Gush Anunim originated. It started as a religious movement, but combined with other movements which had the same cause in mind. Now there are a lot of the older-generation Israelis, from the moshavim and kibbutzim, whose ideas coincide with those of Gush Anunim.

In the western part of the West Bank there are only two settlements at the moment. One is east of Tulkarm, and the other is the place where we are now, Pearim, which is, as I said, six or seven kilometres east of the Green Line, east of Kfar Kassem. We chose this particular place because of its strategic importance. You can see the entire coastal plain. You can see planes landing at Tel Aviv. In fact, it's a very strategic place; you can see that Jordanians built an army outpost here.

We are surrounded on all four sides by about four or five Arab villages. How do the Arabs feel about our settlement here? I personally haven't had any personal contact with them, but I don't think there should be any trouble, because as a result of the Six Day War, when there was freedom of passage between the West Bank and the Green Line, the Arabs have been coming and going. Their standard of living has improved.

At the moment there are fifteen Jewish families here, but there will be more. Our particular group now consists of about 500 families, and the government plans, as time passes, to build housing units for all of the group. Once this is done we'll have a city here.

The next stage will be built on the hill to the south of here – that's where the main city will be built. As time passes there are a number of people who have expressed their willingness to set up industries here at their own expense. We hope to set up industries connected to the computer industry. With time we hope that at least the majority of the families who live here will be employed on the spot.

It will not be a kibbutz. There is nothing communal here. Each housing unit will be self-contained. Anybody who sets up an industry here can employ whom he wishes, and the industry will function on a practical basis.

What are the long-term intentions regarding the Arabs and their land? As far as I know, the government has managed to buy 400 dunams on the site where the eventual city will be built. Other than that, I don't know what the government's attitude is at the moment. We have nothing against the Arabs here; they can continue living as they have lived in the past. As soon as industries are set up, I believe there will be no objection if they want to be included.

To me the meaning of being Jewish is, first and foremost, to live in Israel. My way of life should be according to the laws of the Torah. From the Torah you can learn how to approach daily problems, how to live with these problems, what your attitude should be to your fellow neighbour, what your attitude should be in a family sense, what your attitude should be to work, and how to live according to the Ten Commandments.

I hope Jews and Arabs can live in peace. You can see the tranquillity of the area, and by the help of God, I hope it will continue. I personally have no intention of participating in any further wars. I took part in the last two wars, and I think that every normal human being tries to avoid war. If you speak to the Arab who tills his land in the village closest to us, I think he'd say the same as I would say. Live and let live.

Jews have a historical claim to the land. Jews lived here in biblical times, and now they've returned. The claim of Arabs and Jews is equal. Nobody's telling the Arabs to leave the place. I'm an average Israeli and I believe that the views I've expressed are the views of the majority of the Israelis who live in Israel. The motto, as far as I'm concerned, should be live and let live.

Leah Goralsky, *who came to the new Sinai settlement of Yamit in 1974 from the US, where she was born in 1933, is a Zionist who feels strongly that the Jewish people must have a homeland and that the Palestinians can find theirs in Arab countries.*

Palestine was supposed to be divided into two states, one Arab and one Jewish. The Arab state is now called Jordan. They attacked and were defeated, and they attacked again and again. They obviously don't want us here. It seems to me that every country, every people in the world, has a homeland which they can call their own. There are many uninhabited acres in many of the Muslim lands, including Jordan, where there is room for the Palestinians. Why fight for these few measly rotten kilometres that have nothing but sand and rock. They insist that they want this, and I resent it. The Jewish people have no land that they can call their own, where they can be the majority and make their own decisions, whether for right or for wrong. The Palestinians should have a place too, but it shouldn't have to interfere with the Jewish people who also must have a place. There must be a place, in my opinion, where somebody doesn't say, "You dirty Jew, go back to where you came from." Well, where did I come from? New York. Where did my parents come from? Russia. This is now our base.

The Palestinians need a place too, but there is enough land among the Arabs where they can go. There were hundreds of thousands of Jewish refugees from the Arab countries who were accepted and settled and taken care of in Israel. The Arab refugees who went to Arab countries, on the other hand, were kept as political pawns and not accepted. We know for a fact that the children were taught in the schools to hate. You know, the typical arithmetic problem: "If you had ten Israelis, and you shot five, how many would you have left." We don't have this in Israel. The children are not taught to hate the Arabs.

Malka Aviv *lives on a new settlement called Gitit, a kibbutz which will be a moshav, meaning a co-operative. There are eleven families presently living there, and the average age of the adults is twenty-five. In a year there will be thirty families.*

My husband and I wanted to build a new place with other people who wanted to live together and have a good relationship. We contacted the government and the organization responsible for the settlements, and they offered to let us come to Gitit. It was an army camp before we came here. Our crops are eggplants, watermelons, melons, and a lot of vegetables. In the future we will have peaches, avocados, and grapes. We have about 2,000 dunams, but we don't work all of it yet.

There are Arab villages, but not around here. This place wasn't settled by the Arabs. We don't take land which was used by the Arabs. This was empty area, and we are the first to work this land. If you believe Israel sits on Arab land, then all Israel is on Arab land, even Tel Aviv. But if you believe the Jews came back to their own land, it's a different story.

Afraid? No, not at all. Well, not more than in Jerusalem, or, let's say, in London or Belfast. I suppose it's the same with bombs and kidnapping all around the world. But we are not afraid. It's hard to live in Israel. You have to be very strong, mentally. It takes mental and emotional strength to be an Israeli because of the war, because of the economic problems, and because you don't know what will happen tomorrow.

The story of the Arab and Jewish war began a hundred years ago at the time that the Jews came back. It will take another hundred years to be finished. It's a matter of educating a new generation of Arabs. Maybe in a hundred years something will be changed.

I wouldn't say I am a religious Jew, but I know the tradition, and I love the tradition. I don't believe in God, or anything like that, but I love the tradition, the Israeli tradition. It's the oldest nation. Egypt is not the same Egypt and Rome is not the same Rome. The Jews are the only nation left from biblical times.

Shula Malka *was born in 1957, a decade after her parents came from Morocco. Her grandfather was a rabbi, who wanted to go to Israel as soon as he heard that the "Israeli country" was going to be born. Shula lives on Kibbutz Itav, a new settlement near Jericho. Although she feels the country is Israeli land, she does not mind sharing it with the Palestinian Arabs.*

This kibbutz was started seven years ago by the army. It was an army camp. Six months ago it returned to being a citizens' settlement. Everything here is very small. We have about forty people, all of them single, between the ages of eighteen and twenty-five. I feel that I am doing something for the country, being in a settlement on the border like this or helping people in other settlements. The best thing is working with the youth movement.

We have been here six or seven months. It's a happy life, but it's very difficult, because it's a small group, and you're with the same people all the time. We enjoy it. When you get to know each other, it's like a family. Sometimes, we are in danger here, because the terrorists from Jordan come across the border, and we have to be careful. We have guards watching all night. It is not easy to live in this land. That's why so many Jewish young people leave.

For my grandfather it was very important to live and die, even if only to die, in Israel. He wanted to be buried in Israel. No, I am not religious like my father was. I don't think he is disappointed in that, because I think he would change here. In Morocco everybody was religious because they had to be religious. If they were not Jewish they would get mixed up with the Arabs. But in Israel, because everybody is Jewish, it's not important to stay religious like in Morocco. We're not a religious country. Everybody is not religious. The important thing is to work for the country. For me, being a Jew means being an Israeli. The most important thing for Israelis, whether Jews or non-Jews, is to live for the country, to do something for Israel.

Ib'n Asad *is an Arab born in East Jerusalem in 1945. He is not certain whether he is an Israeli or not because in 1967 when his city was annexed to Israel, his status became unclear. He knows he is a Palestinian and he isn't very enthusiastic about the new settlements on the West Bank which he showed us on a guided tour.*

History is being relived here in the West Bank exactly in the way it occurred before the 1948 war. The Zionist plan of reclaiming the land and establishing Jewish settlements is being done in exactly the same way. Large tracts of land are being taken out of Arab control and are being put into Jewish control, largely with the tacit approval of the Western powers, and all of it inevitably at the expense of the people who live there. What is worse now is that fewer people are exercising more control. For example, in the valley floor directly before us you have a population of about 8,000 people, 1,000 of whom are Israelis and 7,000 of whom are Arabs. Eighty per cent of the land in the valley is controlled by those 1,000 people and the remaining 20 per cent by the native residents.

There are two kinds of settlements that people talk about. There are the so-called legal settlements in the West Bank and those which are illegal. By international law they're all illegal, but I'm using Israeli terms here. The Israelis have established an area, which they wish to retain in the event of any settlement – a so-called security strip between the Jordan River and the West Bank. In order to fortify this boundary they have established numerous settlements.

Some Israelis feel they should be allowed to settle anywhere they wish in the West Bank. So many of these right-wing groups, Gush Anunim for instance, have forced the hand of the government by establishing illegal settlements in largely Arab areas. According to the Israelis a settlement is given the designation of illegal or legal on the basis of whether or not it falls in the government settlement plan.

Compensation for lands taken? Often the question of compensation never arises, because to accept compensation for something is to agree to the legitimacy of the transaction. The Jordanian government has passed a law that makes anyone selling land to the Israelis subject to the death penalty. Accepting compensation is tantamount to selling the land. Therefore, by accepting compensation, you forfeit your citizenship. When your passport expires you have to go to Jordan to get it renewed. As soon as you cross the bridge you'll be put in jail and be subject to execution. So at a practical level there's virtually no incentive to accept compensation.

According to the most generous concession plans in Israel, you would have at the very most two Arab islands, completely surrounded by a Jewish state. The Allon Road links all of these settlements which are at the most westerly edge of the Jordan valley. When they talk about the Allon Plan and the Allon Road in the newspapers, one gets the impression that the settlement line is very near the Jordan River. As you can see, it's some twenty-five kilometres up into the hills. And it's nowhere near the Jordan valley. So it cuts off almost 25 per cent of the West Bank.

The land for a new settlement theoretically comes from three sources: it was Jordanian government land before 1967 – land which is now privately owned or farmed; it was land which belonged to people who have been prevented from returning – the so-called absentee landlords; or it is privately owned village land. Often you have a combination of the three, and in many cases, particularly when it's close to a village, it will all be privately owned land. According to the Geneva Convention, land that was under the government's protection before the occupation comes under the custodianship of the occupying government after the occupation. However, the occupiers may not exploit the land for any purposes such as building, or drilling wells, or anything like that. They are merely the custodians of it. Under the Geneva Convention, the people who fled in war have the right to return, which Israel is refusing to allow. Israel is also illegally taking such land for settlement purposes. If it's land from people who are not allowed to come back, then similar processes are involved. Because those landowners are out of the country, there's no one to inform, and so the land is taken.

I'll give you an example concerning privately owned land. We're coming to the village of Taiyebeh now. One thousand five hundred dunams have been confiscated from Taiyebeh about three months ago. Another 1,500 dunams are just around the corner. The military governor called up the local council of Taiyebeh and asked for a meeting with the council members on such and such a day. The council members heard in advance that the purpose of this meeting was to discuss the closing off of 1,500 dunams of Taiyebeh village land for Israeli security purposes. This obviously meant the establishment of a settlement. So they didn't go to the meeting. The military government acted unilaterally and set up a fence around the areas they wished to confiscate. There was no point in the villagers meeting the military government, because it would only lend legitimacy to a practice over which they had no control or from which there is no recourse. Presumably, if some of the villagers wished to go to the military government and ask for compensation, they would be free to do that, but the Israelis hold all the cards in their hand.

When the occupation began in 1967, Moshe Dayan decreed that a settlement should be built on the bottom end of the Beit Shean valley and that the settlement should have a well to irrigate land in the surrounding area. The Israeli Water Authority brought in hydrological engineers. They told Dayan that the drilling of a deep well would negatively affect the output of six natural springs plus two wells owned by Arabs. Dayan said, "I don't care what it will do to the Arabs. It's a security matter, and I want the well drilled." So they drilled it. It's a very deep well. In 1969 and 1970, the years shortly after the occupation, they pumped from it only minimally. So there was very little effect on the surrounding area.

However, in 1970, when a new Israeli settlement was fully established on land confiscated as necessary for farming, they began to pump very heavily from this well. Immediately the local springs began to decline in value. One of the springs had an output of about eighty cubic metres per hour. From 1970 to 1976, the output dropped from eighty cubic metres to about five cubic metres an hour, a direct result of Israeli pumping. This is admitted by the Water Authority. The water table in the wells owned by the Arab villages fell below the setting of the pumps, and then the village ran out of water. The Water Authority admitted that their system was responsible for the drying up of the well. So they said, "We'll supply you with water from our own well."

The village said it wasn't interested in taking water from the Israelis, because that put them at the mercy of the Israelis who could cut off the water at will. So they said, "We prefer to lower the pump in our well, to where the water table is now, and continue pumping on our own." So the Israelis said, "Well, okay, if you wish to do that, that's fine. As a matter of fact," they said, "we'll pay you for the cost of lowering your pump, 10,000 pounds." The villagers installed the pump, lowered the turbine in the pump to twenty-seven metres from the previous eighteen, and continued pumping. They submitted the receipt to the local kibbutz, which promised to pay them. Two years have passed and they still haven't gotten their 10,000 pounds.

Last summer, when we visited the village, they told us that the water table was falling again about a half a metre a month, and that the pump would run out of water at its present setting of twenty-seven metres. They said, "We're afraid that if we lower our pump again, the water table will fall below that and we'll be out of water entirely, completely at the mercy of the Israelis." The Water Authority has been very blunt and direct. "Look, I'll be frank with you; our plan is to dry up all the wells and springs in this area, and to require all of the Arab villages to connect up to our system, because we can do it more efficiently."

Since the occupation began the Israelis have prohibited all West Bankers from drilling any new wells for agricultural purposes. In the West Bank the Israelis are more concerned about water than anything. To them it is more valuable than gold or oil.

Bialik Belsky *was born in Palestine. He is a hotel manager and a farmer in Matulla, the northernmost Israeli city. He recalls growing up with Arabs.*

I have lived here in Matulla all my life. My parents lived here all their lives. We have more Arab friends than Jewish friends. We played together, we ate together, we slept together, we went to school together, everything together. I learned Arabic in school and I learned Arabic from my friends. We never went to Haifa or Tel Aviv when we were children. We went to Beirut and Damascus. And now that the Good Fence is open, we are seeing all our friends, including Arabs who left this area, after thirty years. (The Good Fence is an opening in the Israel-Lebanese border through which Lebanese workers enter Israel and at which Lebanese wounded receive medical care.)

Yes, they know Hebrew and they know Yiddish. When they were here they talked Yiddish. Today I can go to the border and talk to them. I cannot go beyond the border, but they can come inside here and visit me for a few days. I visit with them in Israel. I take them for a couple of weeks to Jerusalem, Nazareth, and Haifa. Our children have learned to know their children. I am talking about both Lebanese and Palestinians. I know very many Palestinians. They lived in Haifa before 1948. In the war they ran away to Lebanon. I met some of them when they came to Transjordan and some of them in Europe once.

I think that Israel must help to arrange something with the Palestinians outside Israel. This arrangement has to involve the West Bank (with or without Gaza) Jordan, and the other Arab countries. I shall tell you why. The Jews don't have any country, only Israel. That can't be taken from them. So the Israelis must help to provide for the Palestinians in another way.

Thirty, forty years ago life was not like today. Not in Israel, not in any other Arab country. There was a common struggle for a livelihood. I remember when I was a small child and had to leave Matulla, we went to the Arab village, and they gave us a place to sleep, food to eat, and everything.

I have a little paper here dated October 28, 1947, from a time when a Lebanese man borrowed money from an Israeli friend. A year later the war broke out and he couldn't come to Israel to return the money. Now when the Good Fence opened, his son came to Matulla looking for the man who loaned the money. This paper is evidence of his intention to pay back the money. This is how I experienced the Arabs.

Soldiers

"And there will be more war for Israel! I'm sorry to say it, but I think so." –Dan Laner.

Israel is a land of settlers and soldiers. Both agriculture and the military are new experiences and responsibilities for the Jews, but in a few generations they have mastered the double challenge and become expert farmers and fighters. All Jewish Israeli teenagers, both boys and girls, serve in the army for (respectively) three and two years. Thereafter, they are part of Israel's military reserve, whose members renew their training in a yearly return to the camps for a minimum one-month refresher period.

There have been four major wars in Israel's history: the War of Independence 1948-49; the Sinai War in 1956; the June or Six Day War in 1967; and the October or Yom Kippur War of 1973. The minor battles between these wars, including the 1978 strike into southern Lebanon, have virtually joined the wars into a single thirty years' struggle with the Arab states and the Palestinian Arabs. Generals and soldiers, mothers and wives, speak about their unwanted soldiering and their deep desire for a permanent peace.

Ysrael Tal, *a general in the Israeli Defence Forces, has been a soldier since he was a teenager. He reflects mostly on encounters with the Arabs before the state was formed and on the most recent war (1973). A brilliant military strategist, he explains why he is known as a dove in Israel.*

I was born in Safad in 1924 and grew up in Menachain, a kibbutz near Safad. The kibbutz was abandoned by Jewish citizens in 1929 when Arabs carried out raids against Jewish settlements. The Arabs blocked windows and doors. They set houses on fire. My family was almost burned alive. At the last minute we got out. I was five years old, but I remember it. Young Jewish boys managed to infiltrate the mob and rescue us. Jewish refugees concentrated in police stations and in the mountains.

Father worked in southern Palestine at the time. He came back with his revolver and his friends and took us to Beerturnia, sixty kilometres south of Tel Aviv, on the way to Beersheba. This place was destroyed by Arabs in the same raid. Many Jews were killed. We moved to this ruined place and established a new settlement, a moshav or co-operative. At the time it was the most southern Jewish place. We were surrounded by Arab villages and there was no electricity, no roads, no telephone. There was a constant state of struggle with the Arabs. We used to work in the fields with them, but there were no social relations. We were two armed camps. In 1936 there was an Arab revolt once again, and more Jewish settlements were established to the south of us. After that we were not isolated.

I was on guard duty from the age of twelve. We established a signal station, and we, the boys, were signalers with flash-lights. We used kiliographs (mirrors with the light of the sun). We also trained in the use of rifles. At the age of seventeen I joined the British army to fight Germans in the Second World War. At that time the Jewish population co-operated with the British. The Jewish leaders promoted volunteering. Jewish companies, a battalion, and later a brigade were established. We fought in North Africa and Italy. In Europe we were moved from Italy to Belgium and the Netherlands and we were garrisoned with the British army. There we met Jewish refugees and saw concentration camps. We helped gather, organize, and transfer these people to Palestine. At the same time we collected weapons to transfer to Palestine.

I went back to my village and became active with the Jewish underground. At that time the struggle between the Jewish population and the British heated up. Being already a professional soldier with experience, I established courses for commanders in the Haganah. Then came the War of Independence. I was a commander with the Haganah in the new Israeli army, and after that I became a career officer and served as a regular army man. I retired from active service in 1974 and am now serving as assistant minister for defence.

Since I was five years old, I grew up with struggle and engagements. The only war in which I wasn't in the field was the last one. I was with the command staff as deputy-chief of general staff, but it was the most difficult war for me. This was the first war in which my son was a soldier. He was fighting with forward tank units in Sinai and was wounded. He was tank company commander, and as such he took part in the most difficult battles. I knew he was in the southern front where his battalion was.

After the war and the ceasefire there was a war of attrition. There were many disputes among the generals. I assumed command of the southern front in order to impose discipline and to control the situation until the first separation of forces agreement (withdrawal from the western bank of the Suez). The dispute is known in Israeli literature as "the campaign of the generals." It was over how the war was conducted. When I assumed command, these disputes came to an end.

There was also a political struggle in Israel. One group wanted to continue the war and others wanted to discontinue. I opposed continuation. As southern commander, I opposed the instructions of Dayan and carried out my own policy in order to prevent a new war. This was quite a famous dispute. It was public knowledge. Dayan and I became opponents. I carried out my own policy, relying on the loyalty of the troops in the field. All Israeli society was divided after the war, and this was one expression of the division. I managed to prevent a new war. Dayan probably didn't want a war himself, but in my opinion his methods worked against a new agreement and would have created a war. I met the Egyptians, and we had a long discussion about political prospects for the future. I felt that an agreement was really the intention of the Egyptians as well as of the Israelis.

Militarily we won the war. I speak as a professional on the basis of the art of war. It may, in fact, be one of the great military victories. Keep in mind that we were taken by complete surprise. It was our stupidity. We made one of the greatest mistakes. There was both strategical and tactical surprise. We were taken by surprise because our political and military analyses of the situation were completely wrong. On the other hand, Arab strategy and preparation (political, economic, social, military) was very good indeed. So we were taken by complete surprise. And the whole nation was launched into war without any psychological preparation. The majority of our units were not mobilized. They were in the synagogues, or in their homes. On the front lines only small garrisons were deployed. On the Suez Canal there were only 400 soldiers spread over 200 kilometres. There were only eleven artillery batteries, and we had three tank brigades in Sinai far away from the Canal. The Egyptians attacked with five divisions simultaneously. Their concentrated artillery fire could be compared to the biggest battles of the Second World War. They opened this surprise attack by bombing our forward position with 200 bombers. In Golan the situation was similar. It was worse there because there was no obstacle like the Suez.

To be taken by surprise, to be attacked by overwhelming manpower and the most sophisticated modern equipment (tanks, planes, missiles), to manage to survive, and to stop this massive offensive by such a small force was a great triumph. We managed to mobilize the whole nation and to organize a whole army in thirty-six hours, including civilian units. In a matter of days we won all naval battles, destroyed all naval missile boats that took part, shot down hundreds of enemy planes, destroyed most of their armour, and then closed the canal and advanced towards Cairo. We were stopped in this advance only because of the pressure of the big powers. All this is considered by me to be one of the greatest military victories of all time. We completely destroyed about 2,000 enemy tanks. In my view we won in the battlefield. All this was achieved by the courage and motivation of our young generation and by our qualitative superiority in all military respects.

Politically we lost, because the Arabs achieved their main goals of the war. Goals are always political goals. And they managed to gain the support of the big powers, thus promoting the Arab cause, and creating a dynamic political press in the Middle East. Some of my colleagues don't agree, because they don't make distinctions between military and political wars. War is an instrument of politics. The Arabs won everything. We didn't gain a thing.

Everything has happened since then. We were forced into interim agreements. We had to give up part of Sinai. The powers wanted to force us to Geneva without guarantees that the Arabs were going to bring an end to the conflict. The Arabs are now enjoying the support of the powers because of oil. They have the support of the USSR. Our international situation has become worse.

Will there be another war? Basically it depends on the Arabs. It also depends on the big powers and to some extent on Israel. The majority of countries want to please the Arabs. The Arabs, encouraged by the international community, would like to regain most territories without recognizing Israel and without making real peace with Israel. We, the Israelis, suspect the Arabs. While the majority of our nation is ready to recognize Arab rights, they are not ready to recognize ours. Moreover, from time to time they even make declarations that they won't recognize us, won't agree to our national existence, and won't establish real peace. I believe that if political progress doesn't take place there will be another war.

I refer to Arabs as a collectivity, but once agreements are made one can't refer to Arabs in general; there are differences. Our conflict with Egypt and Syria is different from our conflict with the Palestinians and the Jordanians.

Syria and Egypt have territorial claims. These should be discussed, and we should compromise. As for the Palestinians – it is up to them to define themselves. They have a right to self-determination and once they recognize our rights we will recognize theirs. It is up to them to decide whether they want to be a separate nation or attached to Jordan. The real issue at stake is where the borders of Israel should be. Across the borders it is for them to determine what they want. The only concern to me is where the borders should be.

Where? I can tell you in principle but not in geographical terms. When they are ready for peace, the border should be between the nations and the cultures. Israel should remain a democratic, Zionist, Jewish state. The only reason that the Jews established a state was so that they could become a nation, living in freedom, security, and self-determination, free of discrimination and insult. A Jewish state is historically necessary for survival. The question is Jewish liberty. This is the best way to live in peace with mutual respect. If nations mix then conflict is eternal. National security is also important. Compromise should take into consideration the necessity of relatively secure borders. In my opinion though, the most dominant factor is the separation of the two communities – even at the expense of security considerations. Of course, I also take into consideration the potential rights and requirements of the Palestinians. As matters stand, I can't get a national consensus now. The blame for this lies with the Arabs. They don't encourage favourable popular opinion with their extreme statements about throwing Jews into the sea and destroying the Zionist entity. The Arabs are providing very good reasons for continuing suspicion. The only way at this stage of events to expect a rational public opinion is to test a positive Arab proposal – a proposal which recognizes the State of Israel and which has international support. Only with such an event can we expect an Israeli consensus on this matter. Maybe then the rational position will be adopted by the majority of our nation.

Does this make me a dove in Israel? Yes, but I don't recognize the distinctions. I believe in political flexibility and rigid behaviour, otherwise we lose credibility. Those with rigid political positions are considered hawks even if they are soft in behaviour. I do not consider them hawks. On the other hand, those who are flexible are considered doves. According to common distinctions I am a dove. I am a dove as far as political flexibility is concerned. I am a hawk in insisting on clear goals. It is better to be flexible, tolerant, and liberal with political goals and opinions and very rigid in striving to achieve them. And one must persevere.

What does it mean for me to be Jewish? In the first place, I was born Jewish. From the negative point of view, other people call me a Jew and treat me like one. I have no choice. Positively, I am proud to be one. I consider myself to be a member of a great and humanitarian nation with a heritage of universal values and justice. In these respects I belong to a nation which is superior to a lot of other nations. Even when we are fighting for our very existence we do not feel hatred towards our enemies. We treat them like human beings. Others, however, behave in the most cruel way not only with their enemies but also with each other. We have executed only one person, Adolf Eichman. We have not executed the greatest murderers. Look what happens with our neighbours. They kill women and children deliberately. They mutilate and dismember. Execution is a common practice in all those countries. In our most difficult times we do not cease to believe in the most humanitarian way.

We belong to a group of liberal and humanitarian nations. One should be proud to belong to such a category of nations. Also I am proud to belong to a nation that follows the tradition and example of ancient times when our ancestors used to fight for their value and their liberty. I am proud to continue the same tradition, to fight against the many and to survive. Military strength, an efficient war machine, and national motivation are our security. I regard territory as less important. Most of our people believe that everything depends on security.

Ariel Sharon, *a general and a cabinet minister, was born in Palestine on a moshav in 1928. His parents came from Russia in 1920. He joined the Jewish underground at the age of seventeen and worked his way through the ranks of the Israeli army to become a general in 1965. He fought in all of Israel's wars and was wounded several times. In 1973 he was one of the first to cross the Suez Canal.*

We lived with Arabs all our life. As a child I never thought for a minute that we would live without Arabs. For us it's a matter of existence. Arab terrorism did not start in the Six Day War in 1967. Between 1949 and 1957 Israel suffered. Thirteen hundred people were killed by Arab terrorists who came across the borders of the Gaza Strip and the West Bank. In one year, 1953, Arab terrorists – we then used the term "infiltrators" – crossed our border in order to mine or destroy or kill more than 3,000 times. I was the commander of the Israeli commando troops and the Israeli paratroopers. I commanded most, if not all, of the Israeli retaliation raids. This period between 1953 and 1957 was called the time of retaliation. It was impossible for us to succeed with defensive means, because the border was 100 kilometres long, and it was mountainous terrain. We failed because of the terrain, because of the length of the border, and because of the size of the Israeli standing army.

I have many contacts with Palestinians. I don't have any hatred whatsoever. On the contrary, if I have anything against the Arabs it's only their lack of quality. I don't like the way they kill. They are cruel. They are terrible. I have a lot of sympathy towards the Palestinians. When I was still in the army and the advisor to the Prime Minister for a year, I advocated talking to the Palestinians. Even now I advocate talking to the Palestinians. The problem is whether it will be possible to live and exist here with them. I can tell it will be impossible.

To us this is our homeland. This country speaks Hebrew. The place names are Hebrew. They are all biblical names. This is the Jewish homeland. Even though most of the Jews lived in the diaspora and went into exile, there has been a non-stop Jewish existence here for 4,000 years. Jews have been living here all the time.

The Arab Palestinians have been living here for hundreds of years. That's also a fact. The only stranger in this part of the world is King Hussein of Jordan. I believe a realistic solution should start with the state where the majority of the population are Palestinians. That is Jordan. Jordan is a Palestinian state. No doubt our two countries have to solve many things together and these things should be discussed now: the problem of refugees, the problem of political freedom, the problem of open bridges, the economic system, a free port, mutual development of the Dead Sea sources and so on. It can start like that and it can end up in federation.

Here in the Middle East, I think there are only two groups of people whose existence is really threatened. If the Arabs lose the war, the result will be a certain number of casualties, a certain loss of property, and a certain loss of arms. If Israel loses the war, the result is complete extermination. We know about extermination. As Jews we understand the term better than anyone. No one has to teach us the meaning of extermination. We are not going to live in a country where Arab terrorists will hit us in the heart of the country, where they can come and go back in the same night. We will not live in a country where all the centres of population are within the range of artillery and where all the air fields are within the range of surface missiles. We are not going to commit suicide.

"Shalom" is a word we use more than any other word in our language. Shalom means peace. Yet you have to know one thing. Existence here is more important than any contractual peace. What need do we have for a contractual peace if we cannot exist?

Dan Laner *lives in Kibbutz Neoth Mordecai in the Hula Valley just below the Golan Heights. He was born in Austria in 1922 and arrived in Palestine, illegally, in 1940. Except for his parents, who came after him, no other relatives escaped from the Nazis. Laner is presently a general in reserve and works on the kibbutz. A soldier most of his adult life, he hates war, but he sees more of it ahead.*

I was born into a middle-class Jewish family in Austria. I was already a zealous Zionist at the age of sixteen. After Hitler came everything changed, so I joined a transport to Israel, then called Palestine. I arrived in 1940; I joined the kibbutz. Then I volunteered to do something to help in the Second World War. I joined the Palmach. The British were looking for German-speaking people, mostly youngsters like me who left Germany or Austria very late, to work behind the German lines in Europe. I was parachuted into northern Italy in 1943 with radio equipment and three missions – two British missions, meaning sabotage and information, and one Jewish mission, meaning to look for our own people. I joined the Yugoslav partisans and spent over a year near the German lines at the border between Italy, Austria, and Yugoslavia.

Returning to Palestine I rejoined the Palmach. I was made second commander of a battalion which fought the British Mandate government. Then came the War of Independence, in which I fought as a battalion commander and later on as a brigade commander. After the war, I stayed in the army another year, and then I rejoined my kibbutz and my family. As a reserve officer I was put in command of a reserve brigade. In 1963 I rejoined the army and was made second in authority in the northern command. In 1967 I commanded the improvised arms division which went up the Golan Heights. After that war I again stayed on, and in 1969 was made commander of the armoured division which held the Suez Canal in the war of attrition. I stayed there up to October 1972. Then I left the army, because I was fifty years old. Israel likes young generals. I rejoined the kibbutz. But I was asked by the late chief of staff to command an armoured division in reserve. I accepted and every month spent a couple of days in my headquarters.

In 1973 I commanded the armoured tank division, which fought the whole war on the Golan Heights. We reached deep into Syria. I had to stay on for seven months; then the forces were immobilized, and I once more joined the kibbutz, and now I work in the fields. I have a very lovely wife, three children – all of whom have served in the war. My boy was wounded in the last war, but now he is all right.

The most difficult time was the war of attrition. During the War of Independence I think I was too young to recognize the danger and the complications which went on. Now when I think back, I realize we were never in a darker spot. But then I didn't feel it – I mean, we were cocksure. The war of attrition was a war that didn't suit us. It was a blind war. I had a son under my command. That was a little bit of a headache. It was, I think, the worst part.

My most rewarding time? Well, at my age everything rewarding is somehow connected with the children and the grandchildren. The years I spent at home with our family were surely the most rewarding times. I think the most exciting time was the 1973 war; it was really exciting. We certainly did not lose the 1973 war; there's no question about it. My division met the Syrians about four miles from the Kinnaret Sea, and after three days we were at the old border, and in another three days we were twenty-eight miles from Damascus. So you can't say we lost it.

I hate war. War is horrible. Horrible! It's the greatest insult to human intelligence. I don't think that in Israel you'll find a general who would say that war is glorious. There is an absurdity in the military profession. A carpenter has to love making tables, if he is a good carpenter. In the army you hate war and still it's your profession. We really hate it! There's no glory in it! There may be some moments when there's some exultation, I mean, when you succeed in something. But when you see all the people wounded, killed, destroyed, you hate it. But mankind has war always. There hasn't been a time in history when there was no war going on. And there will be more war for Israel! I'm sorry to say it, but I think so.

Israel and the Arabs have no base for believing each other. There is no common ground for us to talk on, so far. I think it will take another generation, something like that. Nobody believes anybody. They are afraid of us; we are afraid of them. Even when both sides speak the truth they don't believe each other. I'm not talking about interim agreements, or ceasefires. Those we have already. But a real peace, which will allow us to reduce the army by 50 per cent, is, I think, very far away. Sorry to say.

I think that the answer to the Palestinian refugee problem is to make some sort of arrangement with an Arab state, like Jordan, to absorb those people who are Arabs. Their language is Arabic, their religion is Islam, so why can't they live, for instance, in Jordan, or somewhere else in the Arab world? This is the only realistic solution. If we are talking about the West Bank, that won't work. Even if they have their own sovereign state in the West Bank, there will be the hotheads who will go on fighting. We will have border incidents. All those very sincere but very funny ideas of demilitarized zones and warning systems just won't work. An independent Palestinian state on the West Bank means that we will have another war in two years or three years. They'll start shooting and bombing our settlements. There are some people who say, "Well, we have now had war for thirty years. We've tried this way and that way, and it didn't work. Now let's try to reach an agreement even if we give back every square inch that we captured in 1967." But we can't afford to make that experiment because the price might be too high.

Being Jewish for me means belonging to a nation which, in my opinion, is a little bit special – not very special, but a little bit special – with a long, very long, history. Very many of the Jewish people in the countries of Europe tried to disappear as a nation, but it didn't work; it just didn't work. I have a very deep feeling towards the Bible as a historical masterpiece and a philosophical masterpiece, and I am proud that my people wrote quite a big part of it. So the feeling of being Jewish, even though I am absolutely not religious, is very deep. I don't think that it can be uprooted.

The strength of Jewish women is absolute.... In the last war our son was in the Sinai. On the third day of the war he was badly wounded. My wife didn't even try to tell me about it. She could have contacted me by radio, but she thought I had enough trouble. Only after about ten days, when it was a little bit quieter, she contacted me to tell me. The first thing that she told me was that "everything is all right." I couldn't even visit my son. But she arranged a big surprise. The war had ended, but we were still busy with the Syrians. One day my second in command asked me, "What would you like to eat?" And I said, "I'd love a cake with lots of cream." He laughed and he went away. But three hours later, he contacted me by radio and said, "Where are you? You never tell anybody on radio where you are." So I said, "Well, you know me... you'll find my tank." So he said, "Okay, I've got a big surprise for you." So I thought, well, that guy's coming out with the cake and cream. An hour or so later, an armoured car came crawling up to my position. And inside was my second in command with my son. That was a big surprise. My wife had sent my son to me. That was far better than cake with cream.

Tirza Laner *is the wife of a general. Born in Austria she came to Palestine early in the 1940's. She reflects on what it means to be a wife and mother in a state where all the men are soldiers.*

What does it feel like to be the wife and mother of soldiers? Nobody asks themselves that. It is natural for us to do all that we can do, each in our place. There are more important things than family life in our house. That's all. What happened when bad news came to the kibbutz? Nothing happened. Nothing happened to me. I am not the only woman; for all the women in the land, it is the same. We have to wait and hope. Sometimes there are deaths, but nothing happens; I can't explain it to you. It's life. It's sad, but so is life.

Each time there was a war I thought it was the worst and that I couldn't stand it. But we stood it. When it was over, we hoped it would be the last one; that's all. Always I hoped it was the last one. But we don't know. I never knew that it wasn't the last war, so I hoped, that's all. You have to have a sense of humour; otherwise it doesn't work. You can't live here without it.

Sam Hirschmann, *whose family arrived from South Africa in 1952, is a student, about to graduate from secondary school and enter the army – reluctantly so.*

I'm not looking forward to going into the army. I think it's a waste of time. Of course, I understand that Israel has problems, but I would prefer not to go into the army. I suppose that Israel is very important for the Jewish nation but I believe that one should be able to live wherever one wants. If I can manage better somewhere else, I won't have any bad feelings about going to live there. But meanwhile, I feel best in Israel.

One of the problems is that we're not wanted here. I think that the Arabs have the right to live exactly as we do, but every country must have its land and be a nation. There's been a Jewish community in Palestine through all the last 2,000 years. And when the Jews started to come back in 1890 they bought land legally. The hostility against the Jews came not from the Arab people but from their leaders. It started for political reasons. Arab leaders lived in a society where the leader had almost all the power; he could do anything he wanted. The Jews brought in socialism and communism, and the Arab leaders didn't want them to come in. They provoked the poor people to fight the Jews, and that's how it started. After Israel became a state in 1948, the Arab nations around us were very happy to use the Palestinians as a weapon against the Jews.

Would I give the Palestinians a state now? Well, as the situation has developed they are a nation now. They're not Jordan. They need a state. But the problem is where to put that state. Perhaps on the West Bank under the control of Jordan, at least at the beginning, and also under the control of Israel.

Dr. Jossy *was born in South Africa in 1938 and came to Israel in 1963. He is a medical doctor and a pilot. As such he serves in the Israeli air force. Dr. Jossy assisted in the rescue of airline hostages at Entebbe in Uganda.*

I have had a number of opportunities to participate in operational medical activity in the field. One particular incident was the 1970 raid on an island in the Red Sea, which served as a commando base for saboteurs and infiltrators in the Sinai. I was part of the medical force that came to evacuate the wounded. We arrived next to a lighthouse where there had been rather a fierce skirmish and shelling was still going on. We came to pick up a young Israeli officer who was severely wounded. The captain wanted to take off immediately because our helicopters are always sitting ducks as targets.

However, one of our medics came running out of the lighthouse, exclaiming, "Just wait; we've got a wounded Egyptian here, as well." The captain had to make a difficult decision as to whether he should wait and, in so doing, endanger the whole crew, including the medical men and the dying officer we had come to save – or whether he should leave immediately and forget the Egyptian. He waited to take this Egyptian soldier, who, it later turned out, was the man holding that fort, and in fact the one who had wounded our officer. We evacuated the two of them on the same aircraft. The Israeli officer did not survive the flight to our base camp. This brought home to me, and I think to many others involved in the particular incident, the fact that medical people transcend all boundaries. Our rescue missions are basically humanitarian.

The Entebbe rescue? The aeromedical evacuation unit stands prepared for any such eventuality twenty-four hours a day, so readiness wasn't a problem for us. The moment we knew that we had to go on this operation, we got together the equipment needed, including resuscitation equipment for children, and flew off. I was in charge of the air force medical team, whose task it was to treat any wounded on the long flight back. On the way there – it was a long flight – we were not full of fear, but full of trepidation. Would we in fact be able to cope with the number of injured? Would the people be in panic and might we have to offer mental first aid?

While waiting in the aircraft for the injured to arrive, we felt like sitting ducks as one often does on these sorts of missions. But soon afterwards the first wave of hostages arrived. At first they appeared to be in a panic, but they settled down very quickly. The problem then became giving intensive first aid to the wounded while working in a very confined space and at the same time keeping the rest of the passengers away. But this is one of the specialties of the aeromedical evacuation unit; we normally do work in confined spaces. Officer Yoni, leader of the rescue and the only fatality, was brought to us literally in death throes. There was nothing we could do for him apart from covering his body in a quiet corner in order to preserve his dignity and prevent further suffering among the hostages who were with us. As you know, it's often the dilemma of a physician to choose between someone who is hopelessly injured and someone who is lightly wounded but thinks that he is severely wounded. This was a problem, but in fact we had sufficient medical teams to cope with any emergency.

Why has the euphoria of the Entebbe rescue not lasted? I think the people of Israel periodically need some sort of boost–almost like an immunizing phenomenon–but between them the country tends to slump into a sort of inertia. We just carry on and everyone exists; some lead a richer and some a poorer existence. At the time of a historic mission like this, your morale goes up; but it doesn't stay up for a long time; it goes back to some sort of base line. I would liken it perhaps to the difference between the qualities of steel and iron. If you try to magnetize steel, it's very difficult, but once it's magnetized it holds. Iron, on the other hand, is very easy to magnetize, but it loses its magnetization quickly. We can compare the people of Israel to the bar which becomes quickly electrified, and very soon afterwards drops back to normal. Maybe we've had too many immunizations. Maybe.

My hope for the future is that some of the historical experiences of the Jewish people will rub off onto the people of the State of Israel and that the next thirty years will see a more mature approach to every different walk of life. I personally am optimistic. I'm optimistic for myself, for my family, for my children, for my neighbours, and when I say "neighbours" I include non-Jewish neighbours in Israel; in other words the Arab, the Druse, and the Christian minorities, and the neighbouring states. I think that the experience of the Good Fence in the north and the open bridges policy on the West Bank has paid off. I think there's hope for the future.

Yaffa Yarkoni *is the most famous singer in Israel. Born in Palestine in 1925 her family arrived from Russia in the 1880's. She sang for the soldiers in all of Israel's wars and is now fighting the image of a war singer because peace is her highest priority.*

My story is the story of my people. I was born here and grew up with Arabs. When I was eight years old we lived not far from Tel Aviv. We were all happy little children and all our neighbours were Arabs. I don't remember my mother going to shop, because Muhammed came every day at eight o'clock with a donkey and a cart full of fruit and vegetables. He gave us what we needed when mother wasn't home without even getting paid. He got paid in due course, and this used to be a part of our life. He delivered produce to us for many years. I don't remember even once thinking of Arabs as our enemies.

I remember myself as a child. You know, I used to write every day in my diary. One day I wrote, "I'm afraid that my dream is going to break, and no more Muhammed is coming to bring the vegetables, and every-

Shifra Fisher remembers a trip to Europe where she found the people "wonderfully silent" and free of the tensions that are common in Israel.

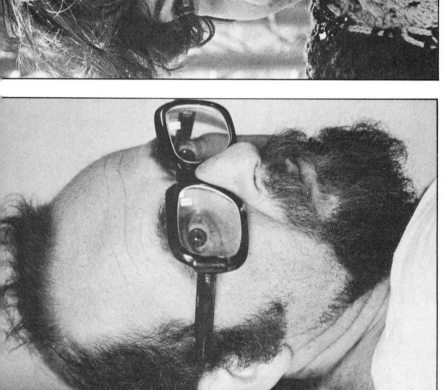

Paul Grossbein moved to Israel from Markham, Ontario, because he felt that in Israel he would not have to worry about his Jewishness.

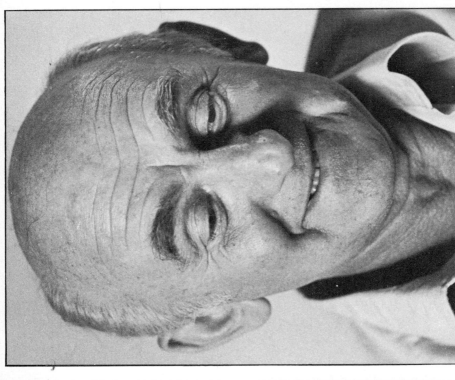

To Sinai Okrent, a Polish survivor of the Holocaust, Zionism means freedom from oppression, freedom from having to live as part of a minority group.

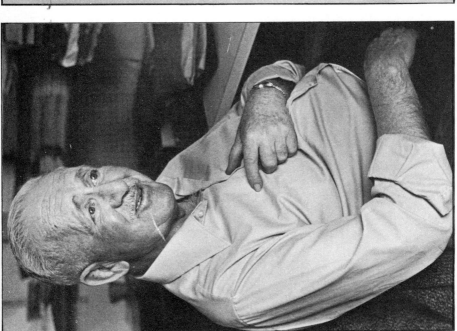

Lionel Pyetan, a native of South Africa, says that Israel has adopted a "sort of voluntary apartheid" separating the Arabs and the Jews.

Josef Gorny, a native of Poland, escaped the Nazi Holocaust because the Russians had banished him to Siberia.

The East Jerusalem campus of Hebrew University.

Professor Yeshria Leibowitz feels that, though desirable, Zionism left many problems unsolved.

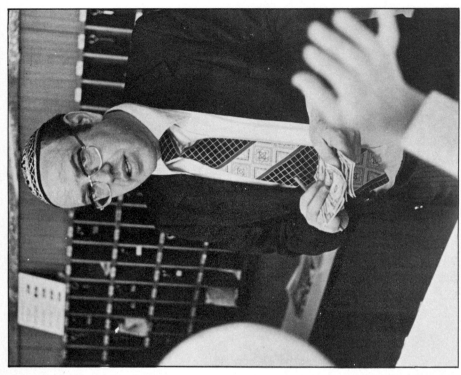

Every Jew should move to Israel, says Mel Heftler, an orthodox Jew and manager of Jerusalem's Central Hotel.

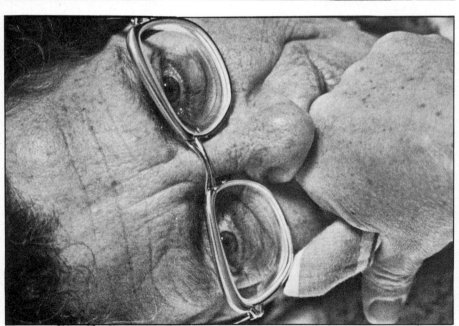

Sara Rahabi, daughter of Golda Meir, says goodwill from the Arabs would solve Israel's main problems.

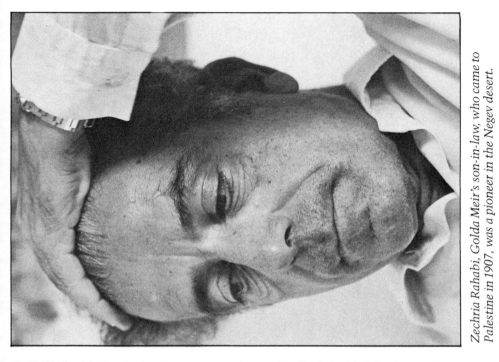

Zechria Rahabi, Golda Meir's son-in-law, who came to Palestine in 1907, was a pioneer in the Negev desert.

Dov Shalgi sits among museum artifacts at Kfar Giladi, one of the first kibbutzim in Palestine.

Malka Aviv is a farmer at Gitit, one of the controversial Israeli settlements on the West Bank of the Jordan.

Ronit Schneidman at Pearim, a West Bank army outpost.

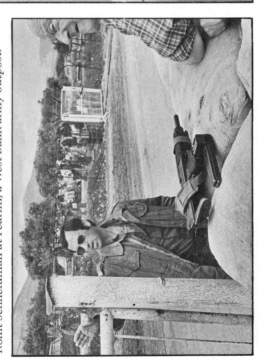

Travel agent Michael DeVries spends his military service giving tours of the Good Fence at the Lebanese border.

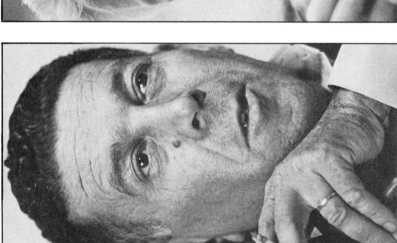

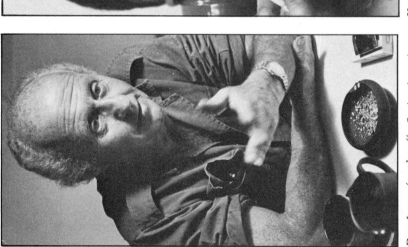

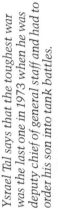

Ariel Sharon, another war hero and former general, is now minister of agriculture in the Begin government, a portfolio with responsibility for settlements in occupied territories.

Ysrael Tal says that the toughest war was the last one in 1973 when he was deputy chief of general staff and had to order his son into tank battles.

Dan Laner fought off a Syrian invasion in 1973 but says, "I don't think that you'll find a general in Israel who would say that war is glorious."

Israeli soldiers saunter through a city square near the location of the famous Wailing Wall.

thing is going to change." Little by little, when I started to get involved in everything and we had the new immigration, I couldn't understand how I used to think another way. But still, all the time I felt sorry about it. We started to have a border and then you could no longer see these people who used to come to us all the time. I couldn't understand that the day would come when the hate would increase so much between these people.

When the Second World War started, I was married to a boy who joined the Jewish brigade to fight the Nazis in Italy. Four days after my wedding, he was killed. I was eighteen at that time. Right after this, we started our war in Israel – the War of Independence – and the opera where I was singing stopped because everybody joined the army. I decided to join the army myself. I was a soldier for two years. We lost many, many boys – my friends. I remember each of them, because we were like one family. Really, everybody knew everybody. My mother opened a coffee house. They used to come and she gave them food. I remember that she went bankrupt. She said, "What can I do? They come every night, and I know where they are going, and I must feed them." We had a piano, and they said, "Why don't you play something?" And I used to sit, play the piano, and sing a little bit. And that's how they discovered that through the microphone my voice was very pleasant. Again and again they asked: "Where is Yaffa? We want Yaffa to sing." And little by little, when I came back to the army, the soldiers asked me to sing.

For two years in the army I was a wireless operator. I had a walkie-talkie on my back. I started to sing when we had the order from the UN to stop the war for twenty-four hours. And we had nothing to do. I had an accordion and so I played and sang. They used to call me by the wire, "Why don't you come and sing for us." I said, "I cannot, because I am doing my job." So I sang for them through the wire. My future husband was at that time a hero in the Haganah. He was one of the biggest fighters. He joined the British army, and as a British soldier he went to Egypt and he brought back arms to the Haganah. They caught him, and they put him in jail for two years. I met him when he was one of the commanders in the Haganah. I was in one brigade; he was in another brigade. We met together during the war, and he said, "I've been through a lot. I've been wounded three times. I would like before the war finishes to get married and have a child." You know, soldiers in Israel, when they talk to you, they never say to you, "I love you," or "I want to marry you," or "I like you." They put it always in a very unusual way. I think that it is the character of the Israeli boys. They don't know how to show their feelings. And sometimes I feel sorry about this, because I myself am very sentimental. But I said, "All right." So we got married in uniform, and after a year I had my child. Soon after I made a record and they discovered me as a singer. I made very many albums. I sang more than I did in opera. And everything I made sold out. Every song was a hit.

Then came another war. They started to bring me back to sing for them, but not as a soldier now, because I already had my child. In the Six Day War I came back and sang for them again. And then in this last war I came back and I sang for them again.

The newspaper called me the "singer of the war," which I hate. I'm fighting against this name. I'm fighting against it because I don't like war. I believe that we must think of living together with the Arabs because there is no other choice. We cannot be dependent on the Americans or on the Russians. We must live in peace and get strong inside. Many people think I am for fighting because of my songs, but it isn't so. This last war I saw some young boys going to war. I stood on the tank and sang for them and said, "I'm waiting for you here; you come back." They used to go with my picture in their pocket. I saw many of them coming back wounded, unable to talk, but they would take the pictures out and show them to me. They had them in their pockets.

There are parties in our country who are looking for war. They must know that Israel is not going to exist if there is another war. I believe these people don't know what they are talking about. They didn't even see the war. They don't know what it is. I know, and when I meet them, I say, "Listen, before you say your ideas, before you talk, go there and see how it is; go as close as you can to the borders; go and see how they live, what they do, how it is; go and listen to the Arabs on the other side." I saw them all. I know. It's not true that they are for war. Today I am walking with a very sad feeling inside, because I believe that something is wrong inside our country. Something is wrong and it must change. It must change.

Meir Pail *was born in Palestine in 1926. His parents had immigrated from Russia in 1921. He spent twenty-eight years in the Israeli army and left after reaching the rank of colonel, because of his radical "peacenik" views. He is one of the leaders of the Moched movement for peace and socialist change.*

I have held various military positions: brigade commander in the Sinai campaign; commander-in-chief of the Israeli Military Academy; deputy commander-in-chief of the general staff college; chief of the operation and tactical department of the supreme general staff of the army, and in the Six Day War, deputy to General Tal in his division. I obtained permission to study at the university to refresh my mind and to finish B.A. and M.A. degrees.

In the army I was considered a radical socialist – which I indeed was and still am – as well as a radical "peacenik." I believed that we should evacuate the territories occupied in the Six Day War. I had to leave the army in September of 1971 because Dayan pushed me out. So I left the army and in 1973 finished my Ph.D. at Tel Aviv University. In the same year we decided to establish a movement called "Moched" in Hebrew, meaning "the focus." The focus of Moched is on peace and socialist change. It's a new movement, a small movement. We have succeeded now in joining hands with some other smaller groups.

I am a rationalist. Our movement is a rationalist socialist movement. We are against rabbis and popes and those who know everything. Our leaders are elected leaders and no one will stay in the Knesset more than two terms. Basically, the army and the army profession should be subject to the politicians. The army is not an aim in itself. It's the politicians who should make the vital and important decisions, not the military professionals.

Before the Six Day War, we had 2.6 million Jews and 350,000 Palestinian Arabs in Israel. So the Palestinians were a small minority, and we could discuss the problem, we could handle the problem. But the Six Day War, unintentionally perhaps, reduced the Israeli political sovereignty. There are now almost 1.5 million Palestinians within the border of Israel. A changed quantity is changing into a new quality. It's a new story. We have a big minority, a hostile minority, composed of human beings. This hostility is a time bomb. If you want to let them have their full spectrum of rights, you must include the right of self-determination. We must find an outlet for their national aspirations. My idea, even after the Six Day War, was that we should help them to maintain political activity, and allow them, after two or three years, to elect a provisional national assembly. The assembly would elect some kind of Palestinian national committee.

With respect to the Palestinians and the West Bank, I think we should consider a four-part deal. The first is ideological: Israel should recognize the rights of the Palestinians for self-determination in an independent Palestinian state, side by side with the State of Israel.

The second part is political: Israel should be ready to evacuate what the Arabs call the West Bank, what we call Judea and Samaria, and the Gaza Strip, and let the Palestinian people establish these territories as a national entity, either as a complete, fully independent Palestinian state, or as an autonomous Palestinian republic, maintaining federative, confederative, or whatever they decide, connections with Jordan.

The third part is that the State of Israel should be ready to negotiate with every competent authoritative representative group, including the PLO, in order to come to terms with and to discuss the final borders and how Jerusalem will be organized. I'm ready to evacuate a piece of Jerusalem. My idea is that there should be a Palestinian municipality, an Israeli municipality, and a border municipality. The border won't be marked, so that the whole border between Israel and Palestine will be an open border. The Palestinian organization that will negotiate with us, in order to prove competence, will declare that they are stopping all terrorist activities.

The fourth part is that we should invite the Jordanian government to join the negotiations. They probably won't, but one must invite them. This is more or less the political project, which I was fighting for even during my days in the army.

Of course, I lean my argument on some pillars. There is, for instance, the pillar of the material change since the Six Day War. I also lean upon the quality of the Israeli Defence Forces and the political moderation among the Arab leaders.

The longer we wait the less likely we are to get any final solution. Sooner or later Israel will explode. You know, in history, the time factor is a dominant factor. Many things that were successful and beneficial two generations ago are ineffective now. I would like Israel to be a light to the nations. For me that means establishing peace with our neighbours and continuing, or perhaps beginning, a new way for Israeli socialism. This is my Judaism.

Zwi Gringold, *the 1973 Hero of the Golan Heights, was born in Israel in 1952. His family arrived from Poland a year before the state was founded. Captain Gringold received the highest medal for bravery for holding back as many as seventy-two Syrian tanks with only two of his own tanks in a twenty-four-hour period. When not a soldier he is an agriculturalist in Kibbutz Lohamey-Hgetaoth.*

I was born, spent my childhood, and for twelve years attended school in this kibbutz. When I was eighteen I went into the army. First I went to the air force. I wanted to be a pilot, but after four months they threw me out of that course and I switched over to the tanks. I did the usual work with the tanks as a simple soldier until I became an officer. They sent me to the Golan Heights in 1971. After two years I became a commander of the company. Two weeks before the 1973 war, I came back to my kibbutz, for a holiday.

The war caught me in the middle of this holiday. I heard about the war on Yom Kippur, Saturday, at three o'clock in the afternoon when a plane flew over in the sky. It was very unusual. So we turned on the radio and heard the news that Arab armed forces had started to attack

Israel in the Golan Heights and in Sinai. I knew that I had a duty to go back as quickly as I could to my unit. I knew that if something happened in the Golan Heights, my unit was involved. So that's what I did; I took a little bag and my uniform, went out to the road, and caught a ride to go to the Golan Heights. I got to the Golan after five on Saturday.

I came to my camp which I had left two weeks before. The picture was not good. Syrian planes had attacked the camp. The few soldiers assigned to the camp were in shock. They didn't know exactly what had happened, and couldn't give me any information about the situation. I spoke into the radio and tried to get my commander, in order to receive my orders. One soldier from my company heard me. Immediately he came from the front with a jeep with a message, "We want you to come and take command of the company, because our commander is dead." He took me with the jeep to another camp, and I met one of the officers from the regiment.

So one of the officers told me: "There are three tanks outside the gate of the camp. Go there and try to do something. I sent two professional mechanics to help you to fix them, and there are the crews of the tanks; do what you can with them." So I went out, and we started work on the tanks. There was a big problem. In two of the tanks there were dead Israeli soldiers. We had to take them out and clean out the blood and everything that we found inside. The soldiers that were not hurt helped me but it was very hard. After a few hours, we saw that we couldn't fix all three tanks. There was only one tank that we had any chance of fixing in a normal time, so it could go to the front. Unexpectedly, someone brought a good tank with only a minor mechanical problem.

At nine o'clock in the evening I went with these two tanks and eight people to the front. On the way to the front, I had a special mission. There is an oil pipe through the Golan Heights, and near the pipe there is a road. My mission was to go down this road to a village, a destroyed village that the Arabs had left in 1967, named Hushnea, to see if there was anything inside, any arms, any Syrians, and if so to fight with them and clean out the area. This was the order. A few kilometres before Hushnea, I ran into Syrian tanks and stopped to fight them. After the first shooting, one of my tanks developed a mechanical problem and couldn't fight any more. I changed tanks. And I stayed alone for a few hours and fought with the Syrian tanks. At the same time I radioed my commander that there were a lot of Syrian tanks. I could see them. Not all of them fought with me, because they were going someplace. Only the tanks that had lost their way, or something like that – I don't understand it even now –

they came by where I was, and I tried to stop them. If the Syrians had known that I was alone, they could have gone past me without any problem. But my luck was that they didn't know exactly what happened and they didn't send a big force to fight with me. And every few minutes I changed my position and destroyed another Syrian tank. This was the situation. In the darkness I could deceive them by frequently changing my position and giving them the impression that there were many.

After a few hours, at twelve o'clock midnight, the first company of the reserves came to the Golan Heights. They were very fast. You must understand that the reserve came from home, prepared the tanks, and then went to the Golan Heights. At twelve o'clock a company came to help me. We tried to push the Syrians back, and then five of our tanks were hurt, my tank also. I jumped out with all my crew, and I had burns on my hand and face. I started running to another tank that was not destroyed, and I got into it. After a few minutes, when I got over the first shock, I asked the commander of the tank what had happened, and he told me. So I asked him to leave me in his tank, and go to another tank, which he did. Five other tanks from this force were taking wounded soldiers back, and after a few minutes I saw that I was alone.

I was alone like before. I reported to my commander what had happened, and he kept asking me all the time, "How many tanks do you have?" But I didn't tell him the number, because I knew very well that the Syrians listened whenever we talked by radio. I didn't want them to know that there was only one tank still on the road. I said to him, "My situation is very bad, but I cannot tell you how many tanks I have." He promised he would send his second commander and another company as quickly as he could, because he understood my bad situation. And for a few hours more I fought. I stayed on the road and I fought. People ask me now: "How many Syrian tanks did you destroy?" I can't answer this question, because I didn't count. I just fought first from one side and then from another side. By changing my position frequently I confused them. In the place where I was fighting there were a lot of Syrian tanks.

In the morning, as he promised, my commander came and his second commander came with another company, and we fought with the Syrians when the sun came up. Everything went well, if I can say that, because we were destroying their tanks one by one and they couldn't get by us. We thought that the situation had improved for us. At mid-day Sunday, we heard on the radio that one of the battalions of the Syrians had gotten around north of us and were attacking the camp where I had been before my holiday. The commander of the division was in this camp which is very crucial to the defence of the Golan Heights. So I turned our tanks around and started to this camp to save them. They told me that the commander, my second commander, and the officer that I spoke with when I came to the Golan Heights were all dead. With two tanks we came into this camp and saved all the people who were still left. I knew that there was no officer in my unit left to command, and so I spoke to the commander of the northern front. And I spoke with one of his officers, and I told him the story. He told me to come to his place, so that they could collect tanks and everything. I met the radio officer and the intelligence officer from my unit, but I was exhausted. I got out of my tank and said to them, "I cannot do any more," and they sent me to the hospital. It was Sunday afternoon around four o'clock. That's my personal history of the battle on the Golan Heights.

Our regiment lost about 150 soldiers in that battle, and a few hundred Arabs were killed. Did I think that I was in danger, too, and that I might be killed? Yes, I think so. Not all the time. In a situation like the one I told you about, you don't have a lot of time to think of this. But you know that you are in danger. If you go to the army, to the war, you know that there is danger. But we know that the Israeli state and the Israeli nation are behind us, and that was the feeling, and because of that we didn't leave our places. And it's true, because of that they gave me the medal.

I hope there won't be another war. But I think there will be. I know that the Israeli nation, the Israeli people, want peace very much. They want peace much more than anything else. But if you understand the reality about the Arabs you will also know why we cannot find the way to make a peace agreement with them. Because in reality, the Arabs have one wish: they don't want Israel here; they don't want the Jewish people here. That's what I think. But I think that we here in Israel, we have to do everything, even what we don't believe we can do, to get peace, and to leave a place for discussion with the Arabs. Maybe we made a big mistake, maybe we didn't catch the point of the Arabs' opinion. I believe that we have to do everything to find a way to make peace.

Minorities

*'"Everything has been done to make me feel a
stranger." –Menachem Cohen.*

Every modern state has its minorities, some of whose members feel
themselves to be second-class citizens. In Israel there are two minority
groups that cannot be overlooked in any treatment of the Israeli people.
They are the Israeli Arabs and the Oriental Jews.

The Israeli Arabs are over 400,000 in number. They are concentrated
in the northern part of Israel, meaning Galilee and such cities as
Nazareth and Haifa. When, in 1948, over 700,000 Arabs left the areas
controlled by the new State of Israel, about 140,000 remained. They and
their descendants became citizens of the state. In addition, there are
nearly one million Arabs in the occupied territories (West Bank and
Gaza), but they have not been included in this portrait.

The Oriental Jews are a minority not in the numerical sense, but in
terms of socio-economic status and political power. The Orientals,
referred to as Sephardic Jews to distinguish them from the European
Ashkenazi, are those Jews who arrived in large numbers –approximately
500,000 –from Asian and African countries, which were mostly Arab
and Muslim. Numerically, the voices of Israeli Arabs and Oriental Jews
in this volume are not proportionate to their number in Israel. This is a
reflection of their status, of the greater accessibility and articulateness of
the Ashkenazi Jews, and of our own linguistic and cultural handicaps.

Eli Eliaschar, *former president of the Sephardic Jewish community and deputy mayor of Jerusalem, was born in 1899. He is a sixteenth generation resident of Palestine-Israel, his family having come from Spain in 1485. Mr. Eliaschar studied medicine and law. He served in the Turkish army during the First World War and occupied an important administrative position under the British Mandate. Then he entered the manufacturing industry. His family has been among the principal leaders of the Jewish community in Palestine-Israel for 300 years, most of them being chief rabbis or influential writers.*

First of all, I am a Jew, I am an Israeli, and I am a Zionist. Whatever in my views may appear to others, or be interpreted by others, as antagonism to Israel or to Zionism is wrong. I am pro-Arab, but I am also pro-Israel. I am an oldtimer, who has lived all his life with Arabs and acquired, by inheritance from my forefathers, a connection with the Arabs—including the Arabs of Palestine, with whom I have day-to-day relations—and so anything you will hear from me is only the result of my idealistic attitude and approach.

As Semites we have aspired for 2,500 years to return to our cradle. Now that we are geographically in the Middle East, we still want to be mentally, socially and culturally in the West, and you can't have it both ways. If you want to live in the Middle East then you have to accommodate yourself to be part and parcel of the Middle East. We must accumulate all possible knowledge from the West, but it is unavoidable that we adjust here to the hundreds of millions of Arabs, and other Middle Eastern peoples. Our survival depends on making ourselves acceptable as part and parcel of the chessboard that is today the Middle East. And how shall we do it? First and foremost by learning to know our neighbours. We don't know them. Not one of our great leaders has ever lived twenty-four full hours of the life of an Arab Palestinian. If they read or write Arabic that doesn't mean that they know how an Arab reacts. And this is one of the greatest defects of the entire establishment today. The ruling power in Israel is Western.

Let me review the history of Arab aspirations. Under Turkish rule there was already the desire and activity for independence in every Arab country. Arabs wanted their independence, and we Jews wanted our independence. In 1911 there was already a great conference of Arab nationalists and Palestinian Jews. Meeting in Paris they settled the question of how to behave if and when Palestine would be liberated from the Turks. The Jews would have their own entity and the Arabs their own entity. What happened afterwards is that we made many, many mistakes. We forgot that we had to come here as Easterners to be accepted by our neighbours. I told the Peel Commission in 1937 that we had to learn to know our neighbours so that we could co-exist together. In my first article on the subject in the 1920's, I warned the Zionist movement that there were Arabs in this country, that the Jews were not coming to a desert. We were not coming to an empty state.

At what points between 1897 and now were there critical crossroads where the deteriorating relationships could have been reversed? If I could go back into history now and turn the thing around, I would go back to 1914 and make every possible effort to understand the Arabs, to know the Arabs, to collaborate with the Arabs. We should have gone a different way to bring forth everything that was common to our two peoples. In history the Jews and the Arabs have the highest achievement. The apogee of the Jewish development is not in the West but in the East with the Arabs. Why? Because 500 years ago the Arabs were tops in science, philosophy, art, music, everything. The Arabs were the greatest mathematicians and philosophers. They introduced Greek and Roman philosophy and science to the West by translating it. The Jews were very, very prominent in this achievement, writing in Arabic. But in 1914, instead of bringing forth what we had in common and instead of opening ourselves to the Arabs and opening the Arabs to us, we became an ivory tower, completely closed, segregated. Even at that time it wouldn't have been easy, but it was possible. And we missed that chance.

Is it now too late? Nothing is too late, but it's difficult. Now we have to establish, first and foremost, an Arab entity. A hundred million Arabs around us will not tolerate it if we expel the Arabs who are living with us today. You have to be crazy to believe in such a utopia. I also don't believe in the idea of the PLO: a secular Palestine. This is also a utopia. You have to take the situation as it is, have approved boundaries, defendable boundaries, and grant the Palestinian Arabs every inch that is theirs since 1967, so that they can have a Palestinian state by their own self-determination. If for economic reasons, nationalistic reasons, political reasons or military reasons they want to join Jordan, this should be their privilege. I believe that if we handle the matter correctly they will join Israel in a federation.

Another thing that I want to make absolutely clear is that if we are weak, if Israel today loses military strength, we are doomed. For many generations to come we will have to be alert and have deterrent power so that we can exist. But if we have open boundaries and can co-exist with an Arab state, then we will be doing something for our future and the future of the Middle East. We'll probably prevent a third world conflagration, which could very easily arise from here.

The war will not be with Arafat but with all the Arabs together. And together we shall have to defend ourselves. In other words, we can obliterate the entire Middle East around us. I don't want that. *Lest We Die with the Philistines* is the title of the book I've written on the situation. It's better to live with the Palestinians than to die with them.

Simon Abergil *is a member of the Black Panther group, representing the Moroccan and other Oriental Jews in Israel. Mr. Abergil was born in Morocco in 1949 and came to Israel in 1961 with his parents. He is married, lives in Jerusalem, and is now fighting for his people and their rights.*

I lived in a room which was two metres by three metres, including the kitchen. The area was the hardest to live in, absolutely the dirtiest part of Jerusalem. It was a nightmare to live there. Because the situation was so bad, five guys got together and decided to do something to make the place better. We went to the Jerusalem police and asked for a permit for a demonstration. That night the police came to our flats and arrested all of us. And when they heard that we were calling ourselves Black Panthers, they said, "It is not possible that this kind of thing should happen in Israel."

And everyone since then has been asking us the question, "Why do you call yourselves Black Panthers?" It was they who gave us the name, because they called us the Yiddish word for black animal. The night that we were arrested, all the people in the area where our flats were came out of their own free will, spontaneously, to the police station and made a demonstration in front of the police station showing that they should be arrested with us. So we were released.

The next day we had a demonstration in front of the home of the mayor. And then a very famous incident happened. The Panthers demonstrated in front of the mayor's home and he came out and told them to get off the grass. It was on television, and everybody in the whole country remembers that day when the mayor told us that we were standing on his grass. From there about 300 people went to Zion Square in Jerusalem and a very serious demonstration ensued. There was a real battle which lasted for seven hours between the police and the Black Panthers. We were beaten and we were arrested. But we said that beatings and prisons and police intervention would not solve the problem of the slums.

Right after that a special session of the Knesset was called, and the finance minister came out and said that he was giving another 90 million pounds for housing in the slums. In other words, after the demonstration all of a sudden 90 million pounds were found. Then Golda said that she wanted to meet us, and we went to meet her–about ten guys–and she started asking each one of us personally, "How's your family? How many kids do you have?" She wanted to have the half hour which was allotted to us filled with nice chat without really getting to the subject we had come to talk to her about. It was winter and it was raining at the time. I said to Mrs. Meir, "We didn't come here to talk about my problems or the problems of any of us. Right now it's raining, and there are a lot of people who have rain coming in their houses now. There are people who don't have anything to eat. It's that we came to talk to you about." Anyway, it ended without any kind of solution from her. And then she came out with another very famous statement. "The Panthers," she said, "they're not nice; they're not nice boys."

We didn't wait, we continued our struggle. In Jerusalem the municipality tried to give us an office provided by them. They told us, "Here, you have an office now; any problems you have you bring to this office, and your problems will be solved." So we got a lot of promises, but we didn't get any solutions. Meanwhile, people were coming to us from all over the country. And other problems from elsewhere in the country came up. People started talking about education, about housing, and about other problems in other places. And we started formulating and working on plans of our own which we sent to members of the Knesset. And to this day, we haven't received any kind of answer. But promises we always have.

The Black Panthers represent at least 40 per cent of the population. These are people who live below the poverty line, young couples with large families who have tiny apartments and who sleep three or four in a bed. But the most important problem for us is education and inflation. Those who really suffer from the price rises are the poor and not the millionaires. "Let's stop crying" is the present slogan of the Alignment. That kind of slogan is whitewashing all the problems that we really have. Slogans like "Let's stop crying" really favour millionaires. They don't have anything to cry about. We'll stop crying the minute there is a solution to the problem. Where would the money come from? They have millions to spend on new buildings and fancy hotels, so we know that there is money that they can bring into the slums.

The conflict with the Arabs? If we want peace, we first of all have to solve our internal problems, because they are more important. Only after we solve our internal problems, can we solve the problem of peace. If there is no peace at home, I don't believe that there will be peace outside.

Menachem Cohen *was born in 1947. A social worker in Jerusalem, he is a fourth-generation Palestinian Jew. His ancestors on his father's side are from Spain, and on his mother's side from Syria. He is spokesman for the Central Committee of the Black Panther movement in Israel.*

The Black Panthers were born six years ago in a Jerusalem slum neighbourhood, known as Mosela, occupied by people from Morocco and from Iraq. The Black Panthers were from nineteen to twenty-two years old. They decided to get organized and fight the authorities because of the discrimination against the black Sephardic Jews. This discrimination took place in all the social life and cultural life of the Sephardic Jews here.

I'll give you some examples. Only 7 per cent of the Sephardic Jews in Mosela are high-school graduates. Thirty-five per cent of the Sephardic Jews, who are 58 per cent of the population of Israel, are living under the line of poverty. Twelve per cent of the Sephardic Jews who were born here are high-school graduates. Only 8 per cent are university graduates. Ninety-three per cent of crimes committed in Israel are committed by Sephardic Jews. Sixty-five per cent of the kids of Sephardic Jews that go to the army aren't accepted. That means there is a policy of discrimination. We don't believe that it happens by accident.

We believe that this whole policy is well guided and well thought out by the government in order to ensure a cheap labour force. Up to 1967 cheap labour was supplied by the black Jews, the Sephardic Jews, and from 1967 on it was supplied by the Sephardic Jews and the Arabs. As I said, when the Black Panthers first started, there was a demonstration in which a lot of people were involved. We had one demonstration of more than 15,000 people, and that's a lot for Israel. That's the first and the last time in all Israel that 15,000 people came together to demonstrate against something. At that time the Prime Minister was Golda Meir. She established a committee and the committee found for the first time that there was discrimination against the Sephardic Jews. They made recommendations. Nothing has happened since. The Black Panthers made a lot of demonstrations, and we ran for the Knesset. We needed only 700 votes in order to get in, that's what we needed. We didn't get in. We got into the Histadrut, which is an organization of workers. We have three members in the Histadrut.

In the current election we are going with the Communist party, the Israeli Communist party. Why? There are three classes of people living in this part of the country: first class is the Ashkenazi Jew, second class is the Sephardic Jew, and third class is the Arab. Now we believe that our fight can be together with the Arabs, because they are being terribly discriminated against by the authorities here. The authorities are expropriating their land; they need special permits in order to move from one place to another; there are very few at work; and they don't get paid like the Jews. They have the same problems as we do in cultural life; and we believe that we should join together with the Arabs, because before 1967 the Ashkenazi Jews looked on us as they now look at the Arabs. They considered us primitive, uncivilized human beings; and that's how they look at the Arabs today. They still look at us like that, but it's less, because they have someone whom they can hate even more.

My own personal history? I grew up in a slum and my parents worked very hard in order to let me finish high school. Then I went to the army. For three years in the army I was in the commandos, sergeant of the commandos, which I'm sorry for now, because I was brainwashed. I was very close to death many times, but I didn't know what I was fighting for. I was going to get killed for things that I didn't believe in. I don't believe that our war here, the Israeli war, is right. I believe we are sitting on land that we took from other people by force, and I believe that their war against us – the Palestinian war I'm talking about – is right.

Muhammed who lives here in a village is more important to me than Lebovitch who lives in Brooklyn. You see, I want to live at peace with Muhammed; I don't give a shit about Lebovitch. If he wants to live in Brooklyn, he can live in Brooklyn. I'm not a Zionist; I am anti-Zionist. For the last six years I have been anti-Zionist. My parents are Zionist.

What has brought about this change in me? First of all, I came close to the leftist group. I have read and I have seen that the Zionist movement is a movement that brought us, the Sephardic Jews, to where we are now. The Zionist movement is a racist movement because they don't want other people to come. They consider this a democratic country, but they won't let people in unless they are Jews. The mission of Zionism is to build a homeland for the Jews. I believe that the Arabs should have a Palestinian state at the side of Israel.

Do I feel alien or a stranger in my own land? No, I don't feel a stranger. I feel that this is my land. But, you see, everything is being done, everything has been done, to make me feel a stranger. We are in no better situation here than we would be in Morocco, Yemen, or Tunisia. I know families that have been separated: half the family came here, and half the family stayed in Morocco. I know that the families over there in Morocco are all well-educated, and the families here are pimps and prostitutes. I know that for sure. I can show you at least fifteen families like that. The same thing in Iraq. The same thing in Syria.

The Palestinians are still being pushed out, day by day. Israel expropriates their land, day by day. So far they have taken up more than a million dunams of Arab land, and what do you think they do with it? They build Israeli kibbutzim on it. How can I as a human being – I don't care what I am, a Jew, an Arab, or a Chinese – agree with them on that? How can I agree that villages of Arabs only five kilometres from a Jewish town, don't have light? For twenty-nine years they don't have light. That's discrimination.

Yes, I believe there will be another war. It's going to be a terrible war. I believe that I will be put in jail, because I'm not going to fight. Me and many of my friends, are not going to fight. We're not going to be tools in their hands. This country, if they won't change their policy, is going to be a catastrophe. In the next war we won't have 3,000 soldiers killed; in the next war we're going to have 30,000. It's going to be a nuclear war. Israel has weapons even though they deny it.

We are fighting all the time. Six months ago the government cancelled subsidized milk products – cheese, milk, and all the things that are from milk. All the prices went up 40 per cent in one night. The people from the poor neighbourhood who didn't have money were affected most. So we broke into the big storage of milk and cheese products, and we stole cheese and milk, and we gave it away in the neighbourhood. We gave it away and we wrote a signed paper explaining why we did it. And it was in all the papers, and they all talked about that. One of our leaders, the one that is going to be in the Knesset, was sentenced for three months to prison. But he's going to get out, because he is going to be a member of the Knesset. So they can't put him in prison. He's going to be out. This is not our way to solve problems, but this is a way to bring it to the people's conscience, to let people know. Our welfare minister walked into the slums with reporters and told them: we are growing here a generation of parasites. That's the minister of welfare. He's calling the black Jews, the Sephardic Jews, parasites. We didn't keep quiet on that. We collected more than fifty big mice, and we knocked on his door at twelve o'clock at night. His guard opened the door. We took him out, and we threw all the mice into his house. We told him, "These are the parasites that are growing in the slums and you should feel for one night what people have been feeling for twenty-nine years."

Ely Ovadya, *born in Libya in 1933, reflects the international and intercultural experience of many Jews. Raised in Africa he studied in Europe, worked in Asia, and got married in North America. But as is the case with so many Jews, Israel is his real home. In spite of his wanderings he has not forgotten his native Arab culture or Arab hospitality.*

My father's parents came from villages around Tripoli. He opened a business and made good money after the war in the clothing business. He also owned a large number of houses, stores, and buildings.

The Jews lived very nicely in Libya. They had the opportunity to build up their business. We enjoyed life in Libya. But we thought of our own homeland. The Jews gave money for the Jewish Agency to help Jews, because they believed in Israel. They gave no thought to the Arabs living there. I think it was blind Zionism. We lived blindly. The generations grew up with that feeling. We didn't know how Jerusalem was, or how Tel Aviv was or what was going on there, or who was living there. The main thing was to go to Zion. It was a blind idea that was cooked in our minds.

The Jewish community in Libya comprised 40,000 to 50,000 people. Now there are 500. The Jewish people kept their culture and their religion alive very well. They read the Bible. They observed the holy days. We, as Jews, believed in going to Israel one day. The excitement was there from the minute I heard that Israel was going to be established. We believed and prayed that all the Jews would be united in one place, in one land, with our own law. Some didn't leave immediately because they couldn't liquidate their businesses. My father, for instance, couldn't liquidate his business, but he lost everything. One day the government just confiscated all the properties, not only the Jewish properties but the properties of the other minorities as well. But it started with the Jewish minority. One day they just took over everything.

Libya had never been an independent state, and the Libyans wanted to be in control of their own country. The Jews happened to be their enemies in a way. They were leaving for Israel already, and the attitude was that if they left the country to fight Arab friends, neighbours, and people in Palestine, they didn't deserve to take their property with them.

Farid Wadji Taberi *is a judge, practising law in Jaffa. An Arab and a Muslim he was born into a family with a 600-year history in Tiberias and with a long tradition of judges and lawyers. He talks about Muslim law in relation to Israeli law and about his optimism for peace.*

I am responsible for Jaffa and the surrounding district, including Beersheba and the Negev, the old and the new Jerusalem, plus the suburbs. How come? The Israeli government does not recognize the old Jordanian court in the old city of Jerusalem. The court is part of the Muslim council in the old city, and the council did not recognize the unification of Jerusalem in 1967. In other words, the Jaffa court has been made central for a wide area. It is the largest Muslim jurisdiction in the country. I am doing the work of three judges There are about five Muslim courts in Israel.

A Muslim religious judge is nominated by the community. Then he applies for appointment. He is interviewed by a committee of nine, including ministers, members of parliament, lawyers, and other judges, Jews and Arabs, mainly Jews of course. And then the final recommendation is given to the minister for religious affairs, who in turn asks the president of the state to appoint him and have him sworn in.

Qualifications? Normally he is supposed to study Muslim law, the Koran, the traditions of the Prophet's life and sayings, the philosophy of Islam, and the law of waqf (Muslim religious trust property law). Such qualifications are very rare now. We have no religious schools for Muslims in Israel at all. Some get qualified at the teachers' colleges.

I am religious, although I like the expression "believer" more than "religious." I'm liberally so. I love God and fear Him. I love man, and I love peace. As a teacher and a humble writer, my theme has always been "God, man, and peace." I'm quite optimistic about peace in the Middle East, generally, and in our country particularly, but not in the near future. It will take some time. But eventually it has to come. The two sides have got to accept each other as they are, otherwise there will be no compromise. We have got to understand each other. I belong to various peace-building societies.

I believe it's necessary for Arabs and Jews to study deeply, mutually, and respectfully each other's civilizations, culture, and history. We should know that we both belong to the land. I believe that we were both included in the promise to Abraham. We are both his children or grandchildren if you like. The promise made to Abraham must have included us. I think both Jews and Arabs should be called the chosen people. Both our cases are equally strong, genuine, and sincere. The only way to achieve peace is to accept each other. Otherwise, may God forbid, we may destroy each other and cause others to be destroyed along with us. And, of course, I do not exempt the big powers from this possibility.

Muslim religious law has been affected by civil legislation in Israel. For example, Islam allows polygamy. It does not advocate, encourage, or urge it. No, it allows it for reasons of necessity. This has been affected by Israeli civil law, which prohibits polygamy. In my opinion this is good. Actually, many Muslim and Arab countries wanted to install this prohibition as well. But due to the ignorance of many people, they could not do it. Turkey was the first to do it.

Other actions allowed in Islam, such as divorce by one side, are no longer possible in Israel. A husband cannot divorce his wife by just uttering the traditional Islamic statement of divorce without the consent of his wife at a competent court. This is, again, in my opinion, a great step towards the improvement of family life. Another problem arises from laws of inheritance. Islam says a boy gets double the share of a girl. A man gets twice as much as the woman. In Islam there are explanations for this. The man is supposed to take care of the family. And there are other social and moral reasons. In Israel this can be so on one condition only. If all the heirs agree to resort to the Muslim court in Israel. If one heir out of 500 says, "No, I would rather go to the district or civil court," the Muslim court has no jurisdiction whatsoever.

This might be progress. But as long as the Muslims are not asked about it, as long as their consent is not taken, this is interference, and I speak both as a judge and as a citizen. I myself am very much for modernization and for the emancipation of women. I lecture on the subject. But this is trespassing on the rights of a certain community in the country.

Another problem has been the waqf property, an institution in Islam of religious trust property, which is similar to benevolent funds or social centres in other religions and organizations. A pious Muslim person would say, in a way, "I leave this house as a waqf." Waqf is from the verb "waqafa" in Arabic which means to stand still, to remain always, without being sold, never to be sold. Usually such gifts are for sick people, foreign students, young but poor couples, etc. The kind of social welfare or charity desired is usually specified. The will is executed or carried out by the Muslim religious judge, who appoints a governor or a trustee for this waqf. During the Mandate, Palestine was well known for immensely rich religious properties in lands and buildings, houses and shops, in various cities and villages which were worth millions of sterling.

When the State of Israel came into existence in 1948, a law was enacted called the Absentee Property Law. Many have criticized this law. Under it, many thousands of Palestinian Arabs were considered absentees as they went to other countries and left their properties behind. But even some who left Tiberias for Nazareth, as we did, were also considered absentees. We had to go to the district court and fight and liberate our property. And very few people succeeded. Many lands that belonged to people who remained in the country were taken for public uses or given to kibbutzim. In this way Arab land became Jewish land.

Another problem is Arab education. Arab education, like other Arab services, has been the victim of neglect, unqualified people, or a lack of policy. What should Israel make out of the Arab children in Israel? Should they be made to forget the Arabs? That's impossible because they're surrounded by Arab countries, Arab radio, Arab television and Arab press. Give them free Arab culture? That would contradict Israeli policy. Make them Jews? That would be neither democratic nor fair. It took Israel some time to allow the teaching of Arab history in the country. Only after 1969 or 1970 was the teacher's college in Haifa allowed to teach anything about the revolution in Egypt and the history of Jamal Abdul Nasser in written lectures.

Actually at elementary school they teach no Arabic history. There's a great stress on Jewish history. Torah is an essential part of secondary school education, for Arabs as well as Jews, but especially for Arabs. The Koran or the New Testament are not taught in spite of the fact that the Koran would provide a great source for excellent high-standard Arabic. So would the New Testament, with its simple and pleasing Arabic and its sublime ideas. Now, when I look at these things as a man of fifty-three, as a judge, as a father, and as a peace-loving citizen, when I look at them very objectively, I do not see bad intentions in the minds of those responsible for the state, but I see short-sightedness, I see little experience, I see the wilderness sometimes. They might be justified in not knowing what to do, but to neglect the basic or essential values of education is something serious.

We both, Arabs and Jews, have no confidence in each other yet. I think of two prominent friends of mine: a fine civil engineer in Haifa, a high-ranking one, who belongs, along with me, to a peace-making society; and a very prominent Arab of the old city of Jerusalem. Speaking to both at different times I got these two replies. The Arab said, "I don't believe a word of what Israel says; not a single word. I can't trust them yet." And that very good friend of mine in Haifa said, "You know, I wish I could trust the Arabs. I wish I could trust them in anything that they announce, declare, or promise us. I don't know why: I just can't trust them." I can't blame my fellow Arab and Jewish brethren. Many factors in history have played a part in creating this situation. Still, I remain optimistic, and I take my optimism from various living examples. Look at what happened between Germany and the Jews. You have mutual representation, trade and commerce, tourism, and an exchange of students and lecturers. What more could you want?

Why not remain optimistic? We can be if we are sincere in our desire to accept one another as we are. I have learned the magic of this as a lawyer, as a teacher, and as a judge. When you meet and accept the other as he or she is, what happens? First, you understand the other person better. Then you start to like and respect him. And then you love the other person. It's not difficult. I don't see why the Jews and the Arabs should not be able to forget their bitterness and work out a new code of relations. I also have some hope in some of the present political leaders of the area, one in particular, Sadat of Egypt. I think he is practical, and I think he will be a good example for other Arab countries. I'm even optimistic about the future mutual relations between Egypt and Russia, in spite of the present misunderstanding. And I think – and here I say it naïvely – I

99

think America and the Western countries should not fear good relations between Egypt and Russia, or other countries and Russia, or Israel and Russia. And if they really mean business and are sincere when they speak about peace, they would all stand to benefit.

Muhammed Na'amneh *is an Arab apprentice to a Jewish lawyer in Jerusalem, having attended Hebrew University for five years. He was born in an Arab village in Galilee in 1945. He has seven brothers and sisters, and his father, like many Israeli Arabs, works in construction. According to Mr. Na'amneh, there were 1,700 Arab students in Israel universities in 1977, which was less than the previous year. He sees Arabs being discriminated against in Israel, especially with respect to land.*

After the first occupation of Palestine in 1948, the majority of the Arab lands were confiscated and the little bit of land which remained was not enough to maintain the population. Therefore, in order to be able to maintain their families, the Palestinian Arabs returned to working in construction.

Land is still being taken away. Confiscation is now concentrated in Galilee. It is cultivated land which is being taken away, land which has plenty of olive trees, and fruits, and so on. It's not uncultivated. Their action is called "Judaizing Galilee." The Israeli authorities are aiming to have a majority Jewish population in Galilee.

Many laws that operate in Israel discriminate in favour of the Jews. I can name the laws: the law of return; the law of land annexation—according to which the transfer of land is done only one way, from the Arabs to the Jews; the laws concerning national security; and the laws concerning family allowances—which are set up in favour of army families, meaning Jewish families, and against large families, meaning Arab families.

Many Arab villages remain underdeveloped. There are villages where there is still no electricity, running water, or schools. Only three years ago an Arab village of 8,000 people was connected to electricity, whereas a nearby Jewish village, which so far has only 1,000 people, had a new road, electricity, running water, and plumbing. Everything was complete when they entered the place. There are many examples of this sort of thing. There are many agricultural problems among the Israeli Arabs. I will give you a very simple and small example. Tobacco is grown in an Israeli Arab village and also in a nearby Jewish kibbutz. One kilo of tobacco from the Arab village is acquired for half of the price that is paid for the same tobacco grown in the Jewish settlement.

100

Ibrahim Samaan, *thirty-eight, is a Palestinian Arab who is a citizen of Israel. His home is in Haifa, and like most Arabs in the area, Samaan believes that his family has always lived there. A time of immigration is unknown. His minority status is multiple as an Arab, as a Christian, and as a Baptist.*

I believe that what is most important these days is the change in the political map of Israel. There are several new parties, and there is a change in the balance of political influence which is a direct result of uncertainty regarding the occupied territories. Should they be returned or not? If they are returned, should anything be retained? Every party is trying to adapt itself to a certain unclear position. Most of the parties are talking about no maps for peace at this stage, and if anybody is declaring maps, he is a prisoner of his declarations. Things are not clear. Israel won the Six Day War because the aim was clear, but the aims for peace are unclear, because Israel is not sure enough or courageous enough to be willing to pay the price for peace. The price is very cheap: returning to the Arabs what belongs to them.

The financial situation is worsening, and many people are thinking of emigration. This is lowering the morale of the people. Maybe the worst enemy of Israel is time. America is realizing that she depends on Arab oil. The Arabs will use the financial weapon of petroleum. Israel will some day find herself alone.

How do the Arab citizens of Israel feel? There is a mixture of feelings. More Palestinian Arabs are declaring their Palestinian identity. The worst position for any person is to be an Israeli Arab. Your own country is in a state of war against your own people. The struggle of two loyalties within you can tear you up. You can't imagine a person who is an Arab, a Palestinian, and an Israeli at the same time. Every time you think about the Arab-Palestinian-Israeli conflict, all of these three are fighting within you. The most that anybody can ask of an Israeli Arab is to be neutral. But even that is not realistic, because you can be neutral outwardly, but not inwardly. At certain points you find yourself completely a Palestinian with no trace of the Israeli; and at another stage, you see yourself as an Israeli. There were occasions when I was ashamed to belong to the Palestinian people, when innocents were killed. That didn't mean that I denied belonging to that people. Any nation includes good people as well as criminals. On other occasions you identify totally with the state in which you live. I'm happy to be what I am. I accept myself as an Israeli, I accept myself as an Arab who belongs to the Palestinian people. And above all, I'm happy to be a Christian.

The educational situation of the Arabs in Israel is poor. A survey was done recently, showing that in western Europe you have something like thirty-four per thousand who have higher education. In Israel, among Jews, the number is between thirty and thirty-two; in the West Bank the percentage is about twenty-eight; in the Gaza Strip about twenty-five; and among Israeli Arabs it's ten or eleven per thousand who have higher education. And then the financial situation. At a certain stage the Israeli Arabs were doing well. When there was a great need for working hands they made a lot of money. There is one plus among the many minuses. The plus is that an Israeli Arab is not obliged to serve in the army, and he gains three years of his life for education or work.

On the other hand, when there is an employment crisis, the first victim is the Arab worker. He goes back to his village, but he has no more means for living from his own land, because a lot of it was confiscated or not sufficiently developed to give him a living. Someone said that we send our Israeli Arab villagers to work in the big cities. They come home full of two things: their pockets are full of money, and their hearts are full of hatred. They can't live in the big cities where they work and they can't make a good living in their own villages.

Are the Arabs in Galilee losing some of their land? Oh, yes. Just last year – the whole world heard about it – the Land Day on March 30 was set up to protest against the confiscation of Arab land and the Judaizing of Galilee. Every state can confiscate land for development. It is very necessary. But to take my land, to forbid me to build on my own land, and at the same time to give it to a Jewish newcomer, that is unacceptable.

This matter of being a Christian among Muslim Arabs is an old problem; it's not a new thing. It surfaces every now and then in Arab history. There are some Arab leaders who would like to see all Christians either convert to Islam or leave. Someone has said that the Muslims cannot tolerate a minority unless this minority proves that it is willing, of its own accord, to accept being second-rate citizens. I cannot and will not be a second-rate citizen, wherever I am, be this in Israel or in an Arab state. I'm willing to struggle against it. Here I am, a minority of the minority of the minority. But first of all, I'm a human being and I belong to the majority of the whole world, which is human beings. And I care more for human rights than for national rights.

What is a realistic solution to the Palestinian problem? We are living in a world where everybody has to say, "This is my home state, my home country." The Palestinians are not different from other people. The Jews kept saying, "Next year in Jerusalem" for 2,000 years, and I think that the Palestinians may continue saying the same for some years to come. Both are Semitic peoples, and both are equally stubborn. I don't believe that in time the whole Palestinian people will be wiped off the map. The Israelis have found the answer to their aspirations by founding the State of Israel. The Palestinians should go through the same experience. Maybe they will decide that it's better to be united with Israel or Jordan. Maybe they can be the glue which puts these three states together – Jordan, Palestine, and Israel.

I think I am in favour of a Palestinian state on the West Bank. I see the whole area – Israel, the West Bank, and Jordan – as one. These three states – I would call them districts – form one geographical and natural unit. Each one of them completes and complements the other in terms of resources. To a great extent they are dependent on each other. I would not call immediately for the uniting of these three units. There has been too much bloodshed. The Palestinians have to go through the same experience as the Israelis went through, that of having their own state, with a transitional period, varying, I should say, from five to ten years. If five years is enough, fine; if not, allow another five years in which the Palestinians would enjoy freedom of thought, the development of a new natural leadership, and the forming of new political parties. Towards the end of this transitional period, two things would take place: general elections for a Palestinian cabinet, and the giving to the Palestinians of the right of self-determination. There are several options open to them: an independent Palestinian state in the West Bank and the Gaza Strip; federation or confederation or union with Jordan; federation or confederation or union with Israel; and federation or confederation with Jordan and Israel. Federation leans more towards unity than towards independence, as I see it, whereas confederation gives more freedom for internal affairs.

A.G. Monsour is a Christian Arab in Israel. He is from a village which is 3,500 years old. He was born in 1918 and works as a mechanic.

Christian Arabs have always had a difficult time in this part of the world. For a long time all the Christian Arabs were protected by the Western Christians. Thus they were hated and considered to be enemies by the Muslims. The Jewish people who have come here, on the other hand, see the Christian Arabs as affiliated with the Arab world and loyal to the Muslims of the East. So, we don't know where we belong, to the West or to the East. We are in the middle. We are between the door and the wall. If they open it, we break, and if they close it, we break too. So, it's not so easy.

Spokespersons

"We've been God's emissaries to mankind
throughout the ages."
–Pinhas Leibowitz.

A spokesperson in Israel is one who speaks for an organization, agency, institution, or government department. Thus, the designation has a specific usage. The word can, however, also be understood more broadly, in the sense that all or most Israelis are spokespersons. They are opinionated, articulate, and outspoken. As someone in the Israeli government Press Office advised us, "You will have no difficulty finding people who will talk. There are 3 million people here waiting to be interviewed as spokespersons for themselves."

It is also said that "for every three Israelis there are four opinions," and again, "Israelis start newspapers and organizations at the drop of a hat." The 1977 election was contested by no less than twenty-two political parties, some of them freshly formed, others representing coalitions of a number of groups. Thus there need to be many spokespersons; and in the final analysis, every Israeli is his or her own spokesperson.

Shlomo Argov *is deputy director-general of the Foreign Ministry. His family has been in Israel since 1800. He was a member of the Foreign Service in Nigeria, in Ghana, in Washington, and in Mexico. He feels keenly the loneliness of Israel in the world.*

My family has been in Jerusalem for many years. I was born and brought up here. I served in the War of Independence. Then I went abroad and studied in the United States for two years. Since 1955 I've been in government service. I was first on the staff of the Prime Minister's Office for four years. I worked with Teddy Kollek, who is mayor of the city. And for just a few months I had the privilege of working with Ben-Gurion; it was a rare opportunity to be in the company of greatness.

I shall always remember his vision, courage, stamina, and decisiveness: all of the qualities of leadership. We have not had the like since. He

104

excelled in various fields. We have had good leadership; but he was a rare combination of many things. And when the country and the people and Jewish history needed him, he happened. It was one of those positive accidents of history that he happened to be at the time when he was. If it wasn't for him, things might have been different, I suspect. It was he who decided that there should be a state. It was his personal life and leadership, I think, that were the instrument.

The state was formed by the people. The war was fought and won by the young people. Had it not been for the brave young people who fought and won in 1948, the vision and the courage would not have been sufficient. But it was Ben-Gurion who drew it out of the people. He inspired us, always. In his later years he was willing to trade land for peace.

You know that our world neighbours have been either with us or against us, but mostly against us. I shall never forget, for example, 1967. Within two weeks Israel found herself totally and utterly alone and abandoned, literally. It was as if the scaffoldings were falling, and we were left stark naked on a stage. And everybody just slipped away quietly. I remember that very vividly. And we are drawing on that lesson today. The world has been with us and against us, but often we've been left alone. I think this loneliness is very much a part of every Israeli today.

I have seen Africa turn its back to us, and I've been deeply offended and deeply upset by that. I remember how much we tried to help them, and really we wanted very little in return, only friendship. We were surrounded by an Arab world that was hostile, and we jumped over that Arab world in order to establish a friendship with a people with whom we felt a great deal of affinity. I felt so myself. Africa was a continent that was unshackling itself. It was a continent that was liberating itself. It was a continent of a persecuted race. We felt we had a great deal in common with Africa. And I knocked myself out, establishing projects with joint co-operation, and so forth and so on. We did very well, and the Africans, I think, appreciated us. I always had the feeling that I had a better understanding of Africans than most other non-Africans who were there, and was given to understand that this was reciprocated. So when in 1967 and later on in 1973 we found ourselves jettisoned by all of these African friends, it was a very offensive act, something that I took very hard personally.

Being Jewish is a unique experience. It involves penalties and it involves hardships. We survive by improving our faculties. We excel as best we can in order to survive in a hostile world. We are a strange people. We are a people who, when offered a bill of rights, so to speak, and a moral code, did not even bother to ask what was in it. The people of Israel said to Moses and to God through Moses, "We shall do and we shall hear." The question's been asked a million times, "Why did you say, 'we shall do,' before you accepted the code?" It's because of the bond between the Jews and God. And that's why God chose the Jews. He could trust the Jews because they accepted His call without a murmur. They didn't check, they didn't even bother to reflect; they accepted.

But I wouldn't change it for anything. Being a Jew means a full life. It's being part of a very remarkable saga. We may be very insignificant little components of that saga as individuals; but we're very much a part of it. I know no more exciting saga than that of the Jewish people. For me, the essential ideas of Judaism form a trinity: God, people, land. God, the God of the Jews, and this land, the land of the Jews, and the Jewish people: that's our trinity.

Yes, there are Jews in the world who support us as best they can and there are non-Jews who support us as best they can. The people rallying to our cause in the United States aren't doing so just because Jews are pushing them, but rather because they feel that they are doing a good thing, a right thing. These senators or congressmen who pitch for us every once in a while do what they do because they believe very deeply that what they are doing is in the best interests of the United States. America is different from many countries. It is not a cynical country. They live by a moral code. They have always lived by a moral code. When the first Pilgrim Fathers landed on Plymouth Rock, they saw themselves as the new Israel. It is not therefore entirely unexpected that Israel enjoys a great deal of support among such a people.

Teddy Kollek, *the internationally known mayor of Jerusalem, arrived in Palestine in 1935 from Austria, where he had been born in 1911. Having been brought up in a home which valued Jewish traditions, though not in the orthodox sense, he joined the Zionist youth movement. When Israel was founded he became a civil servant. From 1952 he was director-general in the Prime Minister's Office and from 1965 mayor of Jerusalem. He is most eloquent when he speaks of the united city over which he has presided since 1967.*

What has happened in the last ten years in Jerusalem? I think we have a great many achievements, and we have a great many more problems. A great achievement is that Arabs and Jews live together with a reasonable amount of tension, not an exaggerated amount of tension. There are different aspirations between Jews and Arabs, obviously. Arabs want their sovereignty, and Jews have finally achieved something they have prayed for for 2,000 years and that's Jerusalem. Until the State of Israel started, the word Jerusalem meant everything that today Israel means.

106

The Jews have to some extent achieved their aim. This hasn't been recognized by many, not by the Arabs, not by many governments. Against great odds we have achieved something of a palatable situation, and we have built a city that I believe is better by far than when it was divided.

Now, the Arabs in Jerusalem do not like this; they see us as an occupying power. The stories that houses have been blown up here isn't correct. Only one house has been blown up. And no house will be blown up because of the intentions of any one individual. A house is blown up only if a large arms cache is found in it. This happened once. Incidentally, the people affected asked for a building licence, and they are getting it. If you wanted to try to divide Jerusalem up again, you would have to send in a few military parachute divisions. This is the one thing against which all the Israelis would fight, because I think that it is of basic importance.

I think we have solved a fair number of problems. Arabs remain Arabs. They all left in the first day after the war because they thought we would do to them what they had been doing to us, but they all came back again. And no Arabs are leaving now with the exception of a few. The schools are run on the Arab League curriculum with a couple of hours of Hebrew. But the youngsters from here can leave and go to Arab universities and come back whenever they like. Arabs are not cut off; they can leave the city every morning, whenever they like, without having to ask for permission. The mosque is under the Arab administration, without Jewish interference. I think a shared sovereignty would bring the wars back, and I think this would be a great tragedy.

Within the city of Jerusalem we can do many things, once the fact that it is the capital of Israel is accepted. There can, for instance, be independent boroughs, not boroughs like in New York – those boroughs are hogwash – but like in London, where the boroughs are not hogwash. All the London boroughs – there are twenty-two of them – have their own budget, have their own mayor, have their own independence, under the Greater London Council. But nobody questions the fact that London is one city under one sovereignty. This could be a model for us here, as long as Jerusalem remains one, and remains the capital of Israel.

Yes we have expropriated a great number of houses for public purposes; this is being done all over. The houses of Arabs in one quarter have been torn down because the whole quarter is being rebuilt. There will be twenty Arab families remaining, and about a similar number of shops in the Jewish quarter. Wherever it doesn't clash with planning, no Arabs will be removed. The fellow who says that there is no room for Arabs in the Jewish quarter is a fool and an extremist, and I don't hold with such opinions, and shall not act by those opinions.

On the other hand, some Arab houses have to be torn down. Now,

Arabs live here under fear of terrorism. One of the men who was forcefully evicted out of his house came to us and said, "I want to leave here; I want to buy myself some land." We agreed on a price. He said, "Under one condition: you have to evict me forcefully because I'm afraid for my life if I come to an agreement." This is the one place where I had a witness; I am told there are other such cases. But I don't see anything morally wrong with evicting people for public purposes.

Somebody asked me on a lecture tour in the United States about the difference between requisitioning and expropriating Jewish property and Arab property. So I said, "The difference is very simple: the Jews call me a bastard, but the Arabs call me a Zionist bastard." I don't think there's anything morally wrong with expropriation. It is happening every day everywhere in the world. It is done much more leniently here than anywhere else, with much higher compensation here than anywhere else.

When Arabs come back here, they are astonished to see that we have Arab street signs. We have Arab street signs in Jerusalem. We are not a particularly tolerant people, but we are a lot more tolerant than anybody else. Not for great moral reasons, but for two practical reasons. First of all, we are a minority. We have lived as a minority all over the world; therefore we know how difficult it is to be a minority. And secondly, we cannot afford to be stricter towards a minority or to give a minority less than we would like to have for the Jewish minorities, let's say, in Russia or in Serbia. So we have two restraints, practical restraints, which make us a bit more tolerant.

Yoram Hamizrachi *of Matulla is a television and newspaper journalist representing Israeli television in the north. Mr. Hamizrachi's father was born in Palestine, his mother in Germany. Yoram was born during the Second World War and brought up by his grandparents, because his father served abroad, first with the British army and then with the Jewish underground, the Haganah. His mother was also a member of another Jewish underground. He speaks for strong defence and for the war which, though regrettable, he thinks is inevitable.*

I cover, for Israeli television, the entire Israeli-Lebanese frontier, the Upper Galilee, the Lower Galilee, and the Golan Heights. I travel a lot in the north. I see a lot of people. In the last year about 50 per cent of my normal routine was to cover the Lebanese frontier. There are no changes along the border. Nobody has moved the security fence to the south or to the north. But there is a new relationship between us and some of the

Lebanese living in isolated enclaves. A hostile frontier, a closed border, became an open frontier. Therefore, the northern frontier has become very important for Israel.

The enclaves – Christian Lebanese villages and areas in the south of Lebanon that are surrounded by Muslim Lebanese areas – are linked today with Israel through the Good Fence. Most of the population of these enclaves are Christians. One enclave is close to Matulla. It has about 7,000 Christians, 4,000 to 6,000 Muslims and a few Jews. They describe themselves as the Lebanese forces, headed by regular army officers.

The outcome will be that the Syrians will have to leave Lebanon. As long as the enclaves can keep themselves alive, as long as they will hold on, they will be the beginning of the fall of the Syrians. Because as far as I know, most of the Lebanese don't tolerate the Syrian presence. Most of the Lebanese remember that for the last fifty years the Syrians have been dreaming about a greater Syria that would include Lebanon. Israel is not going to tolerate the Syrian presence in Lebanon for a long time. I am sure that war is imminent – this year or next year or within three years. We'll have to fight the Arabs again and the next war will also save Lebanon. I don't have any doubt about it.

Israel will not tolerate the terrorist presence along the border. Israel will not tolerate the Syrian presence close to the border. Israel will not tolerate threats to the enclaves, especially the Christian villages, close to the border. I expect that there will be more than one war, and I know that we can afford it and that we will win it. I don't doubt it at all.

I am not happy with the situation, but I don't agree with the Israeli politicians talking about peace. There is no chance for any kind of peace between us and the Arabs. Believe me, I am not a hawk and I am not against peace, but I am also not a dove – just saying okay, peace, peace. I think sometimes nations and peoples have to fight all their lives. I am not afraid of war. I know it is very nice in our time to talk about peace but I don't talk about peace because I don't believe it.

I am a member of a nation whose first lesson was not to trust anybody. Why should I trust the Arabs? I don't trust, and I don't give a damn about what they think about me. My father was always pro-Arab. He likes to eat with them, he likes to sit with them, he likes to drink with them, he talks the language. But he will never forget that he has also fought against them four times. So to drink and to talk with someone is one side of the story, but on the other hand, you have to fight him one day.

My grandfather served in the Turkish army. He was born among the Arabs and raised among the Arabs. But when the order came that they had to recruit 2,000 people, who was recruited? The weak, the poor, and the Jews. He was poor and Jewish. So he had to go to the army. Who sent him to the army? His Arab Muslim friends. He never forgot, so he didn't like them.

Now my grandfather from Germany was a very proud German. He joined the German army in the First World War and even won the Iron Cross. He never went to the synagogue. All his life he didn't eat kosher food. He fought against the British and against the French and against the Russians, everything in the name of God and Kaiser, and he ended the war with some nice medals. He was a very proud German. And when the Nazis came to power, everybody, his Nazi friends, his Gestapo friends and his SS friends came to him and said, "Oh, Heinrich, don't be afraid, nothing will happen to you because you fought with us, you spent nights with us in trenches fighting the French, you are one of us." He was lucky. He married a Russian Jew, my grandmother. She saw what was coming and encouraged her husband to leave Germany. They went from Germany to Vienna. The ambassador in Vienna at that time was a very well known American anti-Semite. He told them, "Your place is not in America; your place is in Palestine." And they came to Palestine.

The experience of my grandparents hasn't raised much hope in me for the kind of peace that people are talking about, this beautiful harmony between Jews and Arabs, kissing and hugging each other in the streets. I don't see any sign of this kind of peace. I don't see any signs of this peace being possible today, tomorrow, day after tomorrow, in a year, in two years, in ten years or twenty years. I have come to the conclusion that the most important thing for Israel is defence, and in defence there are no choices. We are not people of war. We don't enjoy war. We don't enjoy going to war. We don't enjoy even doing our yearly service in the reserves. But this is our fate. This is our way of life. There is no other way.

There is a place for a Palestinian state, but not on this side of the River Jordan. I am not against the Palestinians as human beings. I am not against them as a political unit. I am not against them as a state. But I am against them as a state ten miles away from Tel Aviv.

Orith Shohath, *a spokesperson for a political party, was born in Israel in 1950. Though she knows that Israel is her home and that her family has lived in the country for three generations, she is uneasy about the future because of both the Jews and the Arabs.*

I'm not happy about the fact that my grandparents came here in the first place. I think it was wrong, but I know also that this fact can't be changed. It was wrong because the Middle East had an Arab majority. We came and chased people away. Maybe we could have lived together, but from the beginning we did it the wrong way. We chased them away, took their places, their homes, their territory. I think I can feel at home anywhere where I'm with Jewish people. I don't think it has anything to do with the land. I think we can solve the problem by creating a Palestinian state and getting all the hate out of the people in two or three generations. I think we could live here very happily together. I don't know if it's a solution, but I think it's worth a try. Not doing anything at all is not a solution anyway.

I am not satisfied at all with what is happening here in regard to this problem. The Americans regard us as a democratic country, but they don't know that it's not true. The government feeds us certain kinds of information which saves their policies and it's not true information. Lebanon is an example. I'm sure Israel is involved there, but nobody knows it yet. They don't tell us the facts about the West Bank. Terrible things are happening there now, and they don't show it on television. They try to make everything look nice and beautiful, especially during election time. They don't tell us that there are a million and a half people in the West Bank. They say it's a million, not a million and a half, and the fact that they grow by 60,000 a year, and that in twenty years they will outnumber the Jewish people in Israel is something that they don't tell us.

Where did I get these insights? I was interested in the problem a long time ago. I studied political science and also Middle East history. I was in the States and in Europe. I heard things from a different point of view. I read books that weren't written by Israelis and now I'm comparing and trying to see it in the right way. They never deal with the facts as they are. They always brainwash us and themselves. When you brainwash somebody else for a certain length of time, then you start believing it. The results are going to be very bad. I love Israel and its excellent people. But I am very critical now of the state and its policies. I see Israel facing a pretty bleak future unless something is done here. It could be too late, but I think it's worth a try.

I'm Israeli. I don't feel Jewish. There's a difference between the two, I think. I feel Israeli with specific Israeli problems. I don't feel the problems the Jews had for generations. It's a different kind of hate between the Arabs and the Jews than what we had between the Christians and the Jews. Only when I go abroad do I feel Jewish. People get the feeling that I have these political views because I care about the Palestinians and don't care about the Israelis. And this is not true. I would much rather the Palestinians make their home in New Zealand. But that's not possible. The only place to do it is in the West Bank, and these are the facts of life.

When I was visiting the United States recently I was surprised to discover anti-Semitism. We stopped in a little place in Vermont. The owner of the small hotel was Jewish, but he was afraid to say so. After we said that we were from Israel, he exposed his Star of David. He said, "Now I can show it. Usually I hide it, because clients who come to the hotel don't like a Jewish owner, not in this part of the state and not in Vermont where there are not a lot of Jewish people." I had never considered that problem at all. I don't like that feeling. In the United States I could have a very nice life, since my mother is a doctor. But I don't think I can survive with the feeling of not being wanted as a Jew anywhere. In the States it's just getting worse and worse. I think it's going to get worse because people will be more and more jealous. I had that feeling all the time in America. The people really like Israelis, but I don't think they like Jews. I don't have a problem being an Israeli in the States, but I think I would have a problem being a Jew in the States. The feeling that Jews have of the world not wanting them is very strong.

Pinhas Leibowitz *spent his childhood in Turkey. Although his parents lived in Russia for generations, they held Turkish citizenship to avoid serving in the Russian army. He speaks for the Newspaper Publishers Association of which he is secretary-general. But mostly he speaks for himself. He loves his country which is why he is critical.*

When I was seventeen years old I decided I wanted to leave Turkey and go to Palestine. Without any Jewish background, without being religious, without knowing much about Jewry, or about Palestine, I felt I wanted to live among my own people. That is how I came to Palestine; illegally, of course. It was in 1933 and I have been living here ever since.

Lots of people emigrated from Russia because of the Bolshevik revolution. Some of them went to France, some to the States, some to North and South America. In Istanbul there was a colony of Russian Jews who kept together. They were quite prosperous until nationalism penetrated Turkey. Turks started to say that people should talk Turkish. I suppose that is one of the reasons why there was no future for me in Turkey. Turkish was a language which Europeans did not care very much about. I went to French school, read French, and spoke French. At home I spoke Russian. My people were, in a way, assimilated Russian Jews, who felt that talking Yiddish wasn't so nice. My mother stuck very much to Russian culture, Russian literature, Russian manners. Everything Russian was beautiful in her eyes.

My father died and my mother decided to stay in Turkey with my younger brother. Although I didn't know much about Jewry, I felt I didn't want to live in Turkey. I didn't like the ways. I suppose that maybe I didn't like the kind of Jews that lived in Turkey. I wanted something different, something that had roots. You know, almost everywhere the Jews are merchants. They don't have roots, nothing that has anything solid in it. I wanted a different type of life, something more real. I felt instinctively that I wanted to be among my own people.

In 1942 I joined a Jewish brigade of the British army. I was in the army until 1946. Meanwhile I took on a job with an English newspaper, the *Palestine Post*. I worked at the *Post* until 1952, when I took on my job as secretary of the Publishers Association.

What does it mean to be a Jew? First of all, you must be capable of facing reality. You have to live with it. It is not a matter of choice. It is an accident like any other accident in life. The Jews think a little bit deeper than others do, and they are more inclined to take a philosophical approach to problems. There is a lot of empathy in Jews. We feel other people's suffering; we commiserate with it. We are more sensitive to things, probably because there is so much suffering in our history. We know how much it hurts and that is probably why we are more aware. I suppose we try to be a little bit better, a little more conscious. We try to better things for ourselves and for others. We tend very often to split hairs and create problems where there aren't any problems. On the whole it's just an accident, nothing more. You have got to make the most of it and do what you can with that accident. That's as far as it goes for unbelieving Jews. There are those who are religious and for them the matter is much simpler. They believe in the holy scriptures. Everything is laid out for them and it is so much simpler.

In some respects I probably look at Jews more critically. We are not a nation yet. We are still a massive conglomeration of various cultures. We are a country of immigrants. We mean to bring in as many Jews as we can from wherever they might want to come. This has had a far-reaching effect on life in Israel. Jews coming from North Africa brought habits, manners, attitudes. We started eating a lot of Oriental food. We have a lot more people in the streets. There was a considerable lowering of standards. That is an unavoidable thing. By a process of osmosis, integration, and transformation, we hope to become a nation. Today we are a gathering of various ethnic elements which are not a nation. You can see people everywhere. The streets are not clean.

We have a big problem with Russian immigration. There is not enough awareness or understanding here of what Russian Jewry is. Coming from Russia is coming to an entirely different world. Russian Jews were brought up where the state takes care of everything, where you are told what to do. Getting used to democracy and the ways of democracy is an extremely painful and difficult process for them. If, on top of that, they get the feeling that they are not wanted here, that they are not welcome – that breaks them. And very often it's the result of people dealing with them who are not aware of the realities of the Russian problem. They're just not aware, it's beyond their scope, beyond their understanding. They don't realize how important it is for others. Instead they look at it as a nuisance, a pain in the neck.

This is a critical time for Israel for other reasons. One thing is the dreams. Reality never lives up to the dreams. The dream of a Jewish state is one thing; to live a Jewish state is another. The trimmings of sovereignty or statehood have had an effect. You've got to be very strong, morally strong, not to lose a sense of proportion as a result of being in power. We must remember that it's just sheer accident that we are in a commanding, dominating position. This feeling of power has a debasing effect. It's natural, it's human.

There is also a weakening of motivation. That is a very important element which I'll try to explain. We had people coming here from Europe after the Second World War, people who had been to the concentration camps, who had been through all the horrors of the war. They came here and they rebuilt their lives, they married, they had children. They wanted to spare their children the trauma of what they'd been through. So parents wouldn't talk to their children about what had happened in order that their children could grow up as healthy human beings, without traumas, without fears, without all the things that had marred the lives of their parents.

The pendulum went to the far side. It has come to the point where the children know practically nothing about what brought their parents to Israel, why they were born in this country. And that creates a certain estrangement on the part of the children. They see themselves as children anywhere, in any other part of the world. They don't feel what is very particular, very special, why they are here. So for them to leave Israel, go elsewhere, means nothing. The result of it is that there are over 300,000 Israelis abroad, and some of them are being influenced by other young people and taking drugs. And they try to dress the way people dress elsewhere, without thinking about what is natural, what is in keeping, fitting with the realities of life here, in Israel.

Today you very often find young people who will go abroad without having any uneasiness about it. In other words, their motivation has weakened. And this is really one of the serious things. Without motivation, being here loses much of its sense. My counterpart in the States probably makes about thirty times more than I make here. I live in humble circumstances. But I don't feel miserable about it at all. If tomorrow, instead of driving a car, I have to ride a bicycle, I wouldn't be miserable about it. Only if you have that attitude, can life in Israel make sense.

The Palestinian problem? In the Middle East we are a foreign element. We are a threat to everything that Islam stands for, and to the Eastern way of thinking and acting. We are too dynamic. We have too many ideas. We run counter to the patriarchal way of living. We are a foreign element, which, by the laws of nature, is rejected from the body. They will go on rejecting us until they see that they cannot reject us. We must be so strong that they lose any hope of annihilating us, because that is their aim. There is no doubt about it. And this is why the sweet reasonableness advocated by some nations is the most dangerous thing that can happen to us. They just abhor the idea of our being here. They hate our guts, and the only way we can think of staying on is by not giving them the slightest hope of annihilating us. Nobody wants peace more than we do, but we don't want to kill ourselves. We can't afford to make mistakes. We can't afford to lose one single battle. We shall have to carry on our shoulders the most excruciating financial burden. We are the highest taxed people in all the world. I believe 60 or 70 per cent of our budget goes to security. We must have the most sophisticated hardware.

There is a sense of solidarity here, a community of fate. We were chosen for troubles. We have more than our share of troubles, more than our share, as a nation and as human beings. It's a fact. We've been God's emissaries to mankind throughout the ages. Whenever anything went wrong, the Jews were to blame. This shapes you as a human being and your approach to life. I suppose it even shapes your approach to other people.

Michael DeVries *was born in Holland in 1939 and came to Israel in 1965. He works as a travel agent. During his military service, Mr. DeVries worked as a liaison officer for foreign journalists, TV crews, and other people who visited the Good Fence of Matulla.*

We are seeing here something very, very special. In the Old Testament there is mention of the Dan tribe, which controlled three villages here in the north. One of the villages was called Able, and it was a free city to which refugees could come without being persecuted. Today, in 1976, that is exactly what is happening here. Persecuted people from over the border come to Matulla, which is the site of the former Able, to seek refuge and medical and humanitarian aid. Their own brethren across the border in Lebanon have turned their backs on them. They don't have anyone to turn to but their former enemies, and look what's happening. Suddenly they are finding out that we don't wear horns. We don't have a tail. We are extending a helping hand, feeding and clothing them, and

115

assisting them in fighting our common enemy. That's what makes this a very special thing.

The people who live in the area surrounding the northern border are completely cut off from the rest of Lebanon by warring factions – the Syrian army on the one side and the Palestinian terrorists on the other side. There are all kinds of warring factions putting up roadblocks. The people are left on their own; nobody cares for them. These people come to us and trust us. I hope that in the end we'll come to some understanding with our neighbours in the field of humanitarian acts and in the field of trade. I'm hopeful that people will get accustomed to each other, and will learn to live with each other, difficult as it may be. I hope to see it myself. If not, I trust that my children and my grandchildren will see it and not have to send their sons to war to get killed. Yes, I'm an optimistic realist.

How was the Good Fence opened? It began about fifteen months ago. It first started when the war was still raging in Lebanon. A woman from one of the villages came to the fence to ask for medical help for a child who was very sick. One of our patrols passed by, radioed for help, and a doctor came out and helped the woman. So we decided to open up a medical aid post. A tent was set up. Later it became a hut and later on the semi-permanent buildings that are there now. Today about 500 to 600 people cross daily into Israel to work and approximately 100 come for medical aid. This is the very first time that we have dealt with the population of a neighbouring country on an equal basis. We are not the oppressor, the victor.

M. Bernard Resnikoff *was born in the US in 1918 and came to Israel in 1966. He is the spokesman of the American Jewish Committee in Israel. The committee seeks to apply its expertise in human relations to all the social problems in Israel.*

The American Jewish Committee is the oldest human relations organization on the American scene. It was founded in 1906 by half a dozen people who at the time were concerned with the plight of Jews in Czarist Russia. But the organization has grown since that time to have a much larger, ecumenical thrust. It is now of the opinion that the socio-economic status of Jews in the United States or elsewhere is intertwined with the status of other minority groups. We are concerned that every American, regardless of his race, his colour or his religion, has his fair share of American largesse, and so we have the anomaly of the American Jewish organization fighting for the chicanos in northern California, or the blacks in Detroit. In the same way, but with greater intensity, the American Jewish Committee intends to use their accumulated body of knowledge and skill in Israel to help this country solve some of its problems. What we're trying to do in this country is improve communication between the Jewish majority and the various religious or ethnic minorities.

The American base of the American Jewish Committee consists of chapters in regions throughout the United States. We have a staff of about 300, and we have chapters in many large cities and communities of the United States. We try to seek out men of stature and influence; men with established credentials in occupations or professions; articulate, college-educated men. We don't go in so much for mass meetings, petitions, and rallies as for the scientific method and the gathering of data. We try to use a rational approach to the amelioration of social problems. We are concerned with the protection of all minorities.

Anytime you try to make a change, you have to take into account the social environment and the probable reception of the idea. There are different sets of approaches. We do a lot of work in interrelations between the Jew and the non-Jew, which calls for a different set of techniques from those working, say, between the Jew and the Arab. You have to deal differently with the Western Christian and the indigenous Arab Christian, because, quite naturally, political considerations intrude upon the nature of faith relationships. In the same way, a problem between an Israeli Jew and an Israeli Arab, as you surely know, is different from a problem between an Israeli Jew and a West Bank Arab, a Gaza Arab, or an East Jerusalem Arab. And so we use a variety of techniques, which can include such things as experimentation, laboratory techniques, research, group dynamics, and weekend institutes.

In this part of the world, problems are volatile and multi-layered and not nearly as simple as in North America. In America both the blacks and the whites say that the American experience is good. Both were brought up in the same system, speak the same language. Here it's different. The Jew and the Arab, both of them citizens of this country, have different cultures, different languages, different religions, different histories, different tastes and habits. The things that they share are not as many as members of two different groups in the United States. So here you have to have respect. To understand and appreciate any culture other than your own, you have to look at it in terms of its own value system.

With respect to the Jews from Oriental countries it is true that they are second-class citizens, *but* . . . . The "but" has to do with moderation, it has to do with legislation, it has to do with intent. I don't know of any formal or institutional design to make the Jews of Oriental countries second-class citizens. They are the majority in the country, which is another kind of problem in socio-political terms and I think that if there are any ways in which they are second-class citizens, it's a function of history. By this I mean that the Jews of Oriental countries have come to a highly technological society, twentieth-century in its orientation, political system, and technology, a society which requires a sophisticated knowledge of how to live in a democratic pluralistic system. These people have come from underdeveloped countries, and they have never acquired the technical skill to make their way in a technological society. They were thrust, overnight, from the sixteenth century into the twentieth. This is a pretty tough assignment. If you find more Jews of Western origin in seats of power than Jews of Eastern origin, I think it's a consequence of this historical fact more than anything else.

The Arabs have their own traditions: they have the family system; they have the billet system; they have a cultural system; and they choose, I would say quite understandably, to live among their own number, so that in their togetherness they can pursue their life, which is perfectly proper. As a result, growing up as they do in a twentieth-century technological society, they are falling behind in terms of the acquisition of those artifacts of civilization which make it possible to move forward.

In order to be fair, I have to point out one other thing. The Arab citizens are a minority within a Jewish majority which has a certain Jewish nationalistic aspiration and purpose, with which the Arabs of Israel simply cannot identify. I don't blame them for that. I can't see them getting as excited as the Jews of Israel about the plight of Soviet Jews, or encouraging their reception in the country. They can't identify with that. They can't identify with the spiritual and cultural aspirations of the nationalistic Zionist movement. Theodore Herzl can't possibly be one of their folk heroes as he is a Jewish folk hero.

But I think, given the socio-cultural circumstances, Israel is doing fairly well for its Arab minority in terms of certain fixed guarantees. They are better off economically and sociologically by our standards. But of course there are psychological tensions because they identify with other Arabs whose sovereign states are at war with Israel. I think that is in itself a problem.

There is an asymmetry in the relationship between the Jew and the Christian. Theologically, and maybe historically, the Christian needs the Jew, positively or negatively, whereas the Jew does not need the Christian. Christianity started as a sect of Judaism, and since Christianity had or still has a sense of mission to get the Jew to accept the Christian's Christ, the Christian is inescapably tied to the Jew. Judaism, the older religion, which flourished before Christianity sprang up, and flourished subsequently, is capable of surviving without Christianity. This is what I mean by asymmetry.

I believe that some of the roots of anti-Semitism are found in theology. And I have a gut feeling, which I cannot yet document, that now in the seventies, here in Israel, the Jewish capacity to relate to the Christian who shares this country with him makes possible perhaps for the first time in recorded history, a relationship which is more balanced. You see, in the past, in the Middle Ages, and even in the twentieth century, the Jew, as he approached the Christian in some kind of relationship, came from a position of weakness. Sometimes he shut out the relationship in order to reinforce and maintain his hard-won civil rights and assure his cultural survival. This doesn't apply in this country because the Jews are in the majority and the people of power. Here, the Jew is able to approach the Christian with a mutual appreciation and understanding which makes possible a relationship that is more soundly based. This is one of the reasons for my private conviction that it would be ghastly if this country were 100 per cent Jewish. We would be denying ourselves and the world an opportunity to demonstrate how it is possible for two major monotheistic faiths to be locked together, not in a confrontation, but in an embrace. And I grieve when Christians leave this country, whether they are Easterners or Westerners. We have in this country a large number of Western Christians, Western Christians who choose to share their life with us in the Holy Land. We are making possible at least a beginning of a new kind of ecumenicity that is totally refreshing, and boggling in its dimensions.

Jewish-Arab relations in the Middle East? Personally I happen to think that territory is not an issue – how many yards or acres of ground that we surrender. I don't think the refugee problem is an issue. I think that the basic issue is the unwillingness of the Arabs to accept Israel as a non-Islamic, non-Arab sovereign state in their part of the world.

The only thing that holds promise for peace in the Middle East is the Arab capacity for patience and for learning to live with certain situations. They may never be happy with a non-Arab, non-Muslim state in the Middle East, but maybe given plenty of time they will learn to suffer it just as a person suffers a physical disability or blindness. You're not happy about it, but you've got it, and after all you make your compensations and adjustments. Arabs do have this talent, and this might come into play, but to accept Israel, or to embrace Israel, or conditionally to accept Israel, I don't see it happening.

Duv Friedlander's *family was scattered from Austria, where he was born in 1934, right after the* Anschlusz. *By 1946 they arrived in* Palestine. *Duv subsequently studied psychology in England and Canada and became director of student counselling services at Hebrew University in 1970. He offers a scholarly opinion concerning the effect of war and perpetual conflict on the psyche of the Israeli people.*

When I came back to Israel in 1970, I wondered what type of population I would be returning to after fourteen years. One of the things that concerned me was how a nation could survive three decades of war without there being some impact on the whole psyche of the people and their outlook on life.

I find that the Israelis are quite normal. Their overriding concerns have to do with the economic situation, with the cost of living, with bureaucracy, with inefficiency. Israelis seem to be terribly thirsty to find culture, and to get on with activities for which there is no time in war. The average Israeli wants to travel a lot. We are great tourists.

The Israeli seems to have a tremendous ability a few days after the war to get back to "normal." We did a study after the war on students at Hebrew University. We took a population of 300 students who had been in combat. We defined combat very objectively including data about the number of days in a combat zone, the number of hours of shelling or casualties in the company.

Our results, surprisingly enough, show that exactly one year after the end of the war, business was back to normal for these students. We made comparisons with American veterans from the Vietnam War or the Korean War and concluded that the Israelis had made a remarkable adjustment. The only signs of change we could find were much higher identification with the Israeli nationality and much more commitment to the country. My objective perception as a psychologist working with students is that in one way or another Israelis are making a remarkable adjustment to this conflict situation. I don't think that you can objectively say that the "Israeli personality" is a direct consequence of being in conflict. I think it is much easier to say that the characteristics of the average Israeli are due to difficulties of the economy, the bureaucracy, the polyglot of people gathering here, the intermingling of different ethnic groups at different levels—the difficulties of living in Israel generally.

The Israelis, I think, take a fairly realistic view of life. If they want to survive, they're going to put up and live with a very hazardous type of security situation. They adjust very quickly to the fact that their handbags are checked at every movie house or supermarket and that they themselves are frisked. They seem to appreciate that this is being done for their own safety. I am also impressed with the fact that the security situation is not a cause of havoc in the whole economic, cultural, and social life of the country. Nothing comes to a halt because somebody goes off for forty days for reserve duty. Somehow we find a way of wading around it or making up for it. It's par for the course.

There are so many conflicts and tensions in Israel. There is conflict between the observant religious Jew and the non-religious Jew; there is a conflict between the Zionist religious Jew and the non-Zionist religious Jew. There are a whole bunch who have decided that the Messiah hasn't come and that therefore there is no State of Israel. On the Day of Independence they put up black flags. There is a lot of tension between various ethnic groups, namely the Oriental Jew and the European Jew, which is becoming more of an economic tension, the disadvantaged versus the advantaged. There is tension between groups who differ on what's holy and what isn't, which historic borders are more authentic than others. One of the most incredible things about Israel is the degree of tolerance and democracy in a country that's been in combat for thirty years. There is less tolerance in peaceful countries than there is in Israel.

The tension strongest inside of me has to do with what is real and what is ideal. This war has been going on for thirty years. We paid a lot in blood and assets to create this state. For what purpose? Just to be another state in the world? What should I bleed for? I might sound a bit naïve or idealistic, but I feel that if at the end of all this conflict we are just another state on the map, we won't have done very much. The Zionist idea was to create a model, an ideal, a democracy that could be a light to the world. Today you ask yourself, what has Israel given the world since its conception? It has given the world the concept of the kibbutz and a model for some form of communal living. I certainly see radical differences between a communal settlement in Israel and a commune in Russia. What else have they given? I don't know whether one should be proud of this – but they've given a model of military force in a small nation.

Believers

*"The Jewish people, as God's chosen people, returned to the
Holy Land to pick up at the point where we should never
have left off."*
–Nachman Kahana

One of the surprises in Israel is to discover how many people who call
themselves Jews claim, at the same time, not to be religious. Indeed, the
real surprise is the eagerness and the emphasis with which this information is volunteered and insisted upon as important and correct. The
disclaimer must, of course, be understood in its proper context lest its
meaning be distorted. What non-religious Jews claim is that they are not
religious in the way in which religious Jews are defined in Israel. Religious Jews, it is assumed, are orthodox Jews who adhere to rules and
rituals representing the historic practices of Judaism. Where such a
specific interpretation of religion is understood it becomes quite evident
that even so-called non-religious Jews are actually religious, given the
philosophy and ethics, the values and attitudes which they espouse. As a
matter of fact, the new Judaism or the new expression of Judaism is Israel
for many Jews. Nationalism is itself a religion.

Be that as it may, there are religious Jews, and there are rabbis who
speak for the varieties of religious expression in Judaism. Among the
believers are also "converts," though that term must be used advisedly
given the fact that almost every conversion (i.e. every acceptance of
Judaism by a non-Jew) stands by itself. In other words, the variety of
religious believers covers a wide spectrum.

Mordecai Piron *has been a rabbi with the Israeli Defence Corps for
twenty-nine years. Now he is chief rabbi. He grew up in Vienna and
succeeded in escaping when Hitler invaded Austria in 1938, but his
parents lost their lives there. Rabbi Piron studied at Hebrew University and at London University. He speaks about Judaism and the
military.*

It is not a contradiction to be both a religious and a military man.
According to Jewish philosophy, we abhor war. Our philosophy is anti-

militaristic because war is one of the worst things that can befall mankind. It's a disaster, a catastrophe. According to Jewish conviction, if somebody comes up to kill you, you have to defend yourself and not allow yourself to be killed. There is a big difference between the idealization of war, which we are against, and the realistic knowledge that in order to stay alive we have to fight.

Being a Jew in Israel today means creating a new authenticity for Judaism. This means going back to the roots and to the core of Jewish thinking, philosophy, and ethics, and building the nation in the spirit of all this. To be a real Jew means to identify with our history of 4,000 years, and everything connected with it. In every generation we try to find the right interpretation of what is written in the Bible. The meaning of Judaism in all generations has been to give new meaning to the words of the Bible in the context of everyday life.

I would say the essence of Judaism in all ages has been the love of God, the love of mankind, and the love of study. The love of God is the basic concept which has been fundamental to the existence of our nation for thousands of years. God is the centre of our being and our existence. God as a universal power is the basis of Judaism, which is a theocentric conception. The second is love of human beings. That's the basis of Jewish ethics. We speak about the holiness of life, not only Jewish life but all lives. We speak of love and sympathy. And the third is love of studies. We have always seen study, understanding, logical thinking, as the peak of Jewish existence.

It is true that many Israeli Jews are not religious, but that doesn't mean that they are atheists. Not being religious is a phenomenon very common in Israel and all over the world. But many human beings who declare themselves not to be religious are in reality religious. They just don't know it. Sometimes a moment comes, maybe during battle or in some adversity, when they discover that the only power they can turn to is God. Then they change their mind, their feelings, their emotions. They change their being. Some may remain irreligious all their lives. From the Jewish national point of view that's a very difficult situation.

I do not feel the slightest feeling of hatred against Arabs. If I felt a hatred somewhere in my heart, I would try immediately to root it out. There is a dispute, a very tragic dispute, going on between us and the Arabs all over the world. It's a miserable situation. It's madness. I'm sure that a way can be found.

What led to the Jewish passion for learning? If you read the Bible carefully, you will find that many passages state very clearly that knowledge of God and of things is most important. The Prophets speak always of knowledge of God. That means not only knowledge of Him but of His creatures and of nature.

123

If you carry out an indoctrination over thousands of years, you can create a certain mentality and a thirst for knowledge. The Jews have that mentality and thirst. Jews see in intellectual achievement the highest human achievement. Among Jews a learned man, even if he is a very poor one, is always respected because of his learning. You have to take into account that in 300 B.C., at a time when most people all around the world were still in a primitive and barbaric state, there were already networks of Jewish schools. Practically all children went to school and knew how to read and to write.

There are two things which, in my humble opinion, are the work of a rabbi in the army. First of all, the creation of a framework that enables a religious Jew to work in the army, to carry out all the commandments of the law of our religion freely without any compromises and with a minimum of friction with those who are non-religious. The other task is to carry to those young men and women who enter the army the message of Judaism, of real authentic Judaism, meaning the significance of being a Jew. This includes explaining the meaning of the State of Israel, the connection between the life of Israel and the nation of Israel, and all this with reference to God. It includes the teaching of Jewish ethics in time of war, the principle of love for all human beings, and to explain to them the apparent contradiction between all this and killing in time of war.

To be a conscientious objector in Israel is madness. I think it's quite impossible. You can be a conscientious objector if your country is going out to invade and to expand. But all the wars we fight here are really wars of survival. All our wars are defensive wars. We are fighting for our existence. Conscientious objection is impossible in such a situation. The cause of the war is clear. There is nothing holier, nothing more ethical, than to defend your home, your house, your land, your field, your forest, against those who come to kill you. That's the holiest thing possible.

Menachem Porush, *a rabbi, heads a political party in Israel and has been a member of the Knesset five times. He was born in 1916, and his family is the ninth generation in Israel, having come from Russia 200 years ago. He believes that God promised Israel to the Jews.*

God promised this land to the Jewish people. That is why, nine genera-tions back, my family came here to Israel: because this land had been promised in the Bible to the Jewish people. Although there had been no Jewish people in Israel for about 2,000 years, we had been expecting all the time to come back to Israel.

For us, separation of religion and state doesn't exist. To be a rabbi, as well as a member of the parliament, is not contradictory. Being a politician is essential for a rabbi. According to our philosophy, religion and nationalism can't be separated. I am in the Knesset to keep religion in the Holy Land. There are some people who, because of these many years in the diaspora, feel it's difficult to fulfil religious demands. But practically, the Jewish state recognizes the Jewish religion as something that cannot be separated from the state.

I am fighting in the Knesset, first of all, so that we, the religious Jews, can be in our land, Israel. We have achieved that. We are satisfied. We are happy. I wouldn't say that we got everything that we would like to have, but Israel is a place where a Jew can live as a Jew has to live. Secondly, I would like to influence the state so that it is ruled according to my ideas. That's why I am in the Knesset. That's why the greatest leaders of religious Jewry are so concerned that Jewish religious members should be represented in the Knesset. But the main principles of religion are already recognized by the secular authorities.

There are many differences among the Jews themselves concerning how far we should go to make peace with the Arabs. In my private opinion, the time hasn't come yet for the Arabs to understand that they have to recognize our existence. I don't think they are ready to talk about peace. They still have the same attitudes that they had fifty years ago. They didn't learn a lesson from what they went through. My solution for the Palestinian problem is that the Palestinians should settle in part of the Jordanian territory.

Nachman Kahana, *a rabbi, was born in New York in 1938. His father was born in Palestine, but left during the difficult years after the First World War, first studying in Germany, and then going to the US. Rabbi Kahana and his wife came to Israel in 1962 with a "real feeling of coming home." His parents and brother subsequently joined them. They believe that all the land from the Nile to the Euphrates belongs to the Jewish people.*

The roots of the conflict between Israel and the Arabs are very deep differences caused by religion and national characteristics. I see the State of Israel, even though it may appear to be secular to the outsider, as a continuation of the Bible. Those 2,000 years of exile I would call an "intermission" in Jewish history which shouldn't have been. I don't believe that it was planned, I don't think that it was God's will. It occurred because the Jewish people sinned. We did not keep the Sabbath the way we should. We did not respect the other laws. Consequently we went into exile. The Jews have come back to take up the biblical story at this point and, if today a Prophet were alive, I'm sure that we would get permission from God to continue to write more chapters. The miracles we have seen in Israel are certainly of the quality of the miracles in the Bible.

The story of the Jewish people here is not a question of the Arab-Israeli conflict. It's a question of the fulfilment of God's will. The Jewish people, as God's chosen people, returned to the Holy Land to pick up at the point where we should never have left off. The presence of the Gentiles here when the Jews came back I see as a very undesirable thing. Their opposition to us is anti-Semitism. It's hatred of the Jews. When you deal with the Palestinian question, fourteen or fifteen Arab nations, stretching from the Persian Gulf to the Atlantic, could have resettled all these refugees with no problem at all, considering the money, the land, and the resources that the Arabs have today.

If the world cannot realize that this is Jewish land and cannot stand firm behind us, then the world will have to pay the price. I think that Jewish trouble is coming to an end. I think that the world is going to pay for the blindness and for the hatred of the Jews that has been going on through all these generations. In other words, the conflict is not a political question. I think this is the old question of anti-Semitism coming from the Arabs, from the Western countries, and from the Communist bloc. I think the only way to find tranquillity in this country is not to return territories or land, but to return Arabs. In my opinion the Jews and Arabs cannot live together. There is the difference of religion and the difference of mentalities. Some way must be found for the Arabs to go to their countries.

The Jews have to continue living their destiny as God's chosen people. This country is ours, all of it. Its presence was promised us by God. The land God promised stretches from the Euphrates River in the north, which is the river which borders between Syria and Iraq, to the Nile in the south, and from the Mediterranean Sea to the eastern part of Transjordan. That's the Jewish promised land. The Jews don't want any more, and I don't believe the Jews will settle for anything less.

It's the age-old conflict between Jews and Gentiles, the Jews claiming to be God's chosen people and the Gentiles denying it. This is the actual conflict of Israel. In every historical period the Jews have had many enemies. Never in Jewish history has there been an enemy which, when he began to go down, rose up again. Except one. That's the German nation. The Germans have yet to pay for what they did to the Jewish people, and I say this not out of hate. I think it's a historical fact.

The world is on the verge of a tremendous calamity. Even though I may not be able to prove it, I have a strong intuition that it is connected with the Holy Land. The Jews living in this country will survive. My only

126

worry is for the Jews outside of this country. I would suggest that they come here as fast as possible. I think the world is going down a one-way collision road, and there is no return. Someone is going to have to pay for the 2,000 years of Jewish suffering.

The miracles I mentioned earlier are the miracles I've seen. It's a little bit difficult to understand what happened in the Six Day War. One morning Rabin announced on the radio that Israel had destroyed 400 Arab planes. Now, these things don't just happen. When Israel is so badly outnumbered, and they are able to conquer a great part of the Jewish promised land in seven days, it's a miracle. These things don't just happen. Wars take years to fight. And when we finish one in seven days, that's a miracle.

And I think that a bigger war was the Yom Kippur War. Israel was caught offguard and unprepared. It was such a terrible political decision that Golda Meir made—not to strike first. We paid for it with 3,000 Jewish boys. If Israel was able to pull the chestnuts out of that fire, to move within 100 kilometres of Cairo, and to surround the Egyptian Third Army, and to come within thirty kilometres of Damascus, with such a terrible starting-off point, that's really a miracle. In the whole history of the world, 3 million people in our situation haven't been able to do what we are doing.

Another miracle I think is the lack of fear among the people here. I think that other nations would break. There's no fear here. There's belief. There's optimism. There's courage here in this country, and I think there's a great deal of faith in God. I think that's the underlying thing in this country. Politics, or what we've seen of politics, is only one-ninth of the iceberg. The real things making people move are the things of religion.

Anti-Semitism is in effect anti-God. I think the Christian world holds it against the Jew for giving them Christianity, but since they can't knock Christianity, they do it in a more sophisticated way by hating Jews. Through the Jews, Christianity and also Muhammadanism were brought to the world, and I think that the Gentiles rebel against that. Hatred of a Jew is the Gentile's hatred of the things they were brought up to believe in. They would prefer to go back to the old free times, the orgy days, the pagan days, and take off this mantle of religion that the Jewish people have given them, which in effect goes with the idea of God's chosen people. The Jews have been chosen to make this world a more civilized place by bringing all these different ideas to the non-Jewish world, and this is in fact, the way I see it, the basis of anti-Semitism. Anti-Semitism is hatred, hatred of God, hatred of God's will. When a Christian says that a Jew killed Christ, in effect he himself would like to kill Christ, but he can't do it, so he says the Jews have done it.

127

Jack Cohen *of the Hillel Foundation at Hebrew University, Mt. Scopus, first arrived in Palestine from the US in 1947. The trip was part of his marriage commitment to his wife, a devoted Zionist. The Cohens fell in love with Jerusalem and returned again in 1961. Since then, Rabbi Cohen has devoted his energies to Jewish religious life in Israel.*

In the long history of the Jewish people, the land of Israel has always played a major role. Obviously, that role has changed over the centuries. Following the exile, the land of Palestine was a sentiment, a very powerful sentiment, in the thinking of the Jewish people. Now, Zionism is compiled of a number of elements. During the period of Hitler, I was able to see the reality of the Jewish position in the world: it meant constantly being at the mercy of the goodwill of other peoples. I'm sure all of us recall the ships that were turned away. The whole problem of being a recipient of the largesse, or the mercy, or the pity, or the goodwill, of others is one element of Zionism.

In my opinion the major element is the fact that people have to be tested by power. The Jewish people have been a minority people throughout their history, except for short periods. If there is any value to Jewish religion as such, and if there is any merit to the moral pretensions of the Jewish people, they have to be tested in a setting where their faith is challenged.

I was drawn to the Zionist movement in the thirties, when we all faced the excitement of radical movements. I looked around for something that I could hold on to, and I felt I had found it in the various social experiments that were taking place here in Eretz Israel. It wasn't the state that attracted me; it was the possibility of building an autonomous existence here, which I felt was one of the options that should be available to Judaism.

Now, right from the beginning my Zionism involved the relationships that Jews ought to establish with the Arabs. I'm very much concerned that the status of minorities in the State of Israel should not only be protected, but should become for them a source of enrichment. That's an objective which is, obviously, very difficult to accomplish, but this is the perspective in which I see things. Zionism is still the movement to ensure the right of the Jewish people to maintain its majority status in an autonomous country. That seems to me to be the main element.

From there on you run into all kinds of differences. As a religious person, or as a person who thinks along these religious lines, I don't consider state nationalism to be the goal of human civilization. I think it's a stage which has to be overcome. I think that the earth is the Lord's and the fullness thereof, and we are all here on more or less long-term or

128

short-term leases. We do not have an absolute right to any soil. I don't argue that the Jewish people have an absolute right to any place any more than another people has. The sentiments that are attached to this land are factors that have to be taken into account, but they in themselves are not, and should not be decisive. What seems to me to be decisive is the opportunity for people to develop their own authenticity, without doing too much harm to someone else. You see, the tragedy of the land of Israel, of Palestine, is that the Palestinians, as they now call themselves, and the Jews, have met at a time when neither is in a position – psychologically, culturally, or historically – to be fully and completely able to empathize with the other.

What does it mean for me to be Jewish? I can give you the things that animate me, that excite me. I grew up in a Jewish home, which conferred on me an anchor in life. There was a rhythm to my week, which still remains. The Sabbath is a great occasion. It's filled with beauty and opportunity for reflection. To me a service with fellow Jews in a synagogue is vastly important. I'm able to share the lives of other people, to give them support in moments when they may need me, and to be enriched and protected by them in moments that are difficult for me. Sharing a joy is also a spiritual moment. And the rhythm of both family and community I find a great source of joy. This is enhanced by my attachment to my great tradition. It's a tradition I do not feel called upon to justify, because I am quite critical of much of it.

Every social group, it seems to me, has to deal with four basic questions. One is which kind of polity and social structure makes sense to help that people to function? We're an international people. What kind of social structure can you have for an international people? Up until the last 200 years you could say there was an international Jewish polity that was based around traditional Jewish law, which was the response of the Jewish people to life in exile during the period when historical revelation was the basis of Jewish tradition. Once that belief in historical revelation was challenged, as a result of modern trends of thought, it could no longer serve as the anchor. So in the last 200 years there has been a search for a new form of polity. That's one problem. The second problem is the polity of Jewish communities where other Jews happen to live. The Jews of Soviet Russia cannot create the kind of polity for themselves which exists among the Jews in America. In the land of Israel they can set it up in the form of a state. Thirdly, every group has to deal with ethical issues. There has to be some form of cult. It evolves, inevitably. Now, it can be a cult rooted in a theology, or it can be rooted in political myth, such as you have in Russia. And then, finally, there is the whole question of the nature of man and the cosmos. People have to face up to these issues. Within Judaism there are many, many different points of view.

129

Anyway, to sum up, you have one objective criterion and one subjective response. The objective criterion will have to be on two levels: the Jewish definition of a Jew (being born of a Jewish mother) and the non-Jewish definition of a Jew. Subjectively, a Jew is a person who feels that he associates himself with the fate of the Jewish people.

Among ethical problems being dealt with here the problem of violence is obviously a crucial one. Israel has engaged now in four wars, five wars if you include the war of attrition. The borders at the moment are quiet, unfortunately for the wrong reasons, because the Arabs are at each others' throats. But the problem of violence has been terribly crucial. Beginning in the thirties, when the Jews had to protect themselves against the Arab riots and the Haganah was developed, the concept of "havlaga," or restraint, was advanced. The principle was that if we have to lift up arms, let us do it solely for defence purposes. Let us not be guilty of attacking Arab villages. And that principle guided us during all those years. After the establishment of the state, this principle of havlaga was transformed into what is called "toho haneshet," meaning the purity of the weapon, which meant that the men were instructed, whenever they went into action, never to shoot a defenceless person. The country is in a very interesting religious ferment. There's more religiosity here than in a great many other places in the world, but you have to look for it.

Now, you mentioned you wanted me to deal with the Palestinian question. I am a convinced believer in the essential humanity of all human beings, regardless of the groups that they belong to. Everybody has equal rights to individuality and to participation in the collectivities that go to make up his individuality. I think that the ideal setup is far away from us, as it is from the rest of the world. It would be wonderful to have a common world government, but, you know, let's not be naïve and talk about the Messianic future. That's still the Messianic future. We're talking here about a state that is democratic, and struggling very, very hard for its own democracy under conditions that are very disadvantageous.

I separate the Arab-Israeli conflict from relations between Jews and Arabs in the State of Israel. I want to eliminate all semblances of prejudice and inequality. There are prejudices, there are inequalities here, as there are everywhere in the world. We can afford them less than many other places. Now, the matter is an awfully complicated one, and my attitude is to develop as much patience as I can, not only with the Arabs, but with my fellow Jews. I'm very self-critical, and I'm critical with my own people, and my problem frequently as a Jew is to catch myself, and be as sympathetic with my fellow Jews as I am with the Arabs. But, I'm learning to be as critical of the Arabs as I am of the Jews, and maybe I'm becoming normal here.

130

I believe that the State of Israel must and will eventually broaden its democracy. It's been heading, unevenly, in the direction of greater involvement of Arab citizens in the life of the country. I think we have a very passionate desire not only to live in peace with the Arabs but to have a very genuine relationship with them. We belong together. I think that history has fated us to be together.

One of the most tragic verses in the whole Bible is in the twenty-fifth chapter of Genesis, where we are told that Isaac and Ishmael buried their father in the cave. It's a very tragic sentence, because one is completely unprepared for it. After Hagar and Ishmael were sent out into the desert they lived their own lives. They had no relationship with Abraham, at least not one that is recorded in the Bible. And then, suddenly, there he is at the funeral of his father–Ishmael with his brother Isaac. It's kind of mind-boggling, actually. I would hope that we won't have to wait for that kind of an event before we can begin to realize the degree to which we belong together.

David Hartman, *a professor of religion and philosophy at Hebrew University, is a former rabbi from Montreal. He came to Israel in 1971 because he needed to work out his Judaism in the context of people, land, and nation.*

I was a rabbi for seventeen years both in New York and in Montreal. My fundamental concerns within Judaism were primarily existential: the struggle for individual man to be authentic in the modern world; how he relates to his tradition; and what value a tradition has in a changing modern world. My religious quest was personal and individualistic. What does Judaism say to me, David Hartman, as a modern person? The people I read were Kierkegaard and Freud, and I was very much involved with existential psychoanalysis as well. I was always seeking to clarify my own inner struggles, my own inner dynamics, as a person.

However, there has been a shift in my whole philosophic outlook as a result of the effect of Israel on my thinking. I was functioning in Montreal as a teacher of philosophy, as a rabbi of a community, and I was successful, and all that goes with it. People were seriously interested in studying with me. And then, suddenly, the Six Day War came. And I didn't know what happened to me. Suddenly, Israel, which had been present in my consciousness as a fact, made a deep penetration into my psyche. Suddenly I had to face it, to confront it, to clarify my relationship with it. I realized that if there was another Holocaust I could not really be a Jew anymore, and suddenly the existence of this community was a necessary condition for me to continue functioning as a Jew. I think this happened to all the Jews. The whole destiny of Jewish history, the whole future destiny of what Judaism was about, and the role of the covenant people called Israel, suddenly became very much tied up with the living, physical reality of this country, and the people living here. Once this happened, I couldn't live in peace until I came here. For the first time in my life I was really drunk, literally drunk, with exhilaration, with vitality. I went through a great crisis, because there's a difference between a romantic falling in love during a visit and actually living in this land.

Eventually, I came to the realization that the authenticity of my Judaism was found, not in my individual position, but in the collectivity of Israel that was remaking the possibilities of Judaism. I was cast out of the matrix of thought of the existentialist who lives in his own navel and in his own individualism. Suddenly, the reality of a people and their destiny became the primary organizing category, the organizing principle in my own individual spiritual quest. "Where are we?" became much more important than "Where am I?" I realized that Israel was too important to be left to the Israelis, and that Israel was not just a country of 3 million Jews. Israel really represented Judaism having to confront its own authenticity. To me, authenticity is the ability to translate dreams into reality. In other words, was Judaism to be a sermon that I gave on the Sabbath or was it to be tested by the living reality of the way a people lived? I had the feeling that Judaism was on trial.

We have an opportunity here to see what Judaism can really be. Elsewhere, we couldn't say any more. We were living among the goyim, so we didn't have an opportunity to translate everything that Judaism was about. We didn't have an opportunity to translate our way of life because we were living in a majority culture which didn't sing our song, and we ourselves could only sing our song in a very minimal way. In Israel, Judaism has an opportunity to sing a total song – not an unfinished symphony, but a total symphony. No one's stopping us. We have an autonomous culture. Previously, our situation was that of a person who says, "I have such a great plan, I just need the money to do it." Sometimes, when you give money to a person like this, he suddenly realizes that his plan is not so easy to realize. But now that we have an opportunity in Israel, we should fully utilize it.

I know in my gut that Israel is going to be the most shattering experience of my life, because I'll have to stop being the articulate dreamer of the Jewish people, in order to share the reality of what Jewish people are about. When I came here I didn't have the language. Although I knew Hebrew, I didn't speak Hebrew, and I didn't think in Hebrew. I thought in English. Language is a real problem, especially for a philosopher. If I were a surgeon or a plumber it would have been easier.

I came here because I knew my Judaism had to be historical. I came here not because I was persecuted, and not because I was a failure, but because my Judaism was on trial. If Judaism means anything in the modern world, it's going to have to transform a society. If it can't, then it's dead. Have I experienced the application of Judaism to an entire society? Have I come to the centre of where the action is, or do I find myself a very lonely person? I'm lonely, but I'm in the centre. Religion can be either a protest against modernity or a way of transforming modernity. I think Israel is Judaism deciding to embrace modernity, and I think Zionism is a secular instrument forcing Judaism not to take on what I would call the inauthentic posture of the Prophet who protests.

In other words, I really believe that God wants His spiritual vision to get dirty. He wants it to get into the world and avoid the dangers of otherworldliness. Religion which becomes individualistic is other-worldly. Religion offering salvation of the soul is otherworldly. Religion offering some sort of personal tranquillity in a tumultuous world is also otherworldly. It's abandoning the street, the marketplace, the factory, and politics, and isolating itself in an oasis in a horrible desert. Now, I think that's actually the end of religion. That's not what Torah is about. Torah was meant to be realized in a land, not in a desert. It wasn't meant for the person who's cut off in society. So-called secular Israel, then, is a very deep source of renewal for Judaism in my opinion. Whether you identify with some specific synagogue or not is not the crucial defining characteristic.

We are a very lonely people because no one understands in a very deep way why "peoplehood" is so important to us as a spiritual category. In Christianity and Islam peoplehood is not an essential category. You stand alone before God, seeking salvation, whatever that may be. A Jew never stands alone before God; he can't. Always he is in the midst of a community. Jewishness is a collective term, not an individualistic term. The covenant principle is not an "I," it's a "we." We begin our story as a "we." *We* were slaves to Pharaoh in Egypt. *We* stood on the mountain of Sinai. *We* lived in a desert. Therefore, *we* need a land.

People don't understand that we're not interested in a heavenly Jerusalem; we're interested in an earthly Jerusalem. We never stopped thinking about returning to Jerusalem. No one listened; no one heard what we were really saying. We're here because "we" are important. We're here because Judaism is the way of life of a people, not because of the Holocaust. Peoplehood is my cathedral, my church. That's the meaning of a chosen people. God chose Israel to be His witnesses, which is to say that God's reality is testified to by the living history of this people. If I am

133

not connected to the God of my fathers, I can't say "my God."

This peoplehood is my burden. I wish I didn't have this burden, because sometimes Jews are difficult to live with. I wish I could just be alone. I wish I could be free – free to build my own psychic existence and my own values the way I want to. I'd like to be free. I have no guilt because of God; God doesn't give me any guilt feelings. The ones who make me guilty all the time are the Jews. I'm not doing enough for them. I'm not realizing their dreams. I'm not realizing their aspirations. I want to live my own life but I have to feel my grandfather in my gut. To be a Jew is to have your grandfather in your gut. That's why the family is the sanctuary of Jewish life. We can get along without rabbis, but we can't get along without the father and the mother who tell the story of the past. The world doesn't understand that. That's why they think we're racists.

I think that if we make it here, there's a future for religion all over the world. I think if we make it, you'll all make it. If we don't make it, then I don't think anybody's going to make it any more. We have a small laboratory here. If we can show that a spiritual message can make the difference in a technological society, then there's hope for the spiritual message throughout the world.

Everyone says that Israel should make the first move. I think that's unfair. I just lost 6 million people. I have 3 million here, and I don't think they're that many. I can't risk that much.... Who should make the first move? Well, I say, my Arab brother, you've got to make that move. You have to teach me to trust you. You have to teach me that you really want to live with me and that you don't see me as an alien import who doesn't belong here. And you have to make me feel at home, make me relax. After I'm made to relax, I'll make a move as well. After all, I don't want to live with the psychology of the stranger, of the one who can't trust, of the one who always gets the feeling that a pogrom is about to come. I don't want that to be in my mentality, but it is there. I'd be lying to you if I said it's not there. So I have to be like this, now. I have to have a strong army and I have to have a strong air force, and my kids have to be in the army. My son is a tanker. My son-in-law is a beautiful soul, a fine pilot. He is brilliant. If he had been living in eastern Europe, he would be a great scholar. Today he's a great pilot. He knows that his people have to live, so his spiritual mission now is not to write books, but to be a great pilot. He loves war like he loves to jump off roofs. He'd rather live in peace. He wants to have a family, he wants to have children; he doesn't want to fight all the time. But he also knows that he wants his people to live. So we're this way. We're stiff and we're tough and we have a tremendous will to live. And we're going to negotiate from power. And we're not going to relax. We're not going to give up an inch, not an inch, until you tell me that I can trust.

134

David Spellman *was an Irish Catholic who came to Israel in 1967 and who now lives in Kibbutz Gonen. He married a girl from England, in Israel; and their three children were born on the kibbutz. They plan to stay in Israel. He explained the attractions and burdens of both Judaism and Israel.*

I worked for a British company in Germany as a representative for a textile organization. While I was there, I became interested in what happened during the Second World War. It was a continuation of contact that I'd had in England with people from the Jewish community. I saw the concentration camps. I spoke to Germans and Jews. I became perhaps abnormally engrossed in the subject. It was something I couldn't grasp. It was clear to me that some time or another I would go to Israel to have a look. In 1967, when the war broke out, I went back to England and got in touch with the Jewish Agency, and, with a group of young people, came to Kibbutz Gonen. After a year I went back to England, back to my job at the same company; but then, after three months I decided to return to Israel and Gonen. By then I'd already come to feel that the way of life in the kibbutz was something that attracted me particularly. I think it's a just way of life, a very just way of life. Also, there's a tremendous magnetism about this country as a whole.

I was brought up by a very conservative Irish Catholic family. I was educated by Jesuits, with all that that entails, and was a practising Catholic up to the age of twenty. At that time I went through the usual internal struggle about whether that was the way of life I wanted to lead. I came to the conclusion that it definitely wasn't. Some of the basic precepts of Catholicism—the theological precepts—were totally unacceptable to me. I could never work them out logically. I could never accept the one overall, overriding point that comes into every theological discussion, particularly in Catholicism: in the end one has to rely on blind faith. A great deal of my feeling also had to do with the fact that I could not identify with the way the Catholic church as a whole dealt with the world throughout history. The part that Catholicism played in, or didn't play, in the Holocaust had a great influence on me. I don't consider the church a moral body that stands up to its own precepts.

I've learnt a great deal about Judaism whilst I've been here. This is not a religious kibbutz. On the other hand, we have people here who are religious to varying degrees. The feasts here have an agricultural background. When we celebrate the feast of the harvest festival, there is no liturgical or ceremonial meaning whatsoever. It's something that's extremely day-to-day and real. We bring in the first crops and are happy about it. It loses all its mysticism, its liturgical side of things. The feasts are very beautifully and significantly celebrated.

135

I'm not Jewish and I'm not Christian. I certainly feel closer to the concepts of Judaism than to those of Christianity, far closer. There's something that attracts me in the democracy of Judaism, the logic of Judaism, even at those times when it's very illogical – the day-to-day rulings given by rabbis for example. The process of decision-making, the lack of hierarchy, the role of learning within the religious side of Judaism, the questionability of everything, the ultra-questionability of everything – these are for me the most attractive parts of Judaism and of this country.

In fact, this is what makes life so tremendously intense here. There's the old saying that whenever you've got three Jews together then you've got at least four opinions and four parties; it's really true. We find this in the kibbutz. I find this in the country in general: a constant questioning of the basics. At first, and for an Englishman particularly, I think, this can be tremendously irritating in day-to-day life. It makes things less orderly. People change their minds all the time. Nobody knows where anybody stands. In the end it creates a very active mind on a day-to-day level, which is very, very healthy. This is what I mean by my attraction to Judaism. On the other hand, I don't think that I would ever convert to Judaism. If somebody is born a Jew, he's born a Jew, whether he likes it or whether he doesn't. If somebody is converted to Judaism, then I feel that he must become a religious Jew, and I can't accept enough of the religious side of Judaism to take such a step. Therefore I remain close to it in day-to-day life and leave it at that.

In a kibbutz you have an added aspect of living, namely the community around you. This is manifested more clearly in times of great stress, or at times of celebration: when people get married, when they have children, when you have wars, when people die. The immediate sense of taking part in a communal effort of one kind or another gives an added integrity to life. One's motivations become a little less questionable in many things. I feel very good about the way I bring up my children. The children in Gonen, by the way, live at home with their parents and not in the traditional kibbutz way. They have their communal living during the course of the day, but in the evening they spend their time at home and they sleep at home.

Our kibbutz is as capitalistic as any business corporation I know. We're after profits. We're after running a good, efficient business. From an internal point of view, social questions are the overriding concerns – whether the work is suitable for the type of people we have in Gonen or whether the shift work will interfere with family life. There's something very satisfying about being businessmen on the one hand, while maintaining social justice and equality on the other.

It's impossible to live in this country, and in a kibbutz particularly, for as long as I have, without identifying with Israeli national life. The kibbutz is very much an integral part of the national community. So my contact with the outside world is very strong. I served in the Israeli army and in the Israeli reserve force. I feel that I can't justify my living in this country, and certainly not in this community, without being prepared to do this.

The Israel-Palestine question? Look at the hills. You have 200 yards away, literally, the old border. For close to twenty years the settlers were at the mercy of the Syrians on the hills. Sometimes they were less fortunate, sometimes more fortunate. I don't think that anybody living in this situation could say that we will, tomorrow, give back the Golan Heights to the Syrians. It would be a suicidal decision. On the other hand, the same thing applies for somebody living in this valley. We can't go on generation after generation living in such hostility with the immediate neighbours.

The Palestinians are not just the refugees. The terrorist organizations are something one has to live with in a different way. We have to guard our kibbutz at night. We have to walk around with weapons. We have to build a fence around the kibbutz. A barbed-wire fence around the Jewish community is, I think, something particularly horrible. I'm not too concerned about the dramatics of Arafat walking into the United Nations with a pistol on his hip, but it does bother me that a large part of the time I've got to walk around near my children with a pistol on my hip.

Nirit Barak *was born in Canada and came to Israel in 1970. Originally a member of the United Church, she converted to Judaism before marrying. She feels that she is doing more with her life in Israel than in Canada.*

Before we got married we had talked about getting to know what a kibbutz was like. We came and ended up staying. It was more comfortable here than in Canada for a number of reasons. I converted to Judaism before we married, and we decided that we wanted to raise our children with a religious Jewish background. I didn't want to bring a child up in Canada with a minority feeling. I wanted him to grow up in natural surroundings, without any kind of minority mentality.

In this moshav there are about thirty families – sixty adults, plus about fifty children – and six single people. Mostly they are younger families. Most of them are Israeli-born. There are a few families like us who have come from England or Canada. The economic base of this moshav is

137

agriculture. We grow cotton and corn and peanuts – that's where my husband works – and we have our own turkeys. We also have a little factory that does welding.

For me, being Jewish means a way of life. For me to be Jewish now means having a strong family life. I've heard of so many families breaking up, kids living in broken homes, and marriage not being secure anymore. Somehow Judaism keeps that security. That's not the only thing. It's a healthy way of living. There are certain things that are written down for you to do that you don't really question. It's hard to get used to, but once you're used to it, then you're in the routine: dietary laws, the Sabbath, and all the different holy days. It's hard to explain. For example, the first time you eat a fruit, the fruit of that season, it's a special blessing before a meal. You think about things before you do them. You can't just sit down and dig into a meal without thinking about what you're doing first.

Am I a Zionist? I believe that Israel is a home for the Jews. I have questions in my mind as far as the territories go, the administered territories, and the settlements that are being established. I don't know if they're trying to push the Arabs out. I think a handful of people are doing it, and that's what bothers me, you know. This was Arab land here, Palestinian land, but at one time it was Jewish land, too. Also, we need this area for security.

Critics

"The biggest problem in Israel is the fact that we are living in a big ghetto. It is a bad thing. You are not free." –Kobi Hass.

I srael is a self-critical society. Consisting as it does of articulate individualists who love differentiation and debate, there is no shortage of people who chastize the state, its leaders, and its policies, and who heap criticism on themselves and their neighbours. In all likelihood, Israel is at its democratic best in the ongoing social and political dialogue. The freedom of expression and the sense of tolerance for opposing opinions are striking. Indeed, non-Jewish critics of Israel have voiced their misgivings with greater comfort in Israel than outside Israel, say in North American cities like Toronto or New York, where strong Jewish communities and Zionist organizations are quick to apply the label of anti-Semitism to even the mildest critics. The liberty with which Israeli dissent is expressed is remarkable for a society under constant siege.

Internal critics fall, basically, into two groups: those within and those without the Zionist consensus. The latter are a very small group, perhaps less than 5 per cent of the population. The vast majority of critics are Zionists. Criticism is perhaps easier for insiders since it springs from their loyalty and commitment to Israel as a Jewish state and from a desire to improve that which has been accepted. The outsiders are loners. They attack the very foundations, the philosophical assumptions, on which the state is based. But in Israel even they are not anti-Semitic or, for that matter, treasonous. They are at worst ostracized and ignored.

Max Ohnnh *was born in Casablanca, Morocco, in 1949, and came to Israel with his family at the age of five. He and many of his friends want to leave the country because they "don't see any future here, they just see the politicians fighting with each other."*

I grew up with the mentality of fighting and war and being afraid. When you hear the alarm you have to run to the shelter. This is not the kind of life that young people want. When we were children we went to school with the fear that the alarm would go any minute. It is not the right life for a normal boy. We are all fed up with this situation. We would like to get peace or get a fight all the way.

My family came here because of pressures. My father had a shop, and people were throwing stones into the shop. If you were Jewish you had all kinds of problems. We heard about it from grandfather's stories.

Now, though, we are interested in a new life. The past is dead; we want the future. All the old people and the government think about is what happened in the past. What about the future? We are the young people. We have to live in the future. Not they. They will die in twenty years. What about us? We should think about tomorrow more than yesterday. Yesterday is dead. If we kill millions of Arabs, it won't help us. It won't bring to life all the Jews that are dead. So why not turn a new page with the Arab countries, friendly or unfriendly, and be human beings, living normal lives. Why do we have to fight?

I would solve the Palestinian problem by talking to the people, not to the politicians. I think that we can have peace easily without Geneva, without America, without the Russians, without anybody else. Only us and the Arabs. We can get to an agreement, if they are willing to talk to us.

As long as I am Israeli, I will love this country. I will grow up and build my life in a different place, but I will come back here when I am old, because this is the most beautiful country I have ever seen. I've been all over it with a pack and my sleeping bag, from the north to the south, and it's wonderful. I will come back here when I have enough money for living. This is an expensive country and prices are going up and up. For me to get married and build a house here would be like giving up my whole life to pay, just to pay. If I just owe five lire, I can't sleep at night. What am I going to do when I owe 75,000 or 80,000? That's crazy. I wouldn't do it for any price in the world. I don't want to live this way. I want to build my own life, make enough money to build my house and to pay for my car and to live. And that's it.

Kobi Hass *is twenty-one years old. His father came to Palestine from Belgium in 1944 and his mother from Czechoslovakia in 1935. Mr. Hass has just finished his obligatory three-year army service and, like many Israeli young people, is wondering about his future.*

I am not sure what I want to do, maybe study, maybe work somewhere. I don't have any money right now, so I have to find myself a job. I'd like to do something that I enjoy. I registered at a few universities, but I haven't decided yet exactly in which direction I want to go. I think that most of the Israeli young people wonder about the future. It's something normal.

Now the situation in Israel is quite hard with inflation and so on.

Politics I don't understand. Every time I talk to someone about the elections I am easily convinced because I don't understand things. What I understand is what I see. The government spends money on things that I don't see. If I don't have money I don't buy anything, but if the government doesn't have money they make money.

The biggest problem in Israel is the fact that we are living in a ghetto, a big ghetto. You have the sea on one side, and you have Lebanon, Syria, Jordan, Saudi Arabia, and Egypt on the other side. It's a ghetto, a big one. I think this ghetto is a bad thing. It makes people nervous. Somehow it gets into the soul. You are not free. You always have your borders. I cannot make a psychological statement about this, but it does something to people. I see people always so distressed and nervous all the time. Maybe it's the nature of the Jewish people.

There is a way out of the ghetto. You just have to buy yourself a ticket to Europe. I'm not thinking about emigration, but I thought of relaxing a little bit, studying in another atmosphere, without army reserve duty. But I don't think I'll be able to do it, because I'm not very ambitious. You need lots of money to go out and study. So I'll wait here.

My friends are like me. Some are more to the left, some less. They are people who think about other people as people, and not just as something to kill with two or three bombs. To them war doesn't look so understandable. I can't understand it myself. I was in the army three years, and I didn't catch it. Really. I never thought of myself as a soldier, and I couldn't understand how war could happen. When I look at a Palestinian I say, "There is a man. I would like him to be happy."

David Shaham *was born of Russian parents in Poland in 1923 and grew up in Israel. He was interested in music as a young man, but joined a socialist youth movement and went to a kibbutz after finishing his studies. In 1948 he went to the US for three years in a Zionist educational capacity. After serving two years in the army, Mr. Shaham opened an advertising agency and began writing. As an editor of the* New Outlook *he is a moderate critic of both Israeli and Palestinian policies.*

I had already published a couple of books of fiction and short stories, but I didn't consider writing a career. I thought one should not expect to make money out of writing. I went to university to study law, and while I was studying I opened the advertising agency just to spend the time. Somehow I became quite successful financially, and instead of opening a law practice I stayed in the advertising agency. Those were years of fast commercial growth in this country. I lost almost all interest in politics. I would accept as the truth what the government would tell us was the truth. Soon my work in the advertising agency gave me a fair knowledge of how the media can manipulate in many ways. For ten years I was completely unaware of media manipulation regarding the conflict. I was a part of the mainstream. Then in 1965 I decided to quit the advertising agency and move into public life.

In 1967 I joined the Labour party and was invited to publish a weekly for the party. Very soon I ran into trouble with Golda Meir and Moshe Dayan, who were not happy about the general direction I gave the paper. I allowed people to express views which dissented from Golda and Dayan.

Later I joined a new party, an independent dovish group. Many of our people met with members of the PLO. It can be admitted, now, that they were doing this, with the knowledge of Arafat to try to find a way of dialogue between Israel and the Palestinians. Our meetings with the PLO were based on the understanding that there is no solution without the readiness of the PLO to recognize the existence of Israel.

The views in Israel respecting the conflict and the future are divided something like this. About 20 per cent hold the extreme ideological view that the territory belongs to us and we are never going to surrender it because we are entitled to have our homeland –the land of our fore-fathers. About 20 per cent say that the territories are not the things we are fighting for. We should be ready to negotiate and exchange territory for a real peace or a true peace. About 60 per cent don't know anything, and they usually will support the government position. Their basic sentiment is, let's keep as much of the territory as possible, but return what we must. So these people are sitting and waiting for the govern-ment. When the government tells them we must return a chunk of territory, they will agree to it. When the government tells them that we should not give back this chunk of territory because our security is going to be jeopardized, they will believe the government then, too.

How does media manipulation occur? Most news emanates from the authorities and they are the source of the news in the paper. A paper that does not want to be cut off from the source of news has to "play ball." It is easy for the government to make a request for something not to be published because it happens to be a state secret or the public interest calls for non-publication. The army, for example, enjoyed tremendous public support until 1973. It was also a tremendous source of informa-tion. So criticism of the army was very rare. The idea was that publishing something negative hurt the reputation of the army and lowered morale. Television was under tremendous pressure from political parties.

There is complete freedom of the press as far as writing opinion

142

articles is concerned, but you can manipulate news stories with skilful placement, follow-up, and interpretation. If you try to kill a story, it is very seldom that you don't publish it at all. Most often you will publish it, but then you won't have any follow-up. You kill it by completely ignoring it.

I just came back from a long lecture tour in the United States. I met many Palestinians and ex-Palestinians. I think that one of the worst things you can do to the Palestinians is to justify their position and not encourage them to progress along a realistic line of peace. I think that an infatuation with justice is contrary to the idea of peace. Peace and justice are sometimes mutually exclusive terms. If you are fighting for justice, you have to continue the fight, and there is no peace; and if you want to achieve peace, sometimes it's at the expense of full justice. I am sure that you can never achieve full justice and have peace, and that if you have peace you have to give up a measure of justice.

Peace is the process in which two sides give up both a part of their rights and their idea of seeking justice as it appears to them. The Palestinians cannot achieve full justice, which for them means going back to the places where they lived before. First of all, most of the places don't exist any more. The fact that the land exists does not mean that the place exists. The houses they left are not there any more. Instead of a farm there is now a superhighway. Where there used to be a little one-family house there is now a big industrial complex or a modern skyscraper or a hotel. For the Palestinians there is no way of turning the wheel backwards. And as for the Israelis–they will have to give up the dream of expanding the borders to such a "defensible" extent.

I resent it when Israelis try to tell the Palestinians that they are not a national entity because they have never been so before. I resent it even more when somebody tries to tell us what we are by defining us in terms of religion and not in terms of national existence. Every group is allowed to define itself in its own terms. The Israeli Jews define themselves in terms of an independent sovereign nation and nobody is going to define us in terms of religion.

We urge Israel to promise a complete withdrawal from all the territories occupied in 1967 and to offer complete recognition of the Palestinians' right to determine their own state if they recognize Israel and undertake to live in peace. Of course the Palestinians should also demand and receive compensation for the property that they lost in the State of Israel. You will find many Israelis saying, "And what about the property that the Oriental Jews lost when they left the Arab countries?" Well, this is a real problem, and they are entitled to compensation, too, but they cannot ask this from the Palestinians.

In our discussions with the Palestinians in Paris and the US we found out that there are reasonable people among them who can express themselves in reasonable terms, and can understand reality. This is contrary to the impression you gain if you just watch their choric theatrics when they make public statements. Some of them impressed us as dedicated to the solution. They stake their personal future and personal survival within the PLO on the success of this policy of rapprochement with the Israelis. So at least we know that there is a pressure group there now, whose political future depends on the success of the policies that they advocate. If we can prove to them that they don't get anything by force, but that they can get much more – maybe not all they want, but much more – through negotiations, then they'll opt for negotiations. The government, of course, did not give its approval to the meeting with the Palestinians in Paris, but it had full knowledge of the fact that the meeting was held.

What does it mean to be a Jew? There is a great debate among the Jewish people. Being a Christian is a matter of joining, but being a Jew is not a matter of joining at all. You can't join Judaism. You are born into Jewishness by being born to a Jewish mother. You can become a Jew if you adopt certain practices. You can belong to a Jewish community. But you don't join. Many modern Jews would like to feel that there are two circles that they belong to: they belong to the Jewish people because of their birth; and they join the Jewish religion as an act of free will when they grow up. The issue is that here in Israel a Jewish nation came into existence, a Jewish Israeli nation. Israeli Jews are a national entity in themselves, no matter what others consider them to be. Here the basic belonging is to the Israeli Jewish community. It's a national community, and you don't belong to anything else. You might have a mystic feeling of belonging to the Jewish people of the world, but you don't belong to anything else but the Israeli Jewish community. You cannot be described in any other terms.

Ygal Laviv *is a Tel Aviv journalist. He was born in Rumania in 1937, and came to Palestine with his parents the following year. He joined a kibbutz in his teens, served in the army for three years, and in 1960 began a career in journalism and politics in Tel Aviv. Mr. Laviv has been an economic reporter for several important Israeli newspapers, and has become known recently for exposing corruption in the country.*

Before the 1973 war nobody paid much attention to stories about corruption. Since 1973 the atmosphere has changed, and by publishing a story on corruption, you can force the establishment to act. Corruption existed very widely in Palestine before 1948, but only now does a

"God promised this land to the Jewish people," says Rabbi Menachem Porush, member of the Knesset.

Eli Eliaschar, a former deputy mayor of Jerusalem, is a sixteenth-generation resident of the area.

A resident of Jerusalem's new quarter suns himself within sight of the landmark mosque, the Dome of the Rock. The quarter was designed with the help of Moshe Safdie, the Montreal architect who created Habitat for Expo 67.

▼ *Teddy Kollek, mayor of Jerusalem since 1965, admits that "the houses of Arabs in one quarter have been torn down" so that a Jewish quarter could be built, but he says that expropriation occurs everywhere in the world for public projects.*

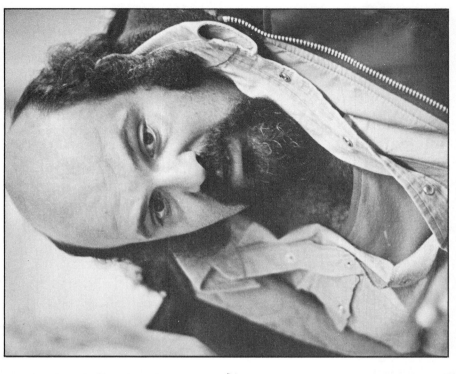

"I am a member of a nation whose first lesson was not to trust anybody," says Yoram Hamizrachi, a TV reporter.

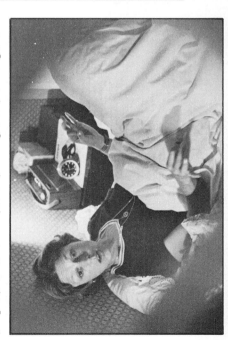

Rachel Rosenzweig (above), a German Christian, converted to Judaism and came to Israel to rid herself of anti-Semitism. Jacquelyne Rokotnitz (below) immigrated from England.

A young gunner relaxes at his post at the Israeli settlement of Pearim, situated on a strategic hill on the occupied West Bank area. The settlement, with its commanding view of a nearby Arab village, is being turned over to settlers.

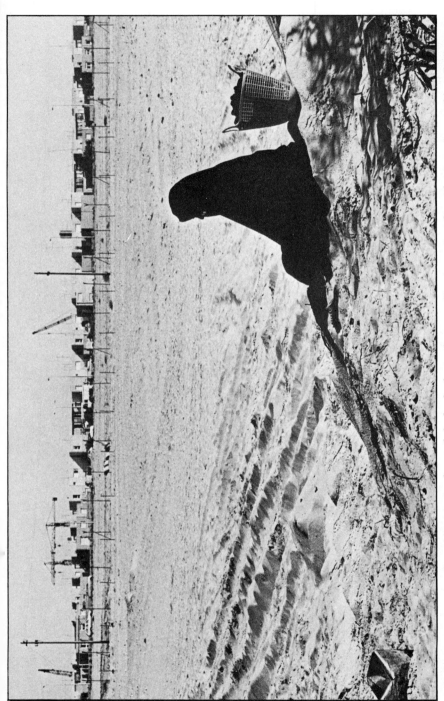

A Bedouin woman watches construction beyond the barbed wire fences at Yamit, an Israeli settlement of several hundred civilians located in the northern Sinai within walking distance of Mediterranean beaches. The Bedouin say the settlement and others like it trespass on their traditional lands, while the Israeli government says that the settlement is needed for security.

"The problem through the centuries was that the Jews were different," says archaeologist Gabriella Bachi.

Avraham Yehoshua, shown at home with his son, is one of Israel's best-known fiction writers.

Zeev Meiri, an immigrant from Poland in 1912, points out a permanent display of mock Egyptian soldiers and describes how the Egyptians tried to invade Kibbutz Yad Mordechai in 1948, the year Israel was born.

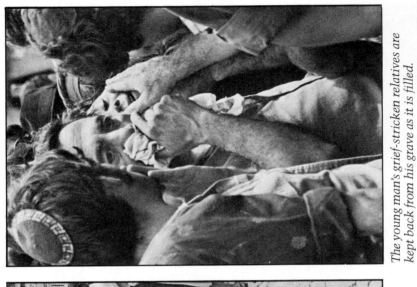

The young man's grief-stricken relatives are kept back from his grave as it is filled.

Solemn pall bearers carry the coffin of an Israeli soldier who was among several killed when a helicopter crashed during military exercises.

published story get results. After 1973 I started to write a series of articles about nation-wide corruption. The first was about the general manager of the biggest building company in Israel. He was also the treasurer of the Labour party, and he used the money of the building company for the party through a bank in Switzerland. I published this story in my newspaper. They checked it out. He was fired. That was the first time in Israel that a man in his position was fired because of corruption. After that I started a series of articles about the man who was appointed to be the governor of the bank of Israel. He took bribes and I brought the proof. I forced the government to enquire. They found the evidence and put him in jail. I have published other stories more recently about political corruption, which will have an effect on the coming elections.

Corruption is normal in any state. The State of Israel is new, and during the first years everybody said there wasn't any corruption. You have to remember though that for those first twenty years, there was a very strong Prime Minister – David Ben-Gurion – and he was really like a dictator. It was a democracy by law but it was a dictatorship. In his day you could not bring any story against him or any of his party. They used censorship.

You cannot hold a million Arabs and still be pure. There is no idealistic military government. Stories of corruption help to break this false image of Israel as ideal. After the war the picture of Israel changed. In Israel we are now in the same situation as the United States. For us it took twenty years to arrive at the same situation as the United States is in after 200 years.

I like my profession. I like what I am doing. But if there is no peace and I see a new war is imminent – war for nothing, war only for keeping the occupied territories – I think that emigration to another country is a possibility. I cannot decide for myself alone. I have to give my two children the opportunity to decide if they want to live or to die. This state was created to solve the problem of the Jew, to put an end to the killing of Jews. Now this state is the most dangerous place for the Jew in all the world. The mood of the young people here in Israel is a little nihilistic. The majority want a life with money and without the army – but here you cannot become independent. You have to go to the army for two years, and when you want to make money, every position is occupied. They want to go to work and succeed but they cannot. So they go abroad.

Israel Shahak *is a professor of chemistry at Hebrew University in Jerusalem. He came to Israel in 1945 from Poland with his mother. The rest of his family was exterminated by the Nazis. Although he was a Zionist in his youth, Dr. Shahak has come to feel that Zionism is an unjust cause.*

I was born in Warsaw, Poland, in 1933. I come from a religious family; as a matter of fact, I knew how to read Hebrew before I knew how to read Polish, but the Second World War interrupted my religious studies. I spent the years of the Holocaust in Europe, finishing in a concentration camp. We made Italy after the war. Several months after the war I came here, in September 1945, and from that time on I have lived in this country, with only two interruptions. These interruptions were connected with my scientific studies: one post-doctorate research period in California and a sabbatical year in London. I was educated here. I finished high school in Tel Aviv. After 1951 I went to the army for two years. I then became a chemistry student at Hebrew University. After a post-doctorate period I became a teacher and I have been a teacher ever since that time.

Do I recollect the concentration camp? Yes, of course. As a child, I remembered things, and now many clear pictures are present, although in between there is no sense of time. You know, a child has clear pictures about any experience, but in between he doesn't know what really happened. In this sense I recollect the Warsaw ghetto and the concentration camp, and everything. As a matter of fact, as I grow older, I think about it more.

I came here with my mother. The rest of my family, especially on my father's side, was completely exterminated. It was a matter of chance, of course. From my mother's side a small branch of the family remained. From my father's family – my father was the eldest of eight brothers and sisters – my mother and I were the sole survivors.

I was a very zealous Zionist until 1956. When I came here I was twelve years old, and I accepted all the Zionistic teachings to which I was subjected, not only as a matter of course but with great enthusiasm.

Now I am an enemy of Zionism. This happened in two stages. The first stage was in 1956, when I was taught by the Suez War in several respects. During the war I began by believing implicitly in Ben-Gurion. I should say that I was a great enthusiast for Ben-Gurion. I admired him very much; and I really believed everything that he and other ministers said: that we were making wars for defensive purposes. Then several days after the beginning of the war, he made a statement in the Knesset saying that the war was really done for biblical and historical reasons, to restore the Kingdom of David and Solomon, with many verses from the Bible,

146

and so on. At the very moment that I heard it and the response of all the Knesset members who stood up and sang our national hymn, I had a sharp reaction. It was because they had lied. Only a few days before they had said the war was defensive and Israel didn't want any territory.

I had begun as an orthodox Jew. At the age of eighteen I underwent a change directed against Jewish orthodoxy, which was then not connected with politics or with Zionism. But in 1956, when I saw this use of Jewish orthodoxy, it became the second factor to make me turn against Zionism. The third one was, of course, the notorious massacre in the Arab village of Kafr Kassem, which was made known to me in the same manner as the truth about the Suez War. I first heard about it, when it was still kept silent, from a friend of mine who lived in the town of Petah Tikvah, not far away from Kafr Kassem. He told me the people of Kafr Kassem had rebelled against the authorities and that therefore they had to be suppressed. It took me a whole week to discover the truth, not from papers, because there was nothing in them, but from another friend. I should say that the military censorship was then much stronger than it is now in Israel.

But what really jolted me into real activity against Zionism was the war of 1967 and its aftermath. First of all, you again had the insistence that it was a defensive war, that we didn't want a piece of territory – several territories in this case. Then I witnessed almost immediately the expulsion of the Palestinians in numerous places. The final turning point for me came from about September 1967 to April 1968, when I really understood that Israel didn't intend to return any of the conquered territories. In a closed meeting at Hebrew University I heard Levi Eshkol telling a Jewish joke about the territories with population. It was like marrying an ugly woman who was rich. He said, "I would prefer the dowry without the bride," meaning the territories without the population.

I joined the League for Human Rights in the fall of 1969, though I had worked for more than a year through various *ad hoc* organizations at Hebrew University. Previously, people had been disorganized. They worked as individuals or through *ad hoc* organizations. Now they are slowly drawing together. This includes not only people inside the Jewish community but all opponents of Zionism, both Arabs and Jews.

After 1956, because of the return of the territories, we had, at least inside Israel, the most beautiful and quiet ten years. Since 1967, however, the situation has been getting worse and worse in all respects, including Israeli society, which is now visibly falling apart. Yesterday it was publicly announced here in the papers that the camp of the general staff of the Israeli army was the centre of trafficking in drugs (hashish and marijuana). I know this society is decaying, decomposing, falling apart,

147

all because of the conquest. The conquest has shown Zionism for what it is. It has made it much more extreme, therefore decomposition is also much more extreme. There is no area that is free from corruption and degeneration. Just look at the number of important officials and members of the ruling party who are now either in prison because of corruption, or who have committed suicide because of a very strong suspicion of corruption, or who are now suspected of corruption.

Before 1961, an important general in the Israeli armed forces called Uri Ben-Ari was caught stealing sugar from his own soldiers in order to sell it. The amount of sugar was not very big, but this act was completely shameful. Ben-Gurion gave orders not to hide it, to put him on trial like everybody else, and to expel him from the army and cancel his rank. And so it was done. After several years, maybe after the Six Day War, or just before it, he was given amnesty. Then he was restored to a position in the government and now he is a consul-general of the State of Israel in New York, which is a very important position, equal to an ambassador. So we have a convicted thief, and a shameful thief – it is much more shameful for a general to steal food from his own soldiers than for an ordinary thief to rob another fellow citizen – being put in such a position.

Economics is the central field in which the corruption is being revealed. Hebrew papers are much more open about economic corruption than about other corruption. The more serious corruption is that attending the conquest. Israeli soldiers or policemen are killing Arabs, but they are either never brought to trial or not given any punishment. Certainly there is no independent enquiry in any killing of an Arab by Israeli security forces. This blood, which literally calls to heaven from earth, like in the story of Cain and Abel, is much more important corruption than anything concerning money. People are much more willing to see corruption in money than in shed blood as long as it is not shed by people of their own community. However, both things are connected.

The Israeli foreign debt is increasing all the time. I mean the debt owed to foreign governments – mainly the United States – and international banks. This state is going bankrupt at a very fast rate. Things are also getting worse in our relations with the Palestinians. You cannot have a military occupation and not have things worsening in terms of human rights or democratic rights. Now you have many reputable figures in Israeli life who are advocating final solutions, expelling all the Arabs, both from Israel and the conquered territories. Here you see real deterioration. I will give you another sign. You will find that most Israelis are completely persuaded that the next war is inevitable. Most of them accept it fatalistically. This by itself is a sure sign of deterioration.

What's happening to the religion of the Jews in the process? I am afraid that you cannot expect an active criticism of its own society from an organized religion which has possessions and officials and money and congregations and so on.

Yes, I am a Jew according to the definition of the Jewish law, the Talmudic law, accepted as the law of the State of Israel. I am a Jew because I was born to a Jewish mother. At the beginning of my activity against the Israeli government the government sent two officials of the Ministry of Internal Affairs to my mother a few weeks before she died to ask her if I was her real son or perhaps an adopted son. As an adopted son I would become a non-Jew. Also by my own definition, I am a Jew because I am devoted to the Jewish heritage and to the Hebrew literature of all ages, because I feel natural and contented when speaking in Hebrew here with my own fellow Jews. You can also say that I am a Jew because the wicked part of the Jewish tradition angers me much more than, let's say, the wicked part of the Chinese tradition. When I read the horrors of our own tradition, like the biblical justification for our treatment of Arabs, I am literally mad with anger. You can say about belonging to a people the same thing you say about love: the proof of attachment is love and hate intermingled. By this definition I am not only a real Jew, but a traditional Jew. You cannot open any great literary creation of the Jews through the ages, beginning with the Prophets, without seeing exactly this characteristic of love and hate intermingled.

I think that, taking all our history as a whole, we have had our periods of great suffering. We have also had periods of relative ease. I don't think the Jews have suffered any more or any less than many other persecuted or minority nations. We have suffered like many of the other peoples have suffered, and speaking generally, no more, no less. There were some times when we have suffered more in the world. Other periods in which we have suffered much less.

I think anti-Semitism is not an isolated phenomenon. There is simply a hatred of minorities. The beginning of all our troubles is our belief that anti-Semitism is something separate, something not connected with the hate and persecution of other minorities, whether national or religious. It is not separate. It is exactly the same, both in form and in extent. I will never forget that in Poland 3 million Jews and 3 million Polish people were killed. I do not forget the 20 million Russians who were killed. I do not forget that in Bergen Belsen, where I saw so very many Jews suffering, I saw hundreds of thousands of prisoners of war of all nationalities being slowly exterminated.

Uri Davis, *an anthropologist and political analyst, is one of very few anti-Zionists in Israel. Born in Czechoslovakia in 1934, he came to Palestine with his family in 1935. He is committed to civil rights and to finding an alternative for the Jewish state.*

My opposition to the Jewish state is rooted in a moral statement or a moral witness. According to my understanding, a Jewish state cannot be democratic in the normal sense of the term. A Jewish state by definition is a state that provides for institutional privileges to Jews by the fact that they are Jews, and therefore must discriminate against non-Jews, specifically against Arabs. Now I know the argument that states always discriminate and favour the interests of one class or one section of the population. Generally speaking this is true, but it's a matter of degree.

If Jews in England were subject to only a fraction of the discriminations Arabs are subject to in Israel, everybody would scream "Anti-Semitism!" I mean, if Jews were not allowed, because of being Jews, to have normal access to intermarriage within England to Christians or whatever; if there were numerous classes against Jews in English universities; if there were massive programs euphemistically called "developments for public interest" that would in fact concretely ensure that 99.9 per cent of all properties confiscated were Jewish properties, and that these properties would almost invariably be transferred to Christian ownership and Christian use: then everybody would, with complete justification, scream "Anti-Semitism!"

The specifics of the Israeli situation are vicious to a whole lot of people, mainly Arabs, because the conception of a Jewish state means that you have to Judaize Palestine, you have to transform Palestine from a territory populated by a native Palestinian Arab population into a territory where there is a Jewish majority. You have to import a Jewish population into the country. You have to gain control over land resources and labour resources.

Remember that the first slogans of the Zionist movement – the so-called socialist Zionist movement – had to do with the conquest of land and the conquest of labour. They did that exactly: they conquered the land and they conquered labour by systematically boycotting and excluding Arabs from participating in the economy of Palestine as far as they could. It was more difficult as long as Jews did not hold legal sovereignty, but once Jewish sovereignty was gained, it went very, very quickly. Within a period of five or six years, through the utilization of state legality and state machinery, most of the Arab lands in the country were confiscated by a whole range of laws passed by parliament, beginning with the defence emergency regulations in 1945 through to the various land acquisition laws and custodianships on refugee properties.

The Jewish Agency and the Jewish National Fund are constitutionally Jewish organizations directed to serve only the Jewish community. Their holdings and properties are constitutionally for exclusive Jewish use. Arabs or non-Jews cannot legitimately sublease or work on these holdings. But the thing is even much more vicious, because there is a covenant signed between the State of Israel and the Jewish Agency in 1961 which gives the Jewish Agency and the Jewish National Fund exclusive rights of cultivation, development, and use of all state lands. This means that the State of Israel, which has authority and jurisdiction over Jews and non-Jews, has given an organization that is constitutionally based on apartheid exclusive monopolistic rights of administration of all state lands. So, even if the Jewish National Fund has, in fact, direct ownership of only 14 per cent of Israeli land, it has effective control of 95 per cent of Israeli land, and thus Arabs are discriminated against, through and through, simply because they are Arabs.

To return to the moral issue, I would simply not support a political regime which, in my opinion, is based upon, and fosters, fascism. The state, at least in terms of my moral values, is not the ultimate value; the state is always an instrument, and must be supported only so long as its uses and benefits outweigh its coercive elements and its negative aspects. Values of equality, equality of civil and political rights for all, are at the top of my value system. Sometimes, by the elementary criteria of human decency, you not only have to withdraw yourself from the state; you actually have to oppose it. And I am one of a very small group of Israeli Jews who are committed to opposing it.

Oriental Jews in Israel are really placed between the hammer and the anvil. They are confronted with systematic and very racist discrimination by the whole range of Israeli state institutions, whether political, educational, social, or whatever. By and large, European Jews in Israel have controlled the more privileged sectors, echelons, and positions within the State of Israel, and Oriental Jews are, in very specific cultural, economic, and political ways, systematically discriminated against and under-represented. The overlap between the ethnic criteria and the class criteria in terms of poverty, levels of education, kinds of employment etc., is really complete. That's the anvil. And the hammer is that within the specific history of the State of Israel they have been thrown into what are called "development areas," which are basically areas out of which the Arabs were driven and not allowed to return. Oriental Jews were flown into those areas—border areas. In other words, they are the victims, the first direct victims, of Palestinian commando, guerilla, and terrorist operations within Israel. So they are really placed between the hammer and the anvil in a very vicious way.

But to recapture the original point. Yes, I definitely claim that the levels of discrimination, of suffering, of systematic mutilation – cultural, social, political – of Palestinian Arabs under Israeli rule are such that they are obviously comparable with colonial situations as we know them in Algeria, Rhodesia, and South Africa. The histories are very different. The legalities are different. But the implications are very similar. And I foresee similar consequences. There is full justification to curb Israeli internal and external policy, by the exercise not only of economic or political sanctions, but by violence if necessary. In fact, the whole range of political opposition and military opposition must come into play to curb it effectively, and even that is not guaranteed. What we do in opposition, anti-Zionist opposition, to Israel is very small.

It's the ultimate irony that the Zionist solution will manifest itself as a complete failure. Zionism will not succeed in altering Jewish fate. The most dangerous place for the Jew today is the State of Israel. The State of Israel will not be a thousand-year Reich; it will not survive, in my opinion, its hundredth birthday. It cannot. And those Jews who will live and continue to live in Palestine will constitute a minority, if not in Palestine then in the Middle East. In fact we are a minority in the Middle East, whatever feelings we may have otherwise. Intentions to establish a political order based on Jewish sovereignties will fail, pragmatically, in my opinion, because they are based on a vicious moral ethics, implying and perpetrating discrimination, apartheid, and violation of every human decency that I know.

"Eine alte Frau," *meaning an elderly woman, wanted to remain anonymous. The operator of a pension (hotel) on Mt. Carmel, Haifa, she was born in Poland in 1901 and came to Israel in 1953. She views Israel as causing the destruction of Jewish morality.*

The situation here is as it was in Germany in 1933. A fog has descended. People here feel that a war will take care of everything. I don't. I'm against war. War is the worst and the most expensive thing. We came back after 2,000 years and we haven't learned. We are educated and we have a history, but what do we bring to this area? Planes and bombs. We could have brought culture and technology. Why should we treat the Arabs as we were treated in Warsaw. We weren't in ghettos or concentration camps because of them. What they said about us in Warsaw we are now saying about the Arabs, namely that they are dirty. They aren't, but even if they are, being dirty isn't as bad as going to war. You can't imagine how the morality of Jews has suffered in Israel because of Israel. Much is being made of our humanitarianism towards the Lebanese at Matulla. But, believe me, much of it is camouflage.

Jacquelyne Rokotnitz *was born in England. Her father was a Hungarian Jew who went to England in 1936 and married an English girl. Jacquelyne was brought up as an English Protestant. Her father died twenty years ago, but the rest of her family still lives in England. Jacquelyne came to Israel in 1970.*

Israel is in serious trouble. It's in serious trouble when morale is considered. There are an awful lot of young people who think to themselves, "What am I doing here?" All my girlfriends have four or five children, all of them. The other day one girl who has one child said, "I don't want any more children; one is enough." And so one of the other girls said to me, "Is she crazy? In Israel? You can't have only one child in Israel, because at least one's going to be killed in the war." Everyone expects part of the family to go down the drain. It's an extraordinary kind of death wish. We have the highest road accident rate in the world. I'm really not sure about it at all. And I ask myself, "What am I doing here? Am I contributing to the Jewish ideal? Am I contributing to the Jewish state? What is the Jewish state? Is there a Jewish state anymore?"

We're being overrun by Arabs, Arabs in our own country. I don't know what the Arab population is, but they're breeding like flies. Soon the population is going to be more Arab than anything. The proportion of Jews from Arab extraction is now more than 50 per cent. The Arab mentality is gradually taking hold in Israel, which makes for a very conflicting society. The odds against survival are enormous.

There was never any connection in my family with Judaism, Israel, and Zionism. My father was a Jewish non-Jew, very professionally non-Jewish, although in fact he was a Hungarian Jew. I discovered by accident that I had Jewish blood in me when I was about eighteen. I went to visit my father's family in America, and slowly it came out. They had all converted to Catholicism, and all of a sudden, out of the blue, somebody dropped a word here and a word there.

I wrote to my mother and said, "How could you let me come to America not knowing I was half Jewish?" She wrote back, "I don't know what you are talking about, my dear." So I said, "I have news for you." She had been married for thirty years to a Jew and didn't even know it. My father never talked about it. And I never forgave my father for doing this. I always felt that it was the unforgivable sin to deny what you were.

As a result, I over-identified. I went around saying, "I'm half Jewish, you know, you'd better know about it." And, since I was old enough when I found out about these things, I became aware that only twenty-two miles of English Channel had separated me from the gas chambers. According to orthodox Judaism I'm not Jewish because my mother is not Jewish, but I would have been Jewish enough to go to the gas chambers. After

153

reading *Exodus* I became interested in Israel and read a lot of articles about the kibbutz. I used to say to friends, "Let's go and work on a kibbutz in Israel, and have a look." Nobody wanted to come. Finally, when I was about nineteen I came. It was only for a short stay, but I met my future husband. After a few years in Tel Aviv and England we settled down in a kibbutz. That's the history of my life in Israel.

Religiously, I don't consider myself to be anything, to tell you the truth. I really am quite agnostic, and Herbert is absolutely atheist, not even agnostic. So we are very, very secular indeed. And of course the kibbutz movement is avidly secular. So religion doesn't really come into our life at all, and if I had to face a religious question with my children, I frankly don't know what I would do. I really don't.

As to whether I'm a Zionist or not, who knows any more what Zionism is? You know, Zionism has been altered and very diluted and in many ways lost. Who knows who is a real Zionist? Is the chap sitting in New York at fund-raising functions, pouring millions of pounds into Israel, more of a Zionist than a lot of the people sitting here and complaining? I honestly don't know. Am I a Zionist? You know, I've spent nearly ten years with Herbert, and he is the classical Zionist. He believes that this is the only place for the Jewish people, and the only place where you can live without feeling like a second-class citizen in some way. I argue with him that certainly in England nobody says, "Oh, she's second-rate, she's a Jew." But maybe he's right; maybe there's an undercurrent of it which I've chosen not to see. Sometimes I say to Herbert, "Oh, who needs it here? Let's go to England." He says, "I don't want to be a bloody Jew anywhere." And in this respect I must accept what he says. Facts are facts. History is history. The Jews have been hounded everywhere. But they're being hounded here, too. Let's face it. Is Israel really such a paradise? Is the Zionist ideal being realized? It's a very good point, because frankly, without America, where would we be? Without the Jewish diaspora, indeed, where would we be?

Cobby Raz *is a hotel worker in Tel Aviv. He is a third-generation Israeli born in 1950. His grandfather was born in Jerusalem and his grandmother in Lebanon. He is working to save money so that he can return to the US, where he recently spent three years.*

I have a lot of friends in the United States, and I think that it is a very nice country to be in. I will tell you something. I'm Israeli, but, except for the weather, I don't like anything in Israel. I can tell because I have been outside the country and met other people. I've been in Europe, Africa, the United States. It's very difficult to have a private life in Israel, because everybody wants to know what you're doing. In Europe or in America the people don't care what you do. You live your private life. You can jump twenty-four hours in your apartment, and nobody says anything. Here, everybody knows what you eat for breakfast. Ninety per cent of the people I know in Israel want to leave the country. Very soon I'm going to leave the country.

No, I'm not sorry that I'm Jewish, but I'm not religious. I know I'm Israeli. I know my religion is Jewish, but I never go to the synagogue or anything like that. I don't believe in religion. I believe in God and in persons. Religion is not important for me.

Activists

"If we cannot establish a big peace, we should establish a small peace." –Kahman Yaron

The "activists" within the state are basically critics of Israel and its policies. However, their criticism goes beyond words. If a broad definition is applied the activists cover a wide range of persons, organizations, and situations. The Black Panthers, for instance, are activists.

Here, the reference is to activists in the fields of peace and human rights. In Israel there are several peace movements and several prominent peace activists. Like the critics outside the Zionist consensus, they are a small minority–and the same is true of the activists who struggle for human rights on behalf of the Arabs in Israel and the occupied territories. Around the world, Jews have been in the forefront of the human rights struggle. Blacks in America, for instance, have known them as leaders and allies in the campaign for civil rights. And the Vietnam War protest movement could always count on some Jewish support. The Jews who have taken up the cause of the Arabs in Israel are, in fact, as alone and lonely as were the first protestors against Vietnam.

They speak best when they speak only for themselves.

Kahman Yaron *is a native of Germany, which he left in 1936 to go to Palestine. He is a specialist in adult education. Education, in his opinion, helps to create a permanent nation for his people and contributes to peaceful relations with the Arabs.*

Since 1967 I have been very interested in Arab-Jewish relations. Several years before that I founded an adult education school in Ramle, a mixed Arab-Jewish town between Jerusalem and Tel Aviv, where we offered evening classes for Jews and Arabs. In 1967 we had the opportunity, for the first time in twenty years, to meet the Arab community from East Jerusalem. As you know, the city was divided with walls and machine guns for twenty years, and the only contact with the Arab population was through the telescope of a machine gun. In 1967, a Dominican brother in West Jerusalem, who knew that I was interested in contacting the Arab population in the old city, brought me to a very famous convent located at the Second Station of Christ.

Mother Superior was waiting for me. She had had a religious experience which told her to wait for somebody like me. I said, "I am the man, perhaps." She said she wanted to build a bridge between East and West Jerusalem. At the same time I was put in contact with a group of Arabs from East Jerusalem by a lady from Hebrew University who wanted to study Hebrew. It was a short time after the war and quite surprising that Arabs should be motivated to study Hebrew. I agreed to teach Hebrew to these people at the convent. Soon we had about thirty students, Arabs from the Via Doloroso and sisters from the convent. It was fantastic for me as a Jew to teach in a Catholic convent to Arabs who just recently were enemies. The convent was located in the Antonia quarters, the last fortress of Judea, where the Roman garrison was located at that time.

Soon many Arabs wanted to study Hebrew and there were Jews from West Jerusalem anxious to study Arabic. So we established an ulpan to teach Hebrew and Arabic at the same time. It was also seen as a good opportunity to bring people together. "Ulpan" is an Aramaic word meaning studio. About 3,000 people have studied Hebrew and Arabic at our institute, now located at Mount Scopus. We have coffee breaks between classes, allowing Jews and Arabs to come together for discussion. We also have folklore programs, outings, group dynamics seminars, and Arab-Jewish encounters. In spite of the political problems and pressures involved, these meetings can fulfil an important human role. The aim of our bilingual ulpan is to achieve better understanding of the two cultures, to have direct contact on the human level, to develop empathy, to uproot prejudices, and to destroy stereotyped conceptions of peoples.

What is my assessment of the results? I am aware of the problem of creating a utopian island in a situation of war and conflict. But, on the other hand, I think that it opens a hope that if the political conflict is solved there will be no great difficulties on the human level in creating understandings between different groups in Israel. I think that there is enmity between Jews and Arabs, but there is no hate. You see, I differentiate. Enmity has a rational base; hatred is more irrational. I don't think it is difficult for Jews and Arabs to come together in spite of the political problem. But I am aware that Israeli Arabs especially have a kind of split personality. It is very difficult in the situation of conflict to be a proud Arab and a proud Israeli. To combine these two in a situation of

157

conflict is quite difficult, it's a kind of schizophrenia really.

Why did I become involved? Because of my own history in Germany. Being a member of a minority group results in a special sensitivity for such groups. After the Six Day War, I concluded that the Arabs keenly felt their loss and that solidarity with a defeated people was called for. After Yom Kippur the situation has changed a little. Now the Arabs are able to speak as equals.

I think that today it is easier for Jews in Israel to meet Arabs than to meet Germans. I have been in Germany several times. I have told the Germans that it is easier to come together with Arabs than to come together with Germans, in spite of the war and the conflict, and the terrorist activities. I feel at ease with the Arabs – maybe because I have the same mentality. There is something in the German character of which I am very afraid. Everything is so perfect and exact. It's very hard for me to explain my feeling in Germany. I feel at home with Arabs, and I think many of us have no real difficulties in coming together with the Arabs, in spite of the fact that my cultural background is closer to the Western world than to the Oriental world.

I think there are cultural differences between Jews and Arabs. Actually they are not differences between Jews and Arabs, but between the Western world and the Oriental world. The same difference exists between Western Jews and Oriental Jews. For example, the conception of time in the Orient is not the same as in the Western world. In the East you don't take time seriously.

I think I am an optimist. We are moving towards the betterment of the world. I think we have a better world than we had twenty or thirty years ago. If we cannot establish a big peace, we should establish a small peace. This is something I believe in very much.

Yes, I am a Zionist. I wouldn't live in Israel if I wasn't a Zionist. It would make no sense to live in Israel without the belief that we're going to be able to live in our own way, in our own Jewish way.

Joseph Abileah, *a violinist with the Haifa Symphony Orchestra, was born in Austria in 1915 and came to Palestine in 1926. A deep believer in peaceful coexistence between Jews and Arabs, he was instrumental in founding the Society for Middle East Confederation in 1972. By "confederation" he means some form of union between Israel and Jordan and Palestine.*

For some time I had the opportunity to study in Jaffa in the French College where Arab students were my schoolmates. I learned quite a bit about the Arab mentality and their special approach to problems. I graduated and was employed by the government in the survey department. This gave me another opportunity for direct contact with Arabs, because in the survey camp we were always together with Arab labourers. I also got interested in the geography of the country and made many extended excursions, mostly by foot, into Transjordan. Next, I entered employment in a bank, but I always studied music and eventually, because it was a family tradition, it became my main profession. My father was a musician and composer. My grandfather was a cantor in the synagogue. My mother was a piano teacher.

My activity on the political level began in the year 1947, when I was invited by the United Nations' Special Committee on Palestine (UNSCOP) to give evidence at Jerusalem. My suggestions were to unite both banks of the Jordan, to implement the irrigation plan, and to limit immigration so as not to harm the local population in any way. I didn't want a single Arab sent from his home or his political rights infringed upon. The majority in UNSCOP asked for partition, and we are witnessing today the unhappy results of that decision.

My father was a Zionist. He was disappointed when he came here and saw how Zionists were. He was a Zionist in the classical sense, hoping for the approaching Messianic age and the return of Jews to this country. When he came here he was also a pacifist, but later he succumbed to prevailing Zionist views.

The main point that brought me to the non-violent approach was an experience I had when I was twenty-one years old. It changed my whole outlook on life. I was on a trip in an Arab region during the disturbances of 1936-39. It was a period of continuous danger for both Jews and Arabs. Although I had been warned not to, I went to an Arab village, where I saw a group of Arabs in the field. I approached them and greeted them kindly. There was no immediate danger, but when they found out that I was a Jew the situation suddenly changed and they threatened to kill me. I said, "If it is your duty, go ahead." I didn't do anything to defend myself. They decided to throw me into a well. I asked where the well was, and they gave me directions. I went to the well and stood at the opening. As they surrounded me, no one had the courage to throw me in. Something happened in their hearts. They started to ask whether it was their duty to kill a defenceless man because he was a Jew or to listen to the voice of their heart and seek to save him. So they found a way to accept me into their community, and I repeated the words they told me and went away. The words were: "I believe today that Muhammad was a great Prophet who brought the monotheistic idea in his age in his geographical region."

I didn't say anything against my convictions. He was one of the people who brought the idea of God to a certain part of the population of the world. The Muslims also accept all the other Prophets including the Jewish Prophets. They accept Jesus as a Prophet. They accept all the teachings. But at that moment, of course, I didn't reason very much. They were pleased with the solution. I saw that they were relieved. I found this power of non-violence before reading the books of Ghandi. If you want to be a pacifist you must be prepared to be non-violent if you are attacked. On all my excursions into the Transjordan, I always went alone without a revolver, without a knife, without any means of defence.

If you ask me about my religion, I would tell you that I try to follow Jewish ethics as practised by the early Christian community. I believe that Jewish values developed especially in the centuries before Jesus. These values stressed forgiveness, love of your enemies, kindness and social responsibility to your fellow man. It was a more humanistic outlook, which eventually culminated in the early Christian teachings. And if we take the Sermon of the Mount as the basis of the Christian teaching, I would say that some of it is a summary of Jewish thinking of that time. You can find all those teachings in Jewish books, in commentaries on the Bible of that time, or in the Talmudic writings. You can find all those teachings, although they are dispersed, not codified.

Jesus was original because he was, I would say, a genius in ethics, and he could absorb in his personality all these teachings and give us an example of a life which made a great impact on future generations. He could live this love. He could forgive the people who put him on the cross. He could live out his ethic to the very end. And this made such an impact. Even today his example gives enthusiasm to people. All these teachings were actually already in the Jewish books, and Jewish rabbis taught them. But there was no personality who could live them. And, therefore, I would say that Jesus was not like others; he was much greater than others. And I believe that if the Jewish people accept such teachings – whether they are personified in Jesus or not is not so important – as well as the Muslims and the Christians, we will reach peace in the world. I do not approve too much of organized religion. I do not share the fatalistic approach which the Jews and Christians share in their eschatology when they say that everything can happen only when the Messiah comes. People who live in this world have to do something about shaping a better one.

I have been a member of the wider Quaker fellowship for more than twenty years. I don't belong to a meeting but my outlook and my daily life are entirely on the Quaker line. In the ethical relationship with our fellow men we must not fall short of what is required in the Sermon on the Mount. It is only by loving our enemy that we can expect the same attitude from him. The strongest hate splits and melts in the sincere sun of love. We can walk along this path more than we believe to be possible.

The Sermon of the Mount was written not for angels but for humans. I am saying all this out of the conviction that comes from experience in life. I further believe in the Messianic age, which will be brought about by the total effort of people of goodwill in the course of generations. So every person should add his share in good deeds, love, and reconciliation during the short time of his earthly life.

I believe that a bridge to peace can be built on four pillars; the first is the brotherhood of man; the second, the sanctity of life; the third, non-violence and truth; and the fourth, that only good ways will lead to good ends. And these four pillars, two on each end of the bridge, must be put on mighty rocks: one is faith and the other hope.

Arabs and Jews can live together now and in the future in spite of everything that has happened. When I was last on the West Bank, my Arab taxi driver said that he was from Haifa. Once they lived near a Jewish family. And he remembered that when he was a small boy the Jewish mother would distribute sweets to Arab and Jewish children alike. The Arab mother did the same, and he said: "Our sorrows were their sorrows and their joys were our joys, and I hope these days will come again." These days will come again, but it must come from the people. The politicians will not do it. We must find the way to each other, and therefore I say that the more we visit each other, the more we have relations with these people on a human basis and on a daily-life basis, the easier it will be to bring this day about.

The war of 1973 made some changes in the general outlook of many people in this country. One section of the Jewish population became aware that Israel is not invincible. They started to realize that army and power politics will not solve our problems. So they began to listen to the proposal of the Society for Middle East Confederation which was founded in 1972. And we had many new members who started to work with us. But there was another section of the population which said, "We are not prepared enough militarily. We have to give more attention to the rearmament and the fortification of the army." So the reactions to the events of 1973 were in two different directions. I myself became convinced more and more by the events of 1973 that a way for co-operation should be found. And we intensified our work. There has been very little progress in peace-making in this country. So we find that our endeavours are very important.

The solution to the Palestinian problem? The Palestinians must have their state, their home country, their passport, their identity, and their roots. This is something they have been looking for for a long time. The question is only if a state on the West Bank and Gaza is viable. I would very much like to see a Palestinian Arab state, whatever the size of its territory, federated with Israel and Jordan. I mention these two countries because geo-politically they are entirely interdependent. It is absolutely a necessity for a West Bank state to have access to the sea. If they have only the port of Gaza, they must pass through an Israeli corridor. Jordan will not be happy because they will be blocked from the sea forever by these two new states: Israel and Palestine. So these countries are entirely interdependent, geographically and economically. They must be united in a confederation.

A confederation gives free development to each of the member states. It does not mix the people together. Instead they educate their children in the way they want. They keep their language, their customs, their religion. Politically there must be union and a common foreign policy. We must have a common orientation. We cannot be, like now, a playball in the rivalries of superpowers. Imagine, from the sea to the edge of the desert in Jordan, there is a distance of not more than 100 miles. In this 100 miles there are supposed to be three national sovereign states. This is a thing that the most elementary logic cannot accept. Therefore, I believe that this national sovereign state for the Palestinian Arabs must be created from the very beginning in the framework of the confederation, whereby Israel and Jordan will also waive part of the absolute national sovereignty and come under the same status as the Palestinians. Everyone will be under the same roof, and everyone will have the same rights.

The Jewish population in Israel? When the state was founded, many people thought that there would eventually be a safe place to live for them and for their children. But we see now that there is no place in the world where the Jews are so much in physical danger as in Israel. We see now that it is not the fulfilment, and it is not the solution for the eternal Jewish problem all over the world. On the other hand, there are many people who came here not because they thought of fulfilment. They just escaped here. They had no other place to go. These people also see that their requirements are not fulfilled, because the economic situation is deteriorating to such an extent now that they don't see any economic future. So gradually people are leaving the country. We can say that about 10 per cent of the people who immigrated, emigrate.

You asked me why the Germans and Jews clashed so disastrously. It was because of three developments along economic, cultural, and educational lines. First, the Treaty of Versailles put great economic pressure on Germany. At a time of much unemployment in an industrial economy, the source of raw materials was shut off. This opened the door for extremism and identification of scapegoats. Second, Germany had civilization but not culture. To find a way to live with one's neighbour in peace means culture. Civilization is something else: it's technology, it's advancement in science, it's a high standard of living.

162

Western civilization in general has neglected culture. The third reason was the sense of duty to the state that had been nurtured in the German people from the time of Bismarck, as well as a feeling of German superiority. Hitler was the representation of all three factors. He was not a sole cause. He was representative of a line of thinking. It wasn't a single madman who made the whole Holocaust.

Reuven Moskovitz, *a school teacher from Rehovot, is one Israeli citizen who has wrestled deeply with the contradiction between Zionism, with its desire for a secure state, and the moral values of Judaism which are concerned about injustice to the Palestinians. He is convinced that catastrophe lies ahead if the latter is ignored. Consequently he has become a worker in the peace movement.*

I was born in a very small village in Rumania on the border of Soviet Russia. For me it's not a question of "why" I came here. When I was in Rumania, I was already in Israel, in Eretz Israel, because my father was a very religious man. My father belongs to a Hassidic family, and when I was three or four I went to the Jewish school where children learn the Torah. Thus every landscape for me was the landscape of Eretz Israel. Every hill for me was the Tabor Hill or a Gilboa. Every big river, of course, was the Jordan River.

It was very natural for my family and I to belong to this land. All its symbolism was my education. At five or six I began to learn the Pentateuch. The stories of all our ancestors, Abraham and Isaac and Jacob, helped us to identify with the presence of the land and with all that happened here. So it was only natural that I should come in contact with the Zionist movement and with the idea that the Jews must have a homeland. After the Second World War I decided to come here. I became a member of a kibbutz in the northern part of the land, on the border with Lebanon. But I must confess that I came into conflict with most of the people I met here. Jewish history taught me that we must have a home for ourselves, but also that we can't be a people like other people.

It was especially clear to me that we couldn't do to other people things that other people did to us. I was shocked, very shocked, when I discovered that Arab people were thrown out of their villages, even in cases when they didn't fight with us. I don't accept that all the Arabs, all the Palestinians, all the refugees, left of their own decision. It isn't true. Many of them were thrown out. Many of them. It's a moral problem because it's impossible to understand Judaism without a moral approach to everything. But for me it's not only a moral problem.

It's also a problem of experience. I was a refugee myself. I was born in a little village. One day the Nazis came and said to us, "Go away." They sent us to the Ukraine. For years I dreamed of coming back to my village. Even after the village was destroyed, I came back. From the very beginning, then, it has been a very important problem for me: the problem of the refugees or the problem of the Palestinians or the problem that we weren't just. I studied the Bible, and I like the Bible very much. Although I was a socialist, my roots are in the Bible, and I know that the Prophets said that Zion can only be saved by coming back with justice.

So in the very beginning I was to some degree an outsider among my people. My opinions weren't agreed with too much, and that was one of the reasons that I had to leave the kibbutz. In 1957 I went to the university in Jerusalem. I believed in the possibility of building a new society, a socialistic society. I studied history and Jewish literature. After that I became a teacher. From history I know that we have never been alone in the land. One of the reasons for the catastrophe of the second temple, in 70 A.D., was that we couldn't manage to handle other people: Greeks, Romans, Syrians, and so on. For me it's clear that every attempt by people to have the land only for themselves must end in catastrophe. The effort today to get rid of the Palestinians and have the land only for the Jews can only bring catastrophe to the Jewish people. You know our society assumes that every Arab child, when he is born, is immediately an enemy. That's unnatural. As a Zionist I understand that the Jewish people had no other way but to come here to build a homeland and a state, but I hope that I am another kind of Zionist—a Zionist who doesn't seek to conquer. If all the Jews came here it would be a land that was impossible to live in.

After the war of 1967 I became a member of the movement for peace and security. We published a manifesto with the title *Peace and Security, Yes; Annexations, No.* And from that manifesto developed a peace movement. I became the general secretary of the movement. And we tried to warn our people that it's not too healthy to become drunk with victory. The territories should only be a guarantee for the signing of a peace pact. With the signing they should be given up. We soon came into conflict with the government and with public opinion.

In my opinion we could have had peace in 1971. The October War was a crime. I was very, very angry. I had a very bad feeling against Golda Meir, because she could have avoided it. Sadat declared himself ready to make peace with Israel, to give up the Gaza Strip—though not in favour of us. He was ready to make peace with us on the borders. It was a good opportunity. The blood of the October War was useless.

Most of our people don't understand exactly how serious our situation is. They are living in a fools' paradise. After the Six Day War, I was sure that it was possible to change things by political activities, by organizing a peace movement. After the October War I decided that the only way to do something was by education. I gave up my job, took a year's sabbatical, and tried to build a small project, a small model, a project where Jews, Arabs, Muslims, and Christians could live together.

The saddest thing is that we, as Jews, have lost our character and reputation as strivers for justice, dreamers, people of vision. We were very proud to be a people of the Prophets. But now, suddenly, we are very pragmatic people. Suddenly we are very realistic-minded. Suddenly we believe only in force, in very cold calculations. Suddenly we are told to give up dreams of a better society, of humanism, of a world of understanding – to forget that it's worthwhile to try to change things in order to live another quality of life.

Maybe I'll fail again; but again and again I'll try to further the dream. The name of the project is Ness Shalom. The founder is Bruno Hussar, a very interesting person. He is a Christian, but he was born a Jew, and he tried to build a kibbutz with Muslims, Christians, and Jews. Every month we organize a dialogue between Jews and Arabs on different subjects. After the meeting, the Arabs, for example, invite the Jews to their village, and they spend one or two days together, and then the Jews invite the Arabs to their village. We have some groups who decide to continue the meetings until they finish school. Already we have cases of very good friendships. I am sure that it will not bring peace. But it can further the attempt to once again keep high the dream of what was the most important thing for the Jews: the vision of a better world.

Rachel Rosenzweig *is a teacher, scholar, musician, and social activist. A native of Germany, she immigrated to Israel in 1964 and converted from Catholicism. She obtained her* Ph. D. *in Jewish Thought at Hebrew University and is now working with a group of friends and associates on solutions to the Palestine-Israeli problem. Their project and its philosophy is called "Partnership."*

It's very difficult for a Christian not to be an anti-Semite. I was born a Christian, and studied theology at the university. One of my teachers dedicated his life to uprooting anti-Semitism in Germany. He opened my eyes concerning what had happened in the Holocaust, and, as a result, I decided that I had to go to Israel in 1960 in order to uproot my own anti-Semitism. It was a time when almost no Germans were coming to this country, and I really was a representative of Christianity and Germany together at the age of twenty-two.

It was a difficult year: the year of the Eichmann trial. The experience had such an impact on me that I really could not fit in anymore in Germany, and I came back here. People in Germany just rejected me. Or perhaps I made myself rejected. At that time I didn't yet know that truth of not blaming.

The same teacher also told me about the man who is now my father-in-law, Franz Rosenzweig. He is the most famous Jewish philosopher known in America today. I got to know his letters, which were published before the Holocaust. They were so helpful to me in coping with life. Somehow I came to find his widow – he died in 1929 – who lived in Berlin at the time. When I came to Israel, it was through her that I got to know her son, who is now my husband. So because of personal events, I married and immigrated to Israel in 1964. I had already converted to Judaism.

I don't think anti-Semitism is inevitable for Christians. As I told you, I was converted from anti-Semitism by a Christian teacher, so that is proof in itself. And I know many people in Germany who are very good Christians and not anti-Semitic. But the traditional teaching of Christianity implies anti-Semitism, because of sentences like, "His blood come over us and over our children." And then there are the symbols. For instance, Christian historians always end Jewish history at the year of 70 or, at the latest, 136. They talk about Late Judaism instead of talking about Early Judaism, and they talk about the Talmudic Time. These things show what they really think of the Jews. They are a people who are a paradox today or maybe shouldn't even exist. This is so entrenched in Christians that even if as human beings they don't feel anything against the Jews, as Christians they still do.

Christianity was composed for me of God and Jesus. The Jesus part broke down for me when I was here during the Eichmann trial. I believed in God for some years, but the more I got involved in things that matter to humanity, the more I understood what Bonhoeffer has said, that we are created by God and have to live as if God doesn't exist, and I had the feeling that in order to really utilize all my own capacities, I should live without relying on Somebody who might complete my own short-comings. That was really the reason that I decided to abandon religion altogether. It's not relevant to what I have to do in this world. I just don't think about everything pertaining to God and the other world, because it's not relevant to what I have to do in this world. So that's how I became a secular Jew.

Ever since I learned about the State of Israel, I realized what its major problem was – the dependence of its physical security and its inner growth on the contentment of its Arab neighbours. Ever since I immigrated to Israel in 1964, I prepared for personally coping with that

166

problem by learning Arabic, making enquiries, writing, discussing, and later being active in one of the so-called peace parties. But every activity seemed to result in failure. Today I know what we are actually doing. We are actually fighting and blaming our own people in order to make peace with the enemy. But how can you succeed in turning your enemy into a partner by turning your people into your enemy? Do you understand that? First of all, go and turn your people into your partners; then you might succeed in creating the conditions necessary for winning over your enemy as a partner.

In 1974, I came across the little pamphlet, *Auto-emancipation* by Leo Pinsker. Zionism, according to Leo Pinsker (this was written before Herzl), is restoring confidence to the Jewish people, so that they can again be masters of their destiny. This is the greatest Zionist ideology that has ever been. A Jewish state is only the first goal and only an instrument whereby people can liberate themselves and accept responsibility for their problems. The problems change but the need for coping with them remains. That this view of the auto-emancipation of the Jewish people does not prevail today is clearly demonstrated by a parable I once heard from an Egyptian journalist: "The Israelis are always arguing about their right to this country. Think of a man who jumped out of the window of the fifth floor because a fire broke out. Would anybody question his right to jump out of the window? No. Unfortunately, the man landed on a passerby and almost smashed him. Now this passerby blames him, threatens him, and later on even attacks him. Instead of coping with this new problem, the man constantly points to the window, trying to convince everybody that he had a right to jump out of the window." It is not relevant what caused the conflict of today. It is only important that there is a problem which questions our future.

After the state was established there was a new problem, and to this day it has never been defined. Israel had concentrated upon furnishing and fortifying a fortress. Maybe a new generation has to emerge, not daunted by the trauma of the Holocaust, a generation that would continue the self-liberation of the Jewish people by recognizing our dependence on others. Recognition of our dependence led to a concrete attempt to create conditions for partnership between Arabs and Jews in March 1977. This formal organizing of Arabs and Jews from all over the country was preceded by two and a half years of intensive experimentation in the concept of partnership. The word "partnership" expresses our goal as well as the means to achieve this goal. The optimum relationship between Arabs and Jews we can think of, in present conditions, can be compared to that between two partners in business. A partnership will evolve if at least three conditions prevail: common interest, mutual trust, and what we call equality of self-respect.

We are forming task forces and youth groups to work on some of the many Arab problems like poor education, the lack of industry, the lack of an Arab channel for TV, or the absence of Arabic in schools. There is a beginning everywhere, not because of us, but because people become aware of it. The Israeli soil is really ready for such a thing. If you don't reproach the people, you can win them over. We are still very small. Of course, you cannot see any fruits yet or any impact on the country up to now. People always expect immediate results, and many people who came and looked turned their backs on me because they didn't see the immediate results. But I myself have grown patient, and I think it will take some years till it will have an impact on the country. We choose the quiet way of winning the trust of all the important people in the government and in the Arab leadership.

Many people who are working with us have always supported the Palestinian state. But we are not talking about that at all today. It's not efficient to take a certain solution and make out of it the purpose, the goal, of all your efforts. I don't want to become the slave of a certain solution, because one of our principles is to always formulate an alternative solution if a certain solution cannot be reached. Even now, I wouldn't say that we have found the ultimate solution, or the optimum solution. There might be circumstances in which this solution is not feasible; then we'll think of something else. The important thing is to be dynamic and flexible in coping with the problem; then all sorts of things might happen. Also, the solution for the Palestinians might be different later on because so many steps which should be taken before that state can be brought into being haven't yet been done. Maybe, by taking the steps we'll arrive at a much better solution than a Palestinian state.

I would like you to understand a little better the method of turning adversaries into partners. We are convinced that the leader's destiny depends on the community's destiny, and that the community's destiny, to a large extent, results from actions and neglected actions. Therefore, to shape our individual destiny for our own good, we have to accept responsibility for the destiny of the community, for the public. We shall not surrender to the overpowering complexity of the problems, nor shall we delude ourselves concerning our power. Our slogan is: "May I have the courage to change things I can change, and the serenity to accept things I cannot change, and wisdom to know the difference day after day." That's really what we are practising, and it's wonderful to act according to this slogan, I can tell you, because it helps you overcome every crisis, and every failure and every mistake, and whatever happens to you.

Our approach is to cope with specific problems in the framework of what I call the citizens' political system. It's parallel to the established political system. We are not establishing a party, not because we don't have the power to be that, but because we think that today we have to activate the people who are not in the establishment in order to complete the work which is done by the government and by the parties. Again this is going back to that phenomenon in Zionist times when every Jew dedicated his life to establishing a home for the Jews. The same thing has to be done today, and that's why we want to establish this network of people who are not in the establishment, but feel responsible for the public good just as the government does.

Felicia Langer *is a lawyer dealing with many civil and human rights cases. Born in Poland in 1930, she came to Israel at the age of twenty. She believes that anyone with a "musical ear for peace" can perceive a change on the part of the Palestinians in the direction of moderation. She believes they will one day recognize Israel's right to exist, if only Israel recognizes their rights as well. The Jewish settlements in Arab areas are wrong from legal, political, and humanitarian points of view.*

I am a woman of law. According to the Geneva Convention every non-military settlement in occupied territories is contrary to international law. That is my judicial point of view. According to my political point of view, it is a political crime to create these settlements. The exact number of settlements is seventy-six so far. The aim is to create a situation that cannot easily be reversed. But this situation might afterwards make the achievement of just peace impossible.

I think that it will be harder to achieve peace with the settlements, and I don't think that they will dictate Palestinian surrender. Even the children are now opposing the occupation with the only weapon left to them, the only remnant left to them from the homeland: the stone. They are fighting armoured cars and trucks with stones. I know the children, personally. While I am speaking with you now, I see faces of children whom I know. They have reached such a point of fighting and hatred against the Israeli occupation that they, the children, are fighting. And now there is no power in the world, not seventy-six new settlements, or even twice that number, that can prevent the Palestinian people from exercising their legitimate political rights. The Palestinian people have paid a terrible price for this war. Comparatively speaking, I think that the price paid so far by the Palestinians is higher than that of the Vietnamese.

For this price what do they want? I think it is a consensus: they want a state in the occupied territories, a Palestinian state. Even if it has not been said up till now explicitly, there is consensus inside the PLO about such a solution.

Of course, the state would have to be guaranteed, and the guarantees would have to be mutual. We, as Jews, also want to feel secure. I feel that this is my homeland. I don't have any other place in the world to go to, and I want to live here in peace rather than at the expense of other people. Therefore, I don't oppose any guarantee for my safety. However, up until now we know that we, the Israelis, have always been attacking. We are crying all the time that they want to swallow us and throw us into the sea, but we are the attackers every time. Except perhaps for 1948, all the wars were initiated and opened by us. The war of 1973, of course, was a war to restore to the Arabs what was taken from them.

I know that some Palestinians want all of their land back. This viewpoint is familiar to me, and I think that it is wishful thinking more than a point of view. Of course, in the future both sides may want to make the solution more ideal. There is a possibility that after some years of co-operation and coexistence the two states could be a federation. Perhaps several states could federate. Arafat is speaking about it as an ideal solution, as a dream. He is talking about a single state, with the consent of the Israelis. I don't think they will use this Palestinian state as a base against Israel. It's not possible physically, geographically, or politically. There would be no international support for that. That this state could be a danger for Israel is ridiculous. If we are not afraid of all these Arab countries, and if we are defeating them all the time, what danger would one small state be? The state of Palestine will be a very weak state, a sub-state.

The Palestinian platform, which is called a Palestinian covenant, explicitly says that Israel has no right to exist. They didn't change it at the Cairo conference, but in their "fifteen resolutions," they have not mentioned a single word about this slogan. All the experts say that the fifteen points show a trend to modify this official point of view. They are opening the door for negotiations. Many PLO people have said, "Nobody has offered us anything; nobody is recognizing our very existence as a people; do you want us to waive, to resign, all that we have, without any sign, any symbolic move, or hint, of recognition?" It is premature to ask them for further concessions in favour of Israel without recognizing that they, the Palestinians, exist. I don't think that it is logical to ask a people who were driven from their homes to recognize those who drove them out only for the sake of their consent to negotiate. It is a very strange demand.

Now, about the official Palestinian platform. I don't agree with it, of course, because I am for the existence of the State of Israel. But Israel has

170

an unacceptable official platform also. The official platform of the Israeli government was stated in the Israeli Knesset about two years ago to the effect that the Israeli people and the Israeli state have legitimate rights to all of Palestine, including the occupied territories. So both sides have platforms unacceptable to the second party.

Israel has gone farther than that. It refuses even to talk with the PLO, because it says the PLO people are scoundrels and not the legitimate representatives of the Palestinian people. In effect, Israel is saying, "We will recognize the Palestinians only on the battlefield." Israel is also saying, "We can do everything against you, and it is moral, pure, and legitimate. But you can't defend yourself. If you don't turn the other cheek, you are scoundrels and anti-Semitic."

I have seen hundreds of Palestinian people tortured by the Israelis, and I want you to note it. Hundreds of people, with marks of torture on their bodies – severe torture, including electricity. The last case was the most terrible thing I have seen in my life. This man had become mad in the prison, mad from the tortures. So they deported him, and the family agreed. I said to them, "Agree, otherwise you know what will happen." He is now in a hospital in Amman. I was not able to see him often, because I felt that I, too, was growing mad. It was terrible to look at this man. He was a shadow, and not a human being. He started kissing all the guards. He didn't recognize me or his children. It was terrible. It was only six months ago, or even less. I don't remember the date. The *Christian Science Monitor* wrote about him.

Lea Zemmel, *a Jewish lawyer with offices in Jerusalem, has a large Arab clientele. She was born in the city in 1945, twelve years after her parents arrived from Poland. The discriminatory practices of her state against its Arab minority have occupied most of her personal and professional life for the past decade.*

There is a double purpose in the confiscation of Arab land. One purpose is to obtain more land for the Zionists, in other words, to build the Jewish homeland, dunam by dunam. As children we used to take to school a penny every Friday to put in the Blue Book. It was not only habit, but a big cause. The pennies were for a certain Jewish fund. We were told that that fund would buy a dunam at a time, and this was how we would build our homeland. That's one purpose, to have more land for the Jews.

The second purpose is to force the Arabs to become a very cheap source of labour power. And we can see it happening. People are taken from the land. The land is taken from them. They have to go to the cities and work cheaply. Every morning you see the buses going to villages in the West

171

Bank, bringing the Arabs to work and returning them again. The Israeli economy is very dependent on this labour. It is cheap labour, without social rights, without taxes, and you don't owe them anything. It's well known that this labour made many people in Israel rich. As a matter of fact, a whole strata of the Israeli population has been moved to a higher level of living. You cannot find a Jewish construction worker today. They are all Arabs. Their labour is cheap. Arabs have no social rights and no union. If you want to fire an Arab you fire him and that's it.

I don't think the problems the Jews are having here are because they are Jewish. White people from Rhodesia would have the same problem. The conflict here is not because Jews are Jews but because the Jews are colonialists. They can use religious justification, but it doesn't mean very much. I have come to the conclusion that the only solution for this conflict can be a state which will promise real equality to both peoples. Such a state can only be a socialist state.

Israelis All

*"I am proud that I am a Jew, and just now I am very, very
happy that I am living in my own state. I am a Zionist. I will
live here till my dying day. There isn't any other way for
Jews." –Julius Berger.*

The preceding chapters have attempted a meaningful categorization
of all the people interviewed. However, Israeli society is too complex and
heterogeneous to cover all the people and all their central opinions in ten
chapters. The languages they speak, the countries of their origin, their
views of Judaism, Arabs, and Israel are too diverse to reduce to ten
groupings.

And yet there is a fundamental homogeneity in Israel, an unmistake-
able unity. Israeli Jews are not all religious in the same sense. Cabinet
solidarity is apparently an unknown doctrine to them. The national
melting-pot has not superceded cultural traditions everywhere, just as
the Hebrew language is not everywhere pre-eminent. Israel is neither
socialistic nor capitalistic but represents a wide-ranging manifestation
of both systems. There is a big and widening gulf between the sabras and
the immigrants. Most of the latter know the world, while the former
know only tiny Israel.

And yet all–young or old, socialistic or capitalistic, right-wing or
left-wing, Ashkenazi or Sephardic, European or Oriental, Russian or
American, religious or non-religious–all are Israelis. With very few
exceptions, all are sufficiently nationalistic and eager for the control of
their own destiny to believe in the state and to be willing to lay down
their lives for it. Israeli nationalism is the new Judaism; that consum-
mation of Zionism which, for the present at least, makes the most sense,
and thus is worthy of every sacrifice.

Julius Berger, *born in Vienna in 1919, left his native Austria after the German occupation in 1938. After a three-year stay in Cyprus, he arrived in Palestine in 1941. He sees the State of Israel as the answer to Jewish destiny, because discrimination against the Jews runs very deep in Christian countries.*

The German people have been anti-Semitic for many generations. My father told me that when he was serving in the army of the Austrian-Hungarian empire, it was the same. Jewish officers always remained Jews. How well you did, and what you did for Germans, didn't make any difference.

Our district was one of the poorest in Vienna. We helped the poor people. I helped my class of boys in algebra, but never got any thanks. And when they came into class, they often took away my lunch. One reason for this was their Catholic background. From their childhood the church taught them that we killed Jesus. And then there were other reasons. If some Jew managed through a lot of hard work to succeed at something they were jealous. The Jews succeeded at every kind of work in the country. If a Jew was a good physician there was always jealousy.

We aren't any super-people. We are just plain people, but we do our best. And we want to do it. I have worked at every kind of work in the country: building houses, cultivating fields, tax collecting, road construction. There isn't any work I didn't do in this country, and I was happy to do it. We are just like other nations, other people. Maybe some Jews are geniuses, just like other people. But we would never say that we are the geniuses of the world...no, never!

Chosen people, I think, yes. We are the chosen people in the true sense of the word. Our prayers, our words, every day and every night assume chosenness. We always say "Shalom," meaning peace, from the morning till the evening. We teach peace to our children from kindergarten till high school; we teach them to be kind to their neighbour. We give everything for peace. We don't want war. We have had enough. But we also have to defend ourselves.

I was born a Jew. I remain one still, because I was taught to be one by my parents and by my grandparents. I don't see why I should be someone else. And if I have to suffer, I have to suffer as a Jew, not as something else. I am proud that I am a Jew, and just now I am very, very happy that I am living in my own state. I am a Zionist. I will live here till my dying day. There isn't any other way for Jews. You see it everywhere – if there is an unemployment crisis, the first one who suffers is always the Jew.

The state has solved the Jewish problem. When I arrived in 1941, there were half a million Jews here. Now there are 3 and a half million. We took all the Jewish refugees from Arab countries. They came without anything except what they wore on their bodies. If you travel over the country now, you may see how they work and how they live. They live their own life.

Jews and Arabs were able to live together for thousands of years. I am a tax collector. Just recently I went over to their villages. They took me in just like another human being, as a friend. We laughed together and talked together. They speak Hebrew fluently. They pay their taxes, and so on. We live together just like human beings should live together all over the world. We can live with them. But they say they want their own country. They don't want to live in a Jewish country. That's their first and last word on it. Jordan is their country. Israel is our country. We want a Jewish country. We don't want a mixture. If they want to live here, we won't throw anyone out. We want peace. Why can't we have it? Do we have to be destroyed twice, once by Hitler and once by the Arabs? The world doesn't understand our problems.

Arie Yaary *was born in 1941 in Tel Aviv. His parents came from Poland in 1936. Mr. Yaary manages an international company. He studied in the US for four years. He thinks the Arab states could and should solve the Palestinian question.*

I have met people and I have seen people everywhere, but I feel that this is the best country in the world. Mind you, we have a lot of problems, but I hope it's going to be all right. We have war all the time, every ten years, but I think you have to look at the basic difficulty here. It's not a question of borders. It's a question of solving the Palestinian problem. You see how Israel has treated the Arabs. You don't find many nations that have treated people the way we Israelis have treated Arabs in occupied territories. The thing is that the Arabs and the Israelis are two entirely different mentalities. We Israelis are more European-minded. The Arabs have their own, Muslim mentality. We are more modern than they are. The way they see things and the way we see things are different.

I have spoken with the other people in the occupied territories. I would say that most of them are not so radical. They are quiet people. They would have been willing to make some kind of settlement, but they don't have any leader. They fight among themselves. They don't know what they want. They think they want to establish a Palestinian state in the West Bank and Gaza – which is a step towards swallowing Israel. This can never happen.

We have to rely only on ourselves, because the rest of the world is a bunch of cowards. The Arabs are rich. They have the oil and they can take the world by the neck. The world is so afraid that they won't consider Israel. Israel is small with only 3 million people. What are we doing? We are fighting for our rights. What are the Arabs fighting for? They have enough land around here. Before the Six Day War in 1967, none of the Arab countries made one step to help the refugees. Look what Israel did in the Gaza Strip. They were living in shacks and in places that civilized people wouldn't even enter. They had no sewers, no electricity, no water, nothing. See what Israel has done, then. We don't have resources, but we have given them houses. We've built roads for them. We gave them electricity. We gave them water. We gave them sewage systems. Where are all the rich countries, like Kuwait and Saudi Arabia? What did they do for them? Nothing.

We have a heavy economic burden. The war, the Yom Kippur War, cost millions of dollars. Fifty per cent of our GNP goes into defence. We have a high rate of inflation. We have to serve in the army every year thirty to sixty days because our army is based on reserves. Yes, I am a family man, married with two kids. Who takes care of my business when I am gone? Nobody. When you get your call to serve you have to serve and that's it. Everyone does it. One is stationed here. One is at the border. Everyone has his own job. I'm a lieutenant in the army.

I am a Jew, but I am not religious. I'm not orthodox; I don't do what the Bible says. But I'm born Israeli Jewish. I don't believe in Jesus. I don't believe in Buddha. I don't believe in Muhammad. I believe in God, not an intermediary.

Emanuel Shaoulian *was born in 1953 in Persia, now called Iran, and came to Israel in 1970. Jews have lived in Iran for about 2,000 years, but they remained Jews. His family was socially part of the middle class. In Israel his father owns a shop. He is a medical student, and his six brothers are also studying.*

I came to Israel before my family for idealistic reasons. I had always heard about Israel, and I felt that I was not a Persian. In 1970 I saw a football game between Iran and Israel. I saw how the Persian people reacted to the Jews, and after I saw their reaction I decided to come here. That was the trigger, but it wasn't everything. I came here because of Zionism.

I don't think the difference between Iranian Jews and Iranians is just training. I have had Jewish training, but I know many people who haven't, and they don't feel like Iranians, either. I don't know what it is. It's not religion. It's something else. My family is religious, but I don't believe in God. I see myself as a Jew, because I think that being a Jew is something more than religion. You belong to such a race and to such a people. That's what I feel.

You know, every people has special qualities. Italians have their special qualities. Arabs have their special qualities. I have my special qualities. I'm not saying that Jewish people are the best–in many points I would prefer to belong to another people–but as a Jew, I can't be myself among others, because of my qualities. I tried it. I was in Italy for three years, and it was very difficult because they were one people, and I was part of another people. Here I feel at home. Jewish people are surprising. In general, they are really ordinary. But there are times when they can do things that they couldn't do normally. In wartime, for example. There was a special spirit in wartime. There was a special spirit in the people.

Yes, I am a Zionist. I feel that this land belongs to me and to my people. I think that every Jew who feels uncomfortable in other places in the world can come here. That's the whole point. I don't believe in forcing people to come here. Everybody who wants to come can come. Living here is not so easy, and yet for us, living in other countries is not easy. An Italian person can take his bag and go to the States and after ten years he is an American. Jewish people can go and remain for four generations, and still remain Jewish. Because we can't be swallowed up in other countries, we have to stay here. But it's difficult. This country has many problems. Many Israelis try to live in other places because of the wars, the taxes, and the constant danger. At certain moments you feel that if you could be a Christian person, maybe it would be better.

Historically, the land belongs to us. I can't accept the statement that this land belongs to the Palestinians. This is the only land that the Jewish people can have. If we can't remain here, we are in danger of not living.

Aaron Mordecai *is a seaman from Beersheba. His ancestors lived in Iraq, and he was born in Burma in 1928. During the Second World War his family moved to India, and in 1952 they came to Israel. Aaron has also lived in England and in South Africa.*

I am Jewish; and a Jew automatically becomes an Israeli. There is no problem with that. Nationality is the place where you were born, and since Burma was a British colony, I have a British passport. I'm allowed to have dual nationality in this country, British and Israeli.

Actually the Jews and the Arabs were the same people originally. I am sure we are from the same stuff as the Arabs. It's just that Jews have been in Europe and they have a different complexion. Their behaviour and their outlook is entirely different from the Middle East or far East Oriental Jews. Arabs say that they are against Zionism and not against Jews, and I'm inclined to believe them. They are envious too, because we've done so much in the land. Now they are getting all the latest weapons, like Israel, and it is not for show. What they want and what we are willing to give up are two different things. We gave up a lot already, the Sinai and the oil fields, and I think we can give up a little more – but not too much.

It's very difficult to solve the Palestinian question. It's a case of land, land, land. Where can you put them? When they left Israel after the war, they were not really driven out. They could have come back had they wanted to. The Jews in Arab countries started to suffer after the State of Israel was born, though, because the Arabs don't want only what was taken in 1967 – land which actually belongs to Israel according to the Jewish Bible. They want the whole country. They want the Jews to be in the minority and the Arabs to rule. That's what they want. This, Israel, of course, cannot accept.

When I was young I thought it was a great thing to be a Jew. I thought the Jews were God's chosen people and things like that. I see now that we are no different from any other nationality. We're not religious, and I don't believe much about the Bible. I think it's a lot of fairy tales. Whether one is a Jew or Christian or Muslim I think that it is all the same. We do the same things, and in the end we just have to die. That's all. We leave this world. So I don't see anything special about being a Jew.

Actually, the State of Israel is a good thing. It shows to the world what the Jews can do, and it's helped develop this country and stamp out diseases. The Jews on the whole are quite talented compared to other races. The thing that brought us back here was religion, the belief in one God – and also the Nazi persecution. These are the two main things I think.

The biggest problem is peace; peace with the Arabs. Once we have peace it will be good for everybody. Money won't be spent on arms and we won't have to borrow money from other countries, and since Israel is way ahead in agriculture and medicine and other things, the Arabs would benefit by it, too. They are bound to benefit. If there was peace you could travel between Israel and the Arab countries freely and exchange views.

Mordechai Nisan *was born in Canada. He grew up in Montreal, and came to Israel in 1972. He finds life in Israel a comfortable contrast to life among non-Jews in Canada, but he believes that in order for Jews and Arabs to coexist separation is necessary.*

My coming to Israel can be explained from two different points of view. I was attracted to the historical homeland of the Jewish people, and I was also beginning to question what kind of full participation in Quebec society a Jew could have. There was a positive as well as a negative motivation in the background of my arrival here. My family wasn't particularly Zionist. Much of what I am was a process of personal development and interest. I was part of that wave in North America in which people sought their personal identity, their own people, their history and culture.

The great opportunity of Israel is that a Jew can be fully himself. This hasn't always been possible in other periods of history and in other countries. Here, we live a traditional Jewish life. We celebrate the festivals and the seasons of the land, and that for me is very important. I can identify with my surroundings. Another advantage is day-to-day living with a community of 3 million Jews. There's an openness a person feels when he is among his own people – people who have the same religion, customs, and ambitions, and who speak the same language.

We have been living for centuries among non-Jews, and we have suffered in many ways as a result of those experiences. Deep down in my soul I often think that I don't want to talk to non-Jews. I want to say we've suffered enough. We've had tragedies enough living among non-Jews for 2,000 years. For fifty years or a few generations, we need to emphasize inter-Jewish living so that we can get to know ourselves again.

The problem of Israel can be formulated very simply. Israel today is a country whose wedge runs from the Mediterranean Sea to the Jordan River. From Tel Aviv to the Jordan River is about thirty-five miles. In that territory we have two separate people: the Jewish people and the Palestinian people. The problem is very simple: how can a million and a half Arabs and about 3 million Jews create any kind of framework of coexistence in that very tiny territory. An examination of relationships between Jews and Arabs in the land of Israel and Palestine in the last seventy to eighty years does not suggest peaceful coexistence between the two peoples.

Jews and Arabs, rather than being brought closer together, have to be separated geographically. I don't live with the illusion that love and brotherhood and all those things somehow flourish as magic formulas for peace. Based on the present historical realities here, I would advocate a solution in which Palestinian Arabs and Israelis would be farther apart instead of closer. Taking into account Israel's legitimate right to security, I can't see Israel withdrawing from the West Bank. I think the world is living under a big illusion, expecting that someday Israel will disappear from the West Bank. I don't think that will happen – in spite of American and Arab pressure. The best Palestinian future lies on the East Bank of Jordan or in other Arab countries.

Nachum Mochiach *is a student in cinema and television in the Faculty of Arts at Tel Aviv University. He was born in Israel in 1953 and represents the common understanding of the younger generation, born after the state was founded and educated in Israeli schools.*

When the Palestinians ran away to Jordan, or to Lebanon, or to Egypt, the Arabs should have settled them there, but the Arabs gave them a place to live in very bad conditions. That is why the Palestinians want to come back to their places here. Even some Jaffa Arabs ran away in 1948. But now Jaffa is part of Israel, it's now Tel Aviv. They can't come back to these places. It was their place of living but not anymore. Nobody told them to leave. It was their own decision.

I don't know what the Arabs really want. I know what we want. We want a real peace. But I still can't believe what the Arabs say about it. Sometimes they want peace, sometimes they want to destroy us, to throw us into the sea. I think we made a very great advance in the last years, after the Yom Kippur War – an advance in a diplomatic and even in a military way. I think all these agreements with the Egyptians and the Syrians are the right things. I don't know how much we have to give them. Of course we can't go back to the borders of 1967, because they're not secure for us. In the War of Independence, the Arabs wanted all of Israel. If we give back all they want, where would we live?

Gabriella Bachi's *family originated in Italy. They left in the late 1930's during Mussolini's regime but her father returned for the latter years of his life. Gabriella, an archaeologist, feels that Israel is her home, but for her being a Jew doesn't necessarily mean being religious.*

What does it mean to be a Jew? I myself am not religious. I was born a Jew. I feel that I belong to the Jewish people. Jewishness is a religion, perhaps, but it is also a people. I try to be rational, and I can't understand all the religious things. You can't place Jewish people alongside Catholics, or Protestants, or Mennonites. Jewishness is a people and it is a religion and it is a country. It is also a group different and separate from other people. Before Zionism the difference was religious habit and culture, and for some it remains the same even after Zionism. For others, Zionism means to become like other people. The main idea was to come back to a land where we would feel at home.

My father felt more at home in Italy. He spent the last four years in Italy in order to write and to get back to Italian literature. He planned to return here but he died prematurely of a heart attack. From him I got the idea that it would be better for humanity if there were no religion and no nationality and not so many languages. But because the world is the way it is, it is better for me to be here than anywhere else. I feel more at home in Italy than in France or Canada, but more at home in Israel than in Italy. My father thought that Israel should exist but after thirty years he wanted something else.

When I was younger I was more patriotic. I was in the army during the Syrian War. I think about the Arab-Israeli conflict but I don't do anything about it. After the Six Day War I was not happy, because I prefer a small Israeli country to a larger one with many Arabs in it. We cannot live forever with soldiers ruling other people. I know that the old border was very dangerous for us, but I would give much of it back. The Palestinians should have some independence, and I don't like those areas to be part of Israel. I like Jerusalem, but I don't care for the Wailing Wall. We'll probably never give back Jerusalem, but I personally wouldn't mind.

The main difference between Jews and Arabs is nationality. I don't think that the Jews are a chosen people. I hate this idea; the Bible is full of it. I believe that we are different, not better or superior, just different, sometimes for the better and sometimes for the worse. I know there is something special – in intellectualism for instance – but I don't know why or from what it comes. Maybe we have studied more.

Mother said it was difficult to be a Jew. I prefer being a Jew if the alternative is to be Catholic or Muslim. If you live abroad among Christians it isn't easy. If you live here with war it isn't easy, either. The problem through the centuries was that Jews were different. They refused to assimilate, and people hate what is different. If you go back into history with the Greeks and the Romans, you know that the Jews refused to worship Greek and Roman gods. I don't think that the Jews suffered only because of the Church and its feeling that the Jews killed Jesus. The Jews always resisted the state and its gods. The rulers liked the Jews when they needed them for medicine and things like that, but they didn't like it when the Jews remained a people apart. When a ruler had troubles he would blame someone else – the Jews.

Meida Rica *was born in the Belgian Congo (now Zaire) and educated in a Catholic school. She came to Palestine in 1944 in order to find out what it meant to be Jewish.*

I did not come to Palestine because of anti-Semitism. I came because I wanted to become a true Jew. I was accepted in my home community. All my friends were Belgian, and I got a very good Christian education. I was accepted by the Christians but I felt that something was missing somewhere. I decided that I wanted to belong to something that was true to myself, to be a Jew in more than just name. I went deeper into it, and I found out that to be a Jew means to belong to a people. So I went back to my people, and I said, "I will help my people to become themselves, so that they can help other people after that." Because you cannot help others if you are not yourself.

To be a Jew means to go back to tradition. Only when you are equal as a human being, can you feel that you are accepted, so I want, first of all, to educate my people to become themselves. I want them to follow their own tradition and be proud of what they have become. When they know where they are, they can contribute to the brotherhood of man. The Jewish people feel that they are equal to the rest of mankind, but the people outside do not feel equal to them. I get that impression from even the most intelligent people. Behind our backs there is always the question of prejudice which makes us feel that we are different if we are Jews. Very seldom can a person get out of his tradition, and history has said that the Jew has slain Jesus, and consequently, without being conscious of it, there is a feeling that the Jew is different–I don't say bad–but different. I do not think that anybody is responsible for this attitude; I think it's a very basic cultural problem. It's the same with the Arabs. I don't blame the Arabs. I don't think there is a conflict because the Arabs do not accept us, or because Arabs are bad, or because Arabs want their rights. I don't think so.

To really join the human race as an equal, I have to go back to my own people. Each people must first find its own priorities and its own culture. I think that in each people there is both good and bad, and that before you can form a community that will eventually become a brotherhood, you have to have a people who are normal and capable of giving something to the world. So I have to make my people a strong people, a people with a lot of value. I want to be a normal person; then I can help you, and you can help me, too.

I believe that Jewish people have values and a faith based in a very deep tradition. This tradition tells them to love their neighbour, to under-stand their neighbour, to help their neighbour. But I believe that a true Arab is the same as a true Israeli. We will come to terms together, because there is no other way. We've got to live on the same piece of land, that's all. We will have to.

I think that the Jews can learn from the Arabs. Arab family ties are very strong. I wouldn't want them to change, because it's very good to have family ties, to have brotherhood within the family. I've been to many villages and this is something I like very much. I think the Arabs love life. They love their children. They love their families. They love to work. We can learn this love from them. Why not? The Arabs can learn from the Jews too. From the Jews they can learn the will to live, and they can also learn not to hate. This is something very important. We have suffered and we have lost people, but still we don't hate. Arabs can kill somebody in my own family and I will not hate them. But if we kill one of them there is very deep hate.

Zeev Meiri, *who was born in Poland in 1912 and came to Palestine in 1935, lives on Kibbutz Yad Mordechai, south of Ashkelon. Zeev went to a religious school until he was seventeen. He was in the Polish military for two years. Then he emigrated to Palestine and joined a kibbutz because it was impossible for him, as a Jew in Poland, to study at the university or to work in the government.*

I had religious parents. My father wanted to make a rabbi out of me, but I didn't like it. I wanted a wider education. It took me about one year to adjust myself to the public school because I didn't know anything. I didn't even know the Polish language. Today I'm not religious, but that doesn't mean I'm not Jewish. I think that a Jew can be a good Jew if he has a conscience of Jewish faith and if he has a relationship with his people, his family, and his nation.

The enemies of the Jews in Poland were not only the Germans who came in, but also the Poles. Why did the Germans build the extermination camps in Poland, and not in other places? Only because they knew that the Polish people would help them. There was a deep hatred of the Poles against the Jews. Political discrimination came out of that hatred. I don't know why, but they didn't have faith in the Jews. They didn't think they could rely on a Jew. I think they got it from Russia. It's probably because they could not compete with the Jews, in business, let's say. Most businesses were in Jewish hands. They were jealous, mostly jealous. Secondly they believed that the Jews were the killers of Jesus. It's a deep belief for the Catholics.

The Palestinians could have a good future, if they could be persuaded to settle in Jordan, and not here in Israel. A state including the West Bank and Gaza would not be good. Israeli borders are not wide enough. It's not possible to have a Palestinian state in a very small country whose dimensions are very long and very narrow; there are places not wider than fifteen kilometres between Jordan and the sea.

Mike Levin *was born in England in 1942 and came to Palestine four years later. He works for the Ministry of Immigration and Absorption, but his views on the Palestinian question are his own. He believes that a coming together of both sides for the sake of peace is possible.*

I feel that Eretz Israel is the land of the Jewish people. They don't have any other land in which to live a sovereign life. Unfortunately, two people are claiming the same land. The fact is that the Palestinians never had their own land in the sense of a sovereign political country. But the same thing can be said about African states and Asian states. I believe that under certain circumstances there is a chance of talking to the Palestinian nationalists, the PLO included. I also believe that there can be division of the land. We don't have to give up our historical feeling about this place, but we also have to be realistic about the political situation. The first thing we should do is recognize the rights of the Palestinians. And the Palestinians have to recognize the rights of the Jews to live in this country. It's a very difficult task, because there is a lot of hatred.

I hope that on the Palestinian side there will be more moderate people. In Israel there is a small moderate group. If we had support from a moderate part on the Palestinian side, it would be easier for the Israeli moderates to convince the Israeli extremists. Unfortunately, I don't see it on the Palestinian side. You see only very small moves on the Palestinian side; very small moves. That's not enough.

How long have I been thinking this way? I would say that I started after the Six Day War. It took me a long time. I think this opinion is growing gradually. If the Palestinians will change their mind it will grow even more. And it will grow if there is pressure from both sides, from America and Russia. I would prefer it to be without pressure from America and the Soviet Union. But you see signs today. You see Israeli correspondents visiting Arab countries. You see Palestinians meeting Israelis in Paris. Those signs are very small, but they are positive.

Yaffa Yshby, *a wife and mother, had special responsibility for the children in her kibbutz near the Jordanian border, an area targeted by Palestinian commandos in the late 1960's. She remembers the help of nearby Arab villagers and how the children adjusted to fear-filled lives.*

A few years ago my job was working with very small children between four days and one or two years old. When the Arabs bombed here we had only one shelter. Now we can take the children to the fields, but at that time we were afraid to go out. The children didn't know for three years what it was like to sleep in a bed in the house. For three years they were only in the shelter where the beds were small and the air was stuffy. I remember that one morning when I was working inside and eight small children were playing outside, we heard a bomb. Near the children's house where I worked was a shelter. Three Arab men came to help me take the children to the shelter. After that, I spoke with them – they could speak some Hebrew – and they told me, "The war is not for us; it's for politicians. We want to work and to live with our children, the same as you do, and we will not fight." An old Arab man took a small baby to him, because the baby was crying and he comforted it.

And so we lived like this for three years. After that, the government helped us with money, and now we have new shelters – very good ones, I think. Now that we have new shelters, we go to sleep every afternoon in them. The children learn to like the shelters and they are not afraid.

Here every young person goes into the army. It's not the same in America where men are afraid to go into the army and they don't have the freedom to go home. Here they come home very often, and the children know. "Tomorrow my father is going to the army for a few days and he will come back," they say. They don't mind it.

Avraham Yehoshua *is one of Israel's best-known writers of fiction. He was born in Jerusalem in 1936. On his father's side his family goes back six generations in Palestine and thence to Greece. His mother arrived from Morocco in 1930. Besides writing, he teaches at Haifa University and he also lectures to the soldiers, this being his duty as a member of the reserves.*

My father is an Orientalist: a teacher of Arabic who is now head of the Muslim and Druse in the Ministry of Religion. I was educated in Jerusalem and at the age of eighteen I started to write. Then I had to go into the army, and I was in the parachute service in 1954 to 1957 during the Sinai campaign. I was nineteen when the Sinai campaign started. During the Six Day War I was in Paris. From 1963 to 1967, I was in Paris for four years as secretary-general of the world union of Jewish students.

In the reserve army, I'm no longer in fighting units. I'm in the unit of lecturers. This is a unique thing in Israel. There is a unit of 400 lecturers from all over society, and they often talk about Zionism, ideology and conflict. The lectures are given by people who are very free to do whatever they want. I want to stress this point. The lecturers openly discuss Israel and the army without any problem. I'm known to be to the left. I've been critical of the government for ten years.

From the point of view of art we are very productive. I would be glad if we could be as productive in energy or in industry as we are in art. There is theatre, and an amazing publication of books. I was speaking to a publisher the other day and he told me there are 3,000 to 4,000 copies of quarterly magazines published in Israel in a population of 3 million. Three-quarters of a million don't read Hebrew, so let's speak about 2 million supporting many publishing houses of poetry and literature. For a first collection of poems, a poet's first book, 1,000 copies will be printed – about the same number of copies as a first book in the States. For any first edition of a novel, 3,000 copies will be printed – the same as any first copy in England or in France. In some ways we are too productive in art. The Arabs are doing the hard labour; the Jews are returning too much to intellectual activities.

To be a Jew for me is connected very much to being an Israeli Jew. If – God forbid it – but if Israel is destroyed, I will be in a very different situation. To be a Jew without Israel would have no meaning. I would have no identity, or else my identity would shrink to almost nothing. To us our Jewish nature is clear and we can feel it, but it is hard to say that the world can understand it. By a certain kind of logic one can even justify this lack of understanding, because when you come right down to it the phenomenon of the Jew is not an easy one to understand. For nations which encounter us in a certain historical situation, like the Germans and the Arabs, our very existence and the uncertainty of our nature in their eyes could provide the spark for whatever kind of insanity was afflicting them at the time. Ultimately, a Jew is a person who identifies himself as a Jew. You can speak about a rabbi in New York, a sabra who knows nothing about Judaism, Henry Kissinger… there is a tremendous mixture. We're not living together, not speaking the same language.

In my opinion, there is something very ambiguous about being a Jew. Because of their ambiguity Jews are provoking to other people. They provoke the insanity of a people in crisis. Saul Bellow, in some of his writings, says neurosis can be graded by the capacity to tolerate an ambiguous situation. Germany after the First World War was a nation whose values and confidence had collapsed. The economic situation was uncertain. The Jews are now in an ambiguous situation, themselves. They can stand it. They can feel it and they can hold it. But to non-Jews in a crisis, ambiguity provokes insanity, hatred, confusion – they can't bear it.

If it had been the Bulgarians who came here rather than the Jews, the conflict would not be so bitter. The Jews didn't know exactly what they wanted. They wanted some land, but they didn't know how much land. There were those who asked for just a little land, to be free. There were those who wanted more land. Then, the question was: what kind of state? One with a prophetic mission? Or an ordinary state like the

186

others? A state as a means to redemption? Or a state by itself? A means, or an end?

Now, the Arabs don't know exactly what we want. Will we be just an ordinary state, or a perfect society to change the region? An independent state run for our own interests, or run by Jews outside? All these unclear things are unclear to both Jews and Arabs. The conflict is taking a bitter direction. The Palestinians don't want to compromise, although all the world is saying that they should compromise. They are scared of living in peace with this kind of society.

Since the Six Day War I have been ready to go back to the 1967 borders, to give up East Jerusalem, and do whatever one could do in order for Israel to be a safe country, living in full peace. A full peace means that Israel has more than intermediary agreements, and that it continues to be both a Zionist country, and a full society with relations with Jews in the diaspora. I'm very hawkish in terms of peace. The ambiguous situation – no peace/no war – is very dangerous. Canada can live without diplomatic relations with Denmark or China, but not with the United States. One must have relations with one's neighbours. For 2,000 years we've had to live with non-Jews. For once, I want to be alone with only Jews.

Schmuel Gringold *was born in Israel in 1949. He is a student in economics and believes that doing everything possible for peace makes more sense for Israel than going to war every few years.*

If we are going to say that Israel is the one and only solution for the Jewish people – and that's what I believe – and if there is a confrontation between the Jews and the Arabs in the Middle East, there are only two situations possible. Either we are going to settle our quarrel by a peace agreement or we are going to fight. For me the second solution is not a possibility, because it raises some questions of morality that I can't forget. Every few years there's a war. The Arabs become much more cruel each time and each time we use much more destructive equipment. The moral issues are too deep a question for me. I prefer to believe that it is possible to find a way to make peace. I am not sure that this possibility of making peace is more real than the possibility of war, but for me it's much more comfortable.

Now, because of this, I think that we have to do everything to solve the problems except endanger our survival as a nation. I don't think that the main problem is the Palestinian nation. The Arabs themselves created the Palestinians, but then I don't think that we should ignore them either. I think we have to talk the same language; and since language in this confrontation forces the Arabs to recognize Israel as a state, then

Israel should recognize the Palestinians as a nation, too. I think that one of the possibilities is to allow them to build their country. I'm afraid that even if Israel does make an effort to solve the Palestinian problem, both the Israelis and the Arabs will not be strong enough to stop the involvement of the Russians and the Americans in this area. If it were only a local problem, the solution would be much easier, because we have a lot of common interests.

Shifra Fisher *is a medical student at the University of Tel Aviv. She was born in Israel but her parents came from Poland. Prior to the national elections in May, 1977, she reflects on what it means to be a Jew, the motivations of young people and the problem of war.*

The main problem here is the war, the situation between the Arabs and us. People must go into the army one or two months of the year, and you cannot lead a normal life. You get used to it, but it's not good. I have been abroad this year in eight countries in Europe. It was just wonderful to see how silent they were – especially Switzerland, with its mountains and lakes, and silent people. It feels so good. Here, we always live in fear. I don't think that I am personally frightened, but war is a problem. It's not such a good feeling, to turn on the radio and to hear that a bus got bombed or people were shot.

In this situation, I think there might be another war, especially if Begin becomes our leader. As a matter of fact, I would like Begin to become our leader. As I heard on television last night, he will do a lot in the field of security. He will have to get together with the Arabs and talk with them. He is not afraid to use force, if necessary. I don't like war, but if it will help us – since the Arabs don't understand any other language – maybe it will be good. Begin will try to do his best to make peace between the Arabs and us, and maybe it will be the answer to the question of safe borders. And he doesn't want to give back lands that our soldiers took in the war.

My parents could have gone to the United States when they came to the country in 1949. They preferred to go to Israel. They were idealistic. I am religious. People who are religious know more about why they are here. For other people, what is there to connect them to the country? This country belongs to us. It was given to us many years ago and we have to live here. Here is our place. God chose the Jews to walk with Him and to be His special people, so that all other people will see what they are doing and will learn from them.

For me to be a Jew means to live here, and to offer all that I can to the country. If there is a happy event, I am happy with all the people. If there is a war or something sad, I am part of that, too.

Epilogue

After many starts and stops, in which the various possible ways of appropriately ending this book were considered, I came to the conclusion that editorial comment was right for *The Israelis* as it had been for *The Palestinians.*

To begin with, I must remind myself and my readers that the context is not only this present volume and the experience that produced it, but also its predecessor, and all that went into the making of that portrait of the Palestinian people. In the Preface to that book it was said: "We present this portrait of the Palestinians without apology to the Jewish people. We intend also to complete our portrait of the Israelis without apology to the Palestinians. We want the world to hear both of them and both of them to hear each other."

Quite frankly, even while I made the commitment to complete *The Israelis*, I doubted whether this undertaking could be carried out. There were questions of available time, energy, and finances. But, more importantly, there was the feeling that "equal time" was not really needed, since the Jewish/Israeli story had become widely known in Western lands. Beyond this was a very personal concern that a rather complete empathy with the Palestinians and an open espousal of their cause had prejudiced a fair hearing of the Israeli Jews.

However, my earlier commitment to listen also to the Israelis was strengthened whenever I remembered the untold Jewish suffering of the centuries, whenever I was reminded how much *Fiddler on the Roof* told the story of my own Russian Mennonite people, whenever I renewed my academic fascination with minority groups, and whenever I returned to my doctoral dissertation and its exposure of anti-Semitism among immigrant minorities in Canada. Joining with Canadian Jews in championing righteous causes also helped. Besides, there could be no reading of history or of the Bible which did not expose the very great debt we owe to the Jewish people. It also became clear to me that if Jerusalem would not know peace, neither would I, my children, or the rest of the world. Thus, a long-standing commitment to international peace also made unavoidable this latest obligation to the Jewish people.

The Israelis made the follow-through rather simple and easy. They helped to remove emotional blockages by opening wide their doors and their hearts. Few were the occasions when a copy of *The Palestinians*, displayed to explain the purpose of our coming, became an obstacle to conversation. Only once was it suggested that we were agents of the Palestine Liberation Organization, and even that suspicion evaporated when I reported how Palestinians in Beirut had accused us of being Israeli agents.

I had determined in advance of my going to Israel to listen and not to argue, except on few occasions and then only as a technique to elicit further response. The willingness with which the people talked and the spell-binding nature of their stories made listening easy. Just to hear Israelis unravel their memories and their feelings became a fascination and a preoccupation. In the process, my goyish heart was melted and intermittently I struggled to hold back my tears. This deep inner reorientation was reinforced in the editing, and more and more I came to believe the Preface of the first volume: "peace lies in the direction of deep, sensitive, and prolonged listening to the peoples on both sides, from both sides, and by both sides."

I heard from the Israeli Jews how deeply written into their soul is their historical experience as a persecuted minority. They were treated as such by the Egyptians, the Assyrians, the Babylonians, the Persians, the Greeks, and the Romans, whose gods they could not accept as replacements for Yahweh. Their own initiatives and dispositions set them apart almost from the beginning. The sense of a special calling, a certain chosenness, a unique peoplehood, and an important task, accompanied the Patriarchs and the children of Israel in the earliest chapters of Jewish history. The ancestral inclination to articulate and symbolize the collective experience with the one and only God strengthened this sense. There is no sociology, no economy, no politics, no law, and no psychology so strong as that which is nurtured and motivated by a strong religion, especially if that religion integrates all aspects of a life which is passed on to every new generation. It was the life-embracing religion of the Jews which made their peoplehood as strong as it was.

The emergence of the people called Christians presented new problems to them. For a variety of reasons most of the Jewish contemporaries did not become enthusiastic about Jesus of Nazareth, the hero and leader of the Christians. Resistance to his reinterpretation of the Jewish writings, as well as varying images and expectations of the coming Messiah, differential political goals, and a measure of conservatism, perhaps even stubbornness, were among the factors that contributed to their detachment.

Christian insistence on being the new Israel, thus pre-empting Jewish identity, history, theology, and the attendant claims to chosenness, helped to put the two minorities within the Roman empire on a collision course. The apparent collusion of the Romans and the Christians in placing collective blame for the crucifixion of Jesus on the Jews, the former by washing their hands and the latter by charging deicide, put into motion a form of eternal punishment for them and their children. For nearly two millennia they have unfairly born the guilt of deicide and suffered to the point of genocide.

The early opposing stance of Christians and Jews with respect to each other set the stage for the disastrous conflicts that ensued in successive centuries. The alliances, which developed between European states and the Christian Church, beginning with the official acceptance of Christianity by the Roman empire, put the Jews at a double disadvantage. Adjusting their lives to the deities of imperial powers and their dictates was one thing. Adjusting to a religion that was rapidly becoming creedal and ceremonial, representing the will of the state more than the will of God, and rarely approaching the complete ethic which was the essence of Judaism, was another thing. In the end the Jews were asked to accept a Christ, who would join them in their ghettos, not as a suffering servant, but as an imperial overlord bearing the sword of the state.

Their resistance was valid and to me quite credible, because it had so much in common with the religious reform movements of my sixteenth century forbears, the Swiss, Dutch, and German Anabaptists. They also rejected the imperial Church, the fusion of clergy and magistrates, the use of the sword in the name of religion, the creedal Christ, and the pomp and ceremony of a religion that had lost its centralities. Like the Jews they knew something of a life-embracing ethic, of a religion that was really a total culture, and of peoplehood which had to be felt before it could be defined.

The Jews resisted Church and state, understandably and properly so, and holy empires and imperial churches resisted them, regrettably and improperly so. The powers found all kinds of ways to keep them in their place. They denied the Jews the ownership of land, and thus they ended up specializing in those vocations and those life-styles which allowed them to survive but which, unfortunately, also stereotyped them. Thus it happened that the Jewish name became a byword among the nations, sometimes for reasons which made them justifiably proud and sometimes for reasons which caused them to hang their heads in shame.

As a minority the Jews pursued their special strengths, as all minorities are wont to do, except that they did it over a longer period of time and with better results. Their love of learning and truth, their need to survive, their desire for recognition, material security, and influence all contributed to those drives which made them an indomitable, and an invincible people. In their weakness they became strong. As a minority

191

they threatened kings and empires. Their ghettos somehow kept shaking the national capitals.

The world feared them and they feared the world. This phobia, a complex of most minority groups, was, in the case of the Jews, so solidly based on experience over such a long period of time that they trembled even when the objective causes for fear had vanished. In these latter days, the old insecurities still run so deep that every criticism, however well-intentioned, reverberates for some Jews with echoes of anti-Semitism and memories of the Holocaust. This is understandable. The psyche of a whole people can be as injured as that of an individual person. Their trust has too often been betrayed, the hand of reconciliation too often rejected.

When new nationalisms swept Europe some Jews tried to embrace the various nation states as loyal citizens, anxious to be not only Jews but also Germans, Russians, Poles, Frenchmen, and Englishmen. Thus they sought to end the enmity that had built up between them and the nations. It worked for some but for Arthur Dreyfus and others the effort was rebuffed. Thereafter they gave their ear to Theodor Herzl who offered them Zionism, a nationalism rooted in their own peoplehood. His plan was backed up by the dreams of many years, the prayers of centuries directed towards Zion, and the undying hope to be "next year in Jerusalem." It was also assisted by various views of prophecy, Jewish and Christian, indeed by self-fulfilling prophecies, and by international circumstances, including the two world wars of the twentieth century.

Now the Jews are in their own land. The same vigour with which they pursued learning, business, and the professions has gone into the development of land–some of it swampy, rocky, and barren–and into the building of a state. Their earlier genius has found new outlets. They are excelling now in agriculture, in affairs of state, and in war. The language of the miraculous, not improperly descriptive of all that has happened in the last thirty years, should in no way detract from their own hard labours and meritorious achievements.

Their strength is not as apparent to them as it is to outsiders. They see themselves under siege, surrounded by alien neighbours linked up to hostile power blocs. The danger of being thrown into the hungry sea is as real to them as is the memory of Hitler's firey furnaces. The fears of the ages are now compounded by the continuing insecurity of the Israeli state, which was intended to end Jewish troubles forever.

From the outside they don't look so weak. They are perceived differently than they perceive themselves. Israel projects the image, not of a David with a sling-shot, but of a military giant fully capable of winning any war over the Arabs in the foreseeable future. As already indicated, their transformation of a land, their commerce, their culture, and their statecraft are well-known. The stream of people who come to Jerusalem to learn how things are done is endless. Outside Israel, the economic success and professional standing of the Jewish people are proverbial in every land. Their voices are prominent in the media and wherever national and international decisions are made.

Critics are loud and vocal, but relatively few in number. As in centuries gone by, so today there are leaders and people whose fears and jealousies concerning the Jews and their activities surface rather easily and which, for the Jews, carry all the overtones of anti-Semitism. That, however, is no longer the dominant or prevailing response to the Jewish people. I think it is fair to say that in most European and North American countries there is now a deep empathy. There is genuine respect for the achievements of Israel. There is a sense of guilt for past neglects which wants, somehow, to offer compensation. There is a new theology, a new politics and a new psychology at work, which should survive any future Arab oil embargoes.

Yet, the Israelis are not without enemies. They now fear the Soviet role and influence and are not entirely certain that Europe and America can be depended upon. They are more than ever concerned about the Arab states, their increasing monetary and military power, though the isolation of Egypt, however temporary this may prove to be, has offered some relief.

As elsewhere in the world, so in Israel there is now an internal awareness that the country's most immediate problem is the Palestinian Arabs – not primarily those who are citizens of Israel, but those under Israeli administration in the West Bank, Gaza, and East Jerusalem, as well as those outside the country. Previously this awareness was muted because of Israeli assumptions that the land was relatively empty and that Arabs were Arabs, requiring no special distinctions. In some, more limited ways, these suppositions still linger. New Jewish settlers on the West Bank, for instance, minimize the Palestinian reality both in terms of land ownership and as a population with any kind of claim. Their conclusions are derived partly from what they have been told and partly from the Palestinian landscape and culture. Nearly a million people reside on the West Bank, yet they can be quite unnoticed because their villages blend so much with the landscape and their way of life is so quiet and unobtrusive. They have no high-rise apartments, no industrial chimneys, few noisy machines. They are not loud or gaudy or forward, but quiet, submissive, patient, and waiting.

In recent years, however, the Palestinian actuality has become increasingly inescapable. Closer contact since 1967 as a result of the Israeli occupation, a high birth rate, guerilla activity, and international politics have all served to bring them into the forefront of domestic Israeli concerns. Indeed, the Begin government has given much attention to the future of both the land and the people.

Israelis are by no means united on this question. Their views include extremes at both ends. Some believe Eretz Israel to contain even more land than is now under Israeli control. Their preference would be to have more land and to have it without the Palestinian people. Thus, the extremists would have no reservations about effecting another expulsion of Palestinian Arabs. At the other end of the political spectrum are those Israelis who would be ready to surrender every dunam of territory, including East Jerusalem, obtained in 1967, and to grant to the Palestinians their full sovereignty in return for peace and the recognition of Israel. There is, of course, also a very small minority, almost negligible, ready to have the State of Israel dismantled as a Zionist state. In between the two extremes are the majority of the people willing to be led in one direction or another. The basic question facing Israel is which direction to follow.

In my opinion, the full recognition of the Palestinians in exchange for full recognition of the Israelis is the most promising direction, both in terms of human idealism and political realism. In many ways, the Palestinian Arabs now have a history similar to that of the Jews. They too have waited for centuries, indeed millennia, to be freed from outside domination. European Christian crusades tortured them as they tyrannized the Jews. When the twentieth century dawned they wanted to shape their own destiny in their own land. The land of Palestine and the city of Jerusalem have always meant much to them. The desire to express themselves as a nation, though vaguely articulated until recently, is as strong as that of the Jews.

They are like the Jews in many ways. They have produced miracles in their land. They have squeezed olive oil out of rocky hillsides. They have pumped water in the desert. They have survived in refugee camps as the Jews have survived in their ghettos. Their love of learning has produced hundreds of university graduates. They now know many languages. They are largely in the diaspora. Their "government" for the most part is in exile. They are in fact, the "Jews" of the Arab world.

Like the Jews, they speak with the same passion about the land. They love their children with the same love. They speak about peace with the same longing. They pick up their weapons only with great reluctance. They would rather send their children to school than to military training. They feel betrayed by the nations of the world, and their fears are very real. Their generosity and hospitality, their laughter and their tears, their determination and fighting spirit, all have their parallels in Jewish history. The similarity, of course, is not total. The two peoples are also

194

sufficiently different in their histories, cultures, and values to be in a position to complement each other.

The present stance of both sides lead to Armageddon, the "final," apocalyptic battle of the nations. An altered course, on the other hand, can mean a New Jerusalem to which the peoples of the world will come to learn how not to make war anymore. What is required now is for the Palestinians and Israelis to hear each other's stories with understanding, to offer each other mutual recognition and statehood. Perhaps, in due course, a confederation could be formed which could grow to include other Arab states and indeed the whole Middle East.

If and when that happens, then the desert will really blossom; the hills and the valleys will dance with joy, the springs will gush forth unendingly, and the fields will produce abundantly. The singular gifts of both the Jewish and Arab peoples will complement each other. The endless wars of all the Semitic tribes will at long last come to an end. And they will all lead the rest of the world in the ways of peace. The chosen race will then be the human race and the promised land will begin to cover the earth.

One final word. The above should not be interpreted as my instructions to the Israelis or to the Palestinians. Outsiders offering all the answers have operated too often in history. But having heard both Palestinians and Israelis, and having walked, as much as was possible, in their shoes, I have come to this conclusion: the Middle East conflict is not so complex that it cannot be unravelled, and peace is not so distant that it cannot be claimed in this generation. A new emotion and a new intention can make the difference. The purpose of these portraits was to identify the emotion, and affirm the intention, and contribute to their early release.

Selected Readings

A. Books

Begin, Menachem. *The Revolt, Story of the Irgun.* Jerusalem: Steimatzky, 1977.

Ben-Gurion, David. *Israel: A Personal History.* New York: Funk & Wagnalls, 1971.

Buber, Martin. *Israel and Palestine: The History of an Idea.* London: East and West Library, 1952.

Cohen, Aharon. *Israel and the Arab World.* New York: Funk & Wagnalls, 1970.

Cohen, Hayyim. *The Jews of the Middle East, 1860-1972.* New York: Wiley, 1973.

Dawidowicz, Lucy S. *A Holocaust Reader.* New York: East and West Library, 1946.

Diamont, Max I. *Jews, God, and History.* New York: New American Library, 1969.

Eliachar, E. and Philip Gillon. *Israelis and Palestinians.* Jerusalem: Gaalyah Cornfield, 1977.

Elon, Amos. *The Israelis: Fathers and Sons.* New York: Holt, Rinehart and Winston, 1971.

Epp, Frank H. *The Palestinians: Portrait of a People in Conflict.* Toronto: McClelland & Stewart, 1976.

————. *Whose Land is Palestine? The Middle East Problem in Historical Perspective.* Toronto: McClelland & Stewart, 1970.

Herzl, Theodor. *The Jewish State.* New York: American Zionist Emergency Council, 1946.

————. *Altneuland, Old-New Land.* New York: Bloch, 1960.

Kollek, Teddy. *For Jerusalem, A Life.* New York: Random House, 1978.

Laqueur, Walter. *A History of Zionism.* New York: Holt, Rinehart and Winston, 1971.

————. *The Israel-Arab Reader.* Toronto: Bantam Books, 1976.

Meir, Golda. *My Life.* New York: G. P. Putnam's Sons, 1975.

Morse, Arthur D. *While Six Million Died.* New York: Random House, 1968.

Parkes, James. *Whose Land? A History of the Peoples of Palestine.* Penguin, 1970.

Peretz, Don. *Israel and the Palestine Arabs.* Washington: Middle East Institute, 1958.

Poll, Solomon and Ernest Krausz. *On Ethnic and Religious Diversity in Israel.* Ramat-Gan, Israel: Institute for the Study of Ethnic and Religious Groups, Bar-Ilan University, 1975.

Sachar, Howard M. *A History of Israel: From the Rise of Zionism to our Time.* Jerusalem: Steimatzky, 1976.

Simon, Leon, ed. *Ahad Ha-am, Essays, Letters and Memoirs.* Oxford: East and West Library, 1946.

B. Periodicals

Facts about Israel. Jerusalem: Ministry of Information. Published annually.

Information Briefing. Jerusalem: Israel Information Centre. Published periodically.

C. Literature Lists
(Available from addresses below)

1. Embassy of Israel,
   Ste. 601-410 Laurier Ave. W.,
   Ottawa, Canada, K1R 7T3.
2. Embassy of Israel,
   1621 22nd Street, N.W.,
   Washington, D.C. 20008

3. Mission of Israel,
   United Nations,
   800 Second Avenue,
   New York, N.Y. 10017
4. Israel Information Centre,
   214 Yafo Road,
   Jerusalem, Israel.

Summary of
Ninety-six Interviews

1. AGE:

Teens	1
Twenties	18
Thirties	20
Forties	24
Fifties	20
Sixties	10
Seventies	3

2. CONTACT:

governmental	18
institutional	28
personal	50

3. COUNTRY OF ORIGIN (29):

Australia	1
Austria	7
Belgium	2
Canada	4
Czechoslovakia	2
Egypt	1
England	3
Finland	1
Germany	7
Greece	1
India	1
Iraq	2
Iran	1
Italy	1
Lebanon	1
Libya	1
Lithuania	2
Morocco	3
Netherlands	1
Palestine	5
Poland	15
Rumania	3
Russia/USSR	15
South Africa	3
Spain	1
Syria	1
USA	9
Yemen	1
Zaire	1

4. OCCUPATION:

agriculturalists	15
arts	4
business	7
civil servants	6
clerical	3
engineers	1
labourers	10
lawyers	4
media	7
military	5
politicians	4
professors	7
rabbis	4
social workers	2
spokespersons	3
students	8
teachers	6

199

5. **PRESENT LOCATION:**
   Rural (22 places)   34
   Urban (13 places)   63

6. **RELIGION/RACE:**
   Jewish   91
   Christian   3
   Muslim   3

7. **TIME OF IMMIGRATION:**
   1970s   11
   1960s   12
   1950s   8

1940s   20
1930s   17
1920s   9
1910s   2
1900s   3
19th century   6
18th century   2
15th century   1
Not applicable   5

8. **SEX:**
   Male   74
   Female   22

Detail of Interviews

Name	Place	Year of Birth	Country of Origin	Year of Immigration*	Occupation
Abergil, Simon	Ramat Hasharon	1949	Morocco	1961	Labourer
Abileah, Joseph	Haifa	1915	Austria	1926	Musician
Adler, Shmuel	Jerusalem	1940	USA	1960	Civil Servant
Argov, Shlomo	Jerusalem	1929	Lithuania	c. 1800	Civil Servant
Asad, Ib'n	Jerusalem	1945	Palestine	—	Guide
Aviv, Malka	Gitit	1953	Russia	c. 1770	Agriculturalist
Barak, Nirit	Mehula	1950	Canada	1970	Agriculturalist
Bar-Ami, Moshe	Tel Aviv	1930	Germany	1950	Spokesman
Bachi, Gabriella	Ramat Aviv	1937	Italy	1939	Archaeologist
Belsky, Bialik	Matulla	1934	Russia	1896	Hotel Manager
Ben-Yosef, J.	Tel Aviv	1931	USSR	1947	General
Berger, Julius	Kadima	1919	Austria	1941	Tax Collector
Bichovsky, Moshe	Maoz-Hayim	1950	Russia	1924	Agriculturalist
Brinker, Menachem	Jerusalem	1935	Lithuania	1905	Editor
Brot, Michael	Lohamey-Hgetaoth	1921	Poland	1950	Argiculturalist
Cohen, Jack	Jerusalem	1919	USA	1961	Rabbi
Cohen, Menachem	Jerusalem	1947	Syria	c. 1800	Social Worker
Davis, Uri	Shmaryahu	1934	Czechoslovakia	1935	Anthropologist
DeVries, Michael	Ramat Hasharon	1939	Netherlands	1965	Travel Agent

*Of individual or ancestors

201

Name	Place	Year of Birth	Country of Origin	Year of Immigration	Occupation
"Eine alte Frau"	Haifa	1901	Poland	1953	Hotel Manager
Eliaschar, Eli	Jerusalem	1899	Spain	1485	Community Leader
Fisher, Shifra	Bnay-Brak	1955	Poland	1949	Student
Friedlander, Duv	Jerusalem	1934	Austria	1946	Professor
Goralsky, Leah	Yamit	1933	USA	1974	Teacher
Gorny, Josef	Ramat Aviv	1933	Poland	1947	Historian
Gringold, Schmuel	Lohamey-Hgetaoth	1949	Poland	1947	Student
Gringold, Zwi	Lohamey-Hgetaoth	1952	Poland	1947	Army Captain
Grossbein, Paul	SDE Nizzan	1939	Canada	1973	Agriculturalist
Grossbein, Sara	SDE Nizzan	1943	Poland	1932	Agriculturalist
Hamizrachi, Yoram	Matulla	1942	Germany	1933	Journalist
Hartman, David	Jerusalem	1931	Canada	1971	Philosopher
Hass, Kobi	Zahala	1956	Belgium	1944	unemployed
Heftler, Mel	Jerusalem	1937	USA	1974	Hotel Manager
Hirschmann, Sam	Haifa	1959	South Africa	1952	Student
Jossy	Herzlia	1938	South Africa	1963	Army Doctor
Kahana, Nachman	Jerusalem	1938	USA	1962	Rabbi
Kollek, Teddy	Jerusalem	1911	Austria	1935	Mayor
Kratz, Rachel	Jerusalem	1934	Rumania	1948	School Principal
Kwiat, Migaf	Pearim	1945	Australia	1965	Technician
Laner, Dan	Neoth Mordecai	1922	Austria	1940	General
Laner, Tirza	Neoth Mordecai	1923	Austria	1941	Agriculturalist

Name	Place	Year	Country	Year	Occupation
Langer, Felicia	Tel Aviv	1930	Poland	1950	Lawyer
Laviv, Ygal	Tel Aviv	1937	Rumania	1938	Journalist
Leibovitch, Eugeny	Tel Aviv	1944	USSR	1971	Seaman
Leibowitz, Pinhas	Tel Aviv	1915	Russia	1933	Publisher
Leibowitz, Yeshria	Jerusalem	1903	USSR	1928	Biologist
Lev, Amnon	Tel Aviv	1916	Czechoslovakia	1938	Civil Servant
Levin, Mike	Jerusalem	1942	England	1946	Civil Servant
Malka, Shula	Itav	1957	Morocco	1947	Labourer
Meiri, Zeev	Yad Mordechai	1912	Poland	1935	Electronics
Meridor, Dan	Jerusalem	1947	USSR	1936	Attorney
Mochiach, Nachum	Tel Aviv	1953	Finland	1920	Student
Mochiach, Ygal	Haifa	1940	Iraq	1950	Technician
Monsour, A.G.	Haifa	1918	Palestine	—	Mechanic
Mordecai, Aaron	Beersheba	1928	India	1952	Seaman
Moskovitz, Reuven	Rehovot	1929	Rumania	1948	Teacher
Na'amneh, Muhammed	Jerusalem	1945	Palestine (Araba)	—	Lawyer
Nisan, Mordechai	Jerusalem	1947	Canada	1972	Political Scientist
Ohnnh, Max	Haifa	1949	Morocco	1954	Bartender
Okrent, Sinai	Lohamey-Hgetaoth	1921	Poland	1948	Agriculturalist
Ovadya, Ely	Tel Aviv	1949	Libya	1933	Businessman
Pail, Meir	Ramat Aviv	1926	USSR	1921	Spokesman
Piron, Mordecai	Bat-Yam	1921	Austria	1938	Rabbi
Porush, Menachem	Jerusalem	1916	Russia	c. 1770	Knesset Member
Pyetan, Lionel	Shmaryahu	1910	South Africa	1938	Journalist
Rachel	Jerusalem	1918	Belgium	1933	Telephone Operator
Rahabi, Sara	Revivim	1926	USA	1921	Agriculturalist

Name	Place	Year of Birth	Country of Origin	Year of Immigration	Occupation
Rahabi, Zechria	Revivim	1921	Yemen	1907	Agriculturalist
Raz, Cobby	Tel Aviv	1950	Lebanon	1900	Hotel Servant
Resnikoff, M. Bernard	Jerusalem	1918	USA	1966	Social Worker
Rica, Meida	Haifa	1925	Zaire	1944	Teacher
Rokotnitz, Herbert	Givat Hayim	1915	Germany	1934	Book-keeper
Rokotnitz, Jacquelyne	Givat Hayim	1940	England	1970	Agriculturalist
Rosenzweig, Rachel	Rod Hasharon	1938	Germany	1964	Teacher
Samaan, Ibrahim	Haifa	1940	Palestine	—	Church Worker
Samoilova, Tanja	Ramat Gan	1951	USSR	1973	Student
Segal, Jonathan	Tel Aviv	1952	USA	1961	Student
Shahak, Israel	Jerusalem	1933	Poland	1945	Professor
Shaham, David	Tel Aviv	1923	Poland	1924	Editor
Shalgi, Dov	Giladi	1914	Germany	1940	Editor
Shaoulian, Emanuel	Tel Aviv	1953	Iran	1970	Student
Sharlin, Lida	Maaleh Adounim	1956	Iraq (via Iran)	1965	Student
Sharon, Ariel	Ashkelon	1928	Russia	1920	General
Shohath, Orith	Ramat Aviv	1950	Germany	c. 1880	Political Spokesperson
Smallman, Robert	Yamit	1928	USA	1974	Businessman
Spellman, David	Gonen	1944	England	1967	Agriculturalist
Taberi, Farid Wadji	Jaffa	1924	Palestine	—	Judge
Tal, Ysrael	Tel Aviv	1924	Russia	1911	General
Yaary, Arie	Tel Aviv	1941	Poland	1936	Businessman

Yarkoni, Yaffa	Tel Aviv	1925	Russia	c. 1880	Singer
Yaron, Kahman	Jerusalem	1925	Germany	1936	Dir. of Adult Education
Yehoshua, Avraham	Haifa	1936	Greece	1825	Writer
Yshby, Haim	Maoz-Hayim	1917	Egypt	1919	Agriculturalist
Yshby, Yaffa	Maoz-Hayim	1927	Poland	1925	Agriculturalist
Yuval, Yoni	Tel Aviv	1931	USSR	1947	Agriculturalist
Zemmel, Lea	Jerusalem	1945	Poland	1933	Lawyer